CONSTRUCTION CONTRACTS AND CLAIMS

Michael S. Simon

McGraw-Hill Book Company
New York   St. Louis   San Francisco   Auckland   Bogotá
Düsseldorf   Johannesburg   London   Madrid   Mexico
Montreal   New Delhi   Panama   Paris   São Paulo
Singapore   Sydney   Tokyo   Toronto

To Linda, Arlyn and Ilyse Simon

Library of Congress Cataloging in Publication Data

Simon, Michael S.

Construction contracts and claims.

Includes index.
1. Building—Contracts and specifications—United States.
2. Construction industry—Law and legislation—United States.
3. Actions and defenses—United States.

I. Title.
KF902.S5   343'.73'078   78-11275

ISBN 0-07-057433-2

1234567890 KPKP 7865432109

The editors for this book were Jeremy Robinson and Joan Zseleczky, the designer was Naomi Auerbach, and the production supervisor was Teresa F. Leaden. It was set in Elegante by KBC/Rocappi.

Printed and bound by The Kingsport Press.

Contents

Preface

Construction Contracts and Claims is intended as a practical text from which the construction, engineering, architectural, and legal professions can gain a better understanding of the legal problems that continually arise during the construction process. All too often construction projects are mired in legal disputes that could have been avoided had the parties been educated as to their legal rights and responsibilities. This book is part of the educational process necessary to aid construction progress by avoiding and deterring litigation.

"The law" is not an absolute. It is composed of legal precedent, legislative pronouncements, administrative rulings, and the ever-changing social needs and demands of our society. These components, even when compiled as "the law," are then subject to the individualistic interpretation of judges and arbitrators. The best way to understand "the law" is to appreciate its complexity, know its parameters and requirements, be cognizant of court decisions, even though they may differ, and be aware of judicial trends. This book studies the status and trends of construction law.

The educational process must begin prior to the dispute. It is too late to avoid lines of entrenchment and litigation after unreasonable contract documents, statements, letters, opinions, or acts are communicated. Negotiation with the uneducated seldom bears fruit. An intelligent person knows when he is right and when he is not; and when he is not, he knows not to claim that he is.

This book represents a new approach to the field of construction law. The attorney must be aware of the practical daily legal needs of the construction profession. He must be able to draft clear construction contract documents and avoid ambiguity. More than technical knowledge of court decisions is required of him. He must be able to act on momentary notice as legal consultant to his client. He must be knowledgeable of the construction process, case law, trends, and probabilities. This is especially true when arbitration or negotiation could be involved. A proper opinion will protect the client and will allow construction to continue without undue costs and delays. The primary concern should be the building of projects, not cases.

The construction attorney will have little or no impact on the construction professions if the members of the construction team are not aware that problems exist. This book, by educating the construction, architectural, and engineering professions as to their legal rights and responsibilities, will broaden their knowledge in order to spot problems, to avoid the planting of seeds which create disputes, to furrow out the roots of potential problems, and to weed out any problems that do occur. This requires an educated construction team, from those who work with their hands to the chairman of the board. This mandates proper legal consultation. A client who knows when and how to use a legal consultant will avoid most litigation.

Not all litigation can be avoided. Honest people have differences of opinion. The right to litigate is one of the foundations of our judicial system, but seldom would it be the sought-after end. However, often litigations are wasted efforts because one of the parties was unaware of its equitable and legal position until it was too late. Hopefully, those who must litigate will have known their rights from the very beginning. If so, they will have a greater chance of success in the adversary proceeding. But if the adversary environment cannot be avoided, this book will enhance the chance for a successful disposition of the claim.

The word "claims" has been added to the title of this book for several reasons. It is my conviction that through education one will realize that being claims-conscious is neither derogatory nor degrading. "Claim" is not a dirty word. A "claim" is defined as that which is demanded "by or as by virtue of a right." A claim is a right. Being aware of one's claims should be a standard operating procedure. I advocate the assertion of rights and, conversely, admonish those who create adversary positions without a right. If all people were claims-conscious and motivated, there would be fewer litigants.

The construction profession does not make money in court. Even if a party is a successful litigant, the award usually comes too late. With the exception of specific situations, even the 100 percent-successful party loses. Even the reimbursement of damages normally does not permit the recovery of any legal fees, the costs expended in the preparation and presentation of the suit, the time and costs of your own personnel, various consulting experts, and witnesses, and the annoyance and other such intangibles. A claims-conscious professional, one who has a working knowledge of its rights before encountering an adversity, can normally avoid adversity, avoid litigation, and avoid being a loser. The choice is one of either being claims-conscious or being loss-motivated.

The topics in this book were selected and the cases reported to make the professional constructor claims-conscious. The topics covered and analyzed are those legal and construction problems most often encountered from estimating and bidding to completion and arbitration. The contents was designed to take the reader from the beginning of the construction project to the ultimate end, the successful negotiation of claims.

Specific acknowledgment is given to *Engineering News-Record*, as the cases which conclude each chapter were previously selected and reviewed by me and published in *ENR's* legal column. The cases were selected to illustrate legal principles and to show how varying factual situations and jurisdictions can affect an outcome. Case awareness is part of the educational process. The taking of a steadfast position based upon a single case or legal precedent can have a devastating effect. Awareness of varying possibilities and probabilities will broaden the chance of success. "The law" is ever-changing, and the reader must continue learning.

I offer my congratulations to those educators and practitioners who have worked so hard in order to attain the long-awaited just recognition of the construction profession and the professional constructor, and specifically to the American Institute of Constructors, the American Council for Construction Education, and the Forum Committee on the Construction Industry of the American Bar Association. I would like to acknowledge my gratitude to all those members of my personal and professional families who have offered their invaluable assistance and encouragement. To Loislee Landis Giambri, for her hours of devoted service and assistance, I extend my sincere appreciation. To my wife, Linda, and my children, Arlyn and Ilyse, for their continuous devotion, I dedicate this book.

Michael S. Simon

ONE

Types of Liability

All too often contractors and their attorneys believe that liability is limited to what is written in the contract. This is a grave misconception. First of all, the responsibilities and liabilities expressly set forth in the contract are not always enforceable. There are many instances when courts will not enforce the responsibilities as written in the contract. On the other hand, there are many areas of contractual liability which are implied and not expressed. This implied contractual liability might be the contractor's obligation to perform its work in a good workmanlike manner. Therefore, even when dealing with contractual liability, the contractor is often subject to a scope of liability different from, and often more comprehensive than, that set forth in the written contract.

Liability, obligations, and responsibilities do not stop with the contract. They are broader and more inclusive. Liability may rest in the field of torts. Although the contract may specify that the contractor is obligated to act in a reasonable manner, even if the contract does not specify it, the law of torts will. Torts are basically divided into two areas, the intentional tort, or wrong, and the unintentional tort, commonly referred to as *negligence*. Under the law of torts, every person owes every other person the obligation to exercise reasonable care and skill. This obligation extends beyond the contracting party. It applies to all persons. The contractor may be liable for its failure to exercise reasonable care in the performance of its duties, even though it is fulfilling its contractual obligations. A contractor who lives by its contract alone is merely inviting potential liability.

The area of tort liability has been expanded with the passage of time, and the area of *strict liability*, or warranty, has evolved. Often the contractor is liable to another for breach of implied warranty or, expressed warranty or is held accountable under the theories of strict liability. Again, obligation is not only to the other contracting party but to third parties. In essence, the standard of care being placed upon the shoulders of the contractor is greater and more comprehensive than the reasonable-care standard imposed by tort liability.

The contractor's prospective liability does not stop with strict liability; in certain circumstances the courts have held contractors liable under the theory of absolute liability. The standard of care and responsibility of the contractor is absolute, and all that need be proved is cause and effect. Since the enforcement of absolute liability is extremely harsh, it is not generally applicable to most construction operations. It has so far been reserved for application to activities which might be deemed ultrahazardous. Most often cited as an ultrahazardous activity in construction is blasting. However, since it is the court which determines the status of the activity, one can never be certain what activity will or will not be deemed ultrahazardous and therefore subject to the theory of absolute liability.

The statement that ignorance is bliss has no place in the law. Far more accurate is the statement that ignorance of the law is no excuse when dealing with statutory, regulatory, and legislative promulgations. All too often a contractor learns the hard way that when it is performing a given act, even in accordance with its contractual obligations, it may be found liable since it is not in accord with, but is in violation of, some law, rule, ordinance, or statute. Whether they are referred to in a given contract or not, the contractor can be liable for breach of its duty to comply with the "laws." A contractor's refusal to testify before a grand jury can be cause for the cancellation of its contracts (Case 1-1). Statutes are inferred to be a part of every contract, and no person has a right to violate them. Such laws might be the Occupational Safety and Health Act, EEO, EPA, or some other well-recognized statute. On the other hand, the contractor must also be fully familiar with enabling legislation and statutes dealing with building codes and public bidding. When dealing with public and quasi-public authorities, the contractor will be held to be legally knowledgeable of the scope and authority of that authority to act. This requires specific knowledge of the enabling legislation which created the public entity for which the contractor is working. Performing work, whether it is a change or an extra, even pursuant to written directions from an authority, may result in an unenforceable and uncollectible item of work if in fact that work was not within the powers of the authority to order or was in contravention of a bidding statute.

Although it is hoped that liability will not arise from the commission of a crime, contractors are no exception to the rule that we are all bound to act in a proper noncriminal fashion. Obtaining a contract by an unlawful method may result in a criminal conviction and forfeiture of all monies received or earned for work performed.

All forms of liability are interpreted or found by the court based upon justice and equity. Contractual rights may be denied when a person has acted in an inequitable manner, e.g., without clean hands. Although our legal system was founded upon separate courts for law and for equity, today they are basically one, and all acts and omissions are judged not only in the light of the law but in the light of justice and equity.

The contractor must also be aware of what its legal rights are against the other contracting party. In certain instances, such rights may be nonexistent. The possibility of a governmental owner's claim of sovereign immunity still exists although its application has been restricted in most instances (Cases 1-2 and 1-3). A contractor may be found liable on the basis of more than one form of liability. There are numerous different types of liability; to perform work on any construction project without knowing the potential scope of liability and without competent legal advice is to invite problems if not disaster. It must be remembered, however, that knowing the extent of one's liability and one's rights is not a single person's function; it is everyone's obligation. Every person within every organization, from the apprentice to the president, should be educated to know the various possibilities for liability. Unless one is educated about the various types of liability and their specific relationship to the construction industry, one will not know when to seek competent legal advice. This role of education is often filled by counsel giving in-house seminars. Proper representation should include education. Too often the attorney is called too late to be of any assistance. It is the obligation of the contractor and its counsel to educate its organization so that it will know when to seek further legal advice.

CASE 1-1 Fifth Amendment Cost Contractor

A corporate painting contractor's present contracts were canceled, and it was prohibited from contracting with any public authority when its president refused to testify before a grand jury on bid rigging.

The contractor was a closely held family corporation. During 1964, the corporation entered several painting contracts with the New York City Housing Authority. The contracts were executed by the contractor's president. The president was also a director and stockholder of the corporation. Each of the contracts contained a standard disqualification clause in accordance with the Public Authorities Law of New York, §2601.

This law requires all contracts awarded by a public authority to provide that upon the refusal of a person to testify before a grand jury, to answer any relevant questions, or to waive immunity against subsequent criminal prosecution such person and any corporation or firm of which he or she is a member, officer, or director shall be disqualified for five years from contracting with any public authority, and any existing contracts may be canceled by the public authority without incurring any penalty or damage.

After receiving the contract awards, the contractor discovered that the district attorney was conducting an investigation before a grand jury on public-contract bid rigging. The contractor's president, having learned that the corporation was included in the investigation, gave up his position as president and director and sold his stock. He remained but only as an employee.

The past president was called to testify before the grand jury. He refused to sign immunity waivers and pleaded the protection of the Fifth Amendment. All the other officers, directors, and controlling stockholders appeared when subpoened and indicated a willingness to sign immunity waivers. However, after the past president refused to sign a waiver of immunity, the Public Housing Authority terminated the contractor's existing contracts and disqualified it from doing any business for five years. The contractor then filed suit contesting the disqualification.

The United States Supreme Court, in affirming the decision of the New York Court of Appeals upholding the disqualification and termination, stated:

> We do not consider the constitutionality of §2601 of New York's Public Authorities Law or the validity or effect of the contract provisions incorporating that section. Appellant's [contractor's] claim is that these provisions operated unconstitutionally to require its president . . . to waive the benefits of his privilege against self-incrimination. But appellant cannot avail itself of this point, assuming its validity. It has long been settled in federal jurisprudence that the constitutional privilege against self-incrimination is "essentially a personal one, applying only to natural individuals." It "cannot be utilized by or on behalf of any organization, such as a corporation." . . . If a corporation cannot avail itself of the privilege against self-incrimination, it cannot take advantage of the claimed invalidity of a penalty imposed for refusal of an individual, its president, to waive the privilege. Since the privilege is not available to it, appellant, a corporation, cannot invoke the privilege to challenge the constitutionality of §2601 of the Public Authorities Law [*George Campbell Painting Corp. v. Reid et al., Members of New York City Housing Authority, et al.* 392 U.S. 286 (1968); see also *Lefkowitz v. Turley,* 414 U.S. 70 (1973)].

CASE 1-2   Contractor Sues State

The Supreme Court of New Jersey has ruled that a contractor may sue the state without its consent, although the court has no power to compel the state to pay a judgment [*P, T & L Constr. Co. v. Commissioner, Department of Transportation,* 55 N.J. 341, 262 A.2d 195(1970)].

The case involved a contractor's attempt to recover a contract balance the state had withheld as damages for delay. The merits of the claim were never litigated because the lower courts upheld the state's defense of immunity.

After failing to recover the money through special legislation, the contractor went back to court asking that the doctrine of immunity be overruled.

The court agreed that the time for change has come. The courts should be open to a person who holds a contract with the state even though satisfaction of a favorable judgment would depend on the legislature, it said.

CASE 1-3   Sovereign Immunity Upheld

The federal government, acting in its "sovereign" capacity, can suspend a project without paying delay damages, the Department of Agriculture Board of Contract Appeals has ruled.

The case involved a road contract in Idaho let by the Forest Service. The contract contained the standard federal suspension-of-work clause that permits an equitable adjustment to be made for unreasonable suspensions [*Appeal of Goodfellow Bros., Inc.*, AGBCA 75-140, 77-1 BCA 12, 336 (1977)].

After the project got under way, the threat of fire prompted the federal regional forester to issue a formal suspension-of-work order to the contractor.

The contractor's request for a special permit to work during the shutdown was denied, and paving operations were halted for twenty-seven days. Subsequently, the contractor filed a claim for additional costs caused by the delay.

Denying this claim, the appeals board held that "actions of a general and public character which implement programs in the national interest constitute sovereign acts and such acts create an immunity to contractual claims against the government."

TWO

Tort Liability

The contractor's obligations and liabilities exceed those specified by contract, statute, and the written word and go into the area of torts. As previously mentioned, a *tort* is literally translated as a "wrong." There are both intentional and unintentional wrongs. The intentional wrong will carry liability in nearly every instance. No party is granted a legal right to do harm intentionally to another. This intentional wrong, whether it is fraud, deceit, assault, or some other act, has created liability on a party even when clauses in the contract would preclude liability in those instances. A clause which seeks to avoid liability for delays and merely grants extensions of time is generally not enforceable when the party seeking the protection of the clause has committed an intentional tort. Therefore, no person can escape the responsibility and moral commitment not to harm another intentionally.

The unintentional tort, or negligence, has followed a wide swing of the pendulum in application. At one time the saying was "caveat emptor," which strictly translated means "let the buyer beware." The manufacturer or builder was apparently cloaked from liability, but this point of view has steadily been eroded. The doctrine of negligence is simply that every person owes to every other person the duty to exercise reasonable care and skill in the performance of its duties to avoid injuring the other person. Each person is compared against, and obligated to live up to, the standard of reasonable care exercised by an average reasonably prudent person. If that standard is not met, negligence is present.

A highway contractor was found liable for failing to exercise reasonable care in the protection of third parties during its construction of a highway. The court specifically noted that the question of reasonable care did not depend upon whether or not the contractor was performing in accord with its contract; instead the liability was strictly dependent upon the contractor's exercising reasonable care toward others. The court stated:

> The primary duty to exercise reasonable care for the safety of the general public using a road or highway during improvements or repair rests on the road contractor, and the road contractor in this respect must act reasonably and with due regard to the rights of persons lawfully using the way and is liable for injuries resulting from negligence in the performance of his work. . . .
>
> The liability, aforesaid, is imposed upon the road contractor not by virtue of his contract with a public authority, or upon failure to perform the work in accord with a contract, but upon the tortious breach of duty imposed upon the contractor by the common law. . . . The road contractor's liability exists regardless of the requirements of its contract with the public authorities and irrespective of any liability on the part of the governmental authority employing the contractor. Thus, a road contractor contracting with a public body is not entitled to avail itself of the immunity of the latter from liability for injuries resulting from either willful tort or negligence in the performance of its public work [*Best v. Fred Weber Constr. Co.,* 525 S.W.2d 102 (Mo. Ct. App. 1975)].

The standards of an architect's implied contractual obligations were set forth when it was denied further compensation.

> An architect is required to furnish plans and specifications prepared with a reasonable degree of technical skill which would produce, if followed, a building without marked defects. . . . Such plans are not required to be perfect; the architect is liable only for his failure to exercise reasonable skill in their preparation [*Stanley Consultants, Inc. v. H. Kalicak Constr. Co.,* 383 F. Supp. 315 (D.E.D. Mo. 1974)].

The obligation to exercise reasonable care might arise by one subcontractor's having to exercise reasonable care with regard to the work of another subcontractor when in fact there is no contractual obligations between them. This obligation to exercise reasonable care might extend from the architect to the contractor when in fact there is no contractual relationship between them. The lack of a direct contract does not mean that a duty is not owed to a third person. The surveyor, like anyone else, is under the obligation to exercise reasonable care to every third party, including the contractor. The failure to exercise average reasonably prudent care and skill creates liability (Case 2-1).

In a leading case a lawsuit was commenced against Levitt & Sons, developer and builder of the house, by the lessee, whose son had been scalded by hot water. The basic action was in negligence for installing a hot-water system without a mixing valve, as well as for breach of warranty. The house was not sold to the lessee but was sold to someone else who then leased it to the person bringing suit. In finding the builder-developer liable, the court stated:

> In fulfillment of the deliberate design of its system for distributing hot water for domestic use, Levitt assembled the ingredients, including the heating unit . . . and directed their installation. In this respect it was not unlike the manufacturers of

automobiles, airplanes, etc., whose products embody parts supplied by others. When their marketed products are defective and cause injury to either immediate or remote users, such manufacturers may be held accountable under ordinary negligence principles as well as under expanding principles of warranty or strict liability. . . .

If there is improper construction such as a defective heating system or defective ceiling, stairway and the like, the well-being of the vendee and others is seriously endangered and serious injury is foreseeable. The public interest dictates that if such injury does result from the defective construction, its costs should be borne by the responsible developer who created the danger and who is in the better economic position to bear the loss rather than the injured party who justifiably relied on the developer's skill and implied representation [*Schipper v. Levitt & Sons, Inc.,* 207 A.2d 314 (1965)].

Probably the most important statement from this case is a good example of the current trend of the law to protect the "innocent." The court stated:

The law should be based on current concepts of what is right and just and the judiciary should be alert to the never-ending need for keeping its common law principles abreast of the times. Ancient distinctions which make no sense in today's society and tend to discredit the law should be readily rejected. . . [ibid].

The trend in the law today is to protect the third party. The contractor must be fully aware that if there is a question of who should bear liability, i.e., the person who in some way was involved in the creation of the harm or the party injured by that harm, the "innocent" party will be protected.

The liability of a contracting party to a third person is not terminated upon the owner's acceptance of the project. Construction professions

are not to be relieved from liability merely because their work has been completed and accepted by the owner. Such liability may rest on architects and engineers on the basis of improper design as well as on contractors for defective materials, equipment and workmanship [*Totten v. Gruzen,* 245 A.2d 1 (1968) (Case 2-2)].

As indicated by the Levitt case, liability exists whether or not there has been reasonable care. Developers' obligations have reached the point of strict liability or breach of warranty, and in this instance the standard of care and degree of responsibility is greater. The specific degree of care required by strict liability or breach of warranty is not defined. Note that it is not based on contract: it is based on the common law and equitable principles of protecting the innocent. Many of these warranties are set forth in the Uniform Commercial Code. Simply put, the contractor cannot rely upon the fact that it has acted reasonably; it can be held to a higher standard.

The ultimate standard is that embodied in the principle of *absolute liability.* The doctrine of absolute liability is applied in situations involving ultrahazardous activities. It is often hard to make a distinction between the application of strict liability and absolute liability. The rule of absolute liability has most often been applied in blasting cases (Case 2-3). Its extension to other situations will obviously be growing and is self-evident by merely turning around and looking at no-fault insurance. In holding a contractor liable regardless of whether it exercised reasonable care or was negligent, a New York Court held:

> the question . . . was not whether it was lawful or proper to engage in blasting but who should bear the cost of any resulting damage—the person who engaged in the dangerous activity or the innocent neighbor injured thereby [*Spano v. Perini Corp.*, 25 N.Y.2d 11 (1969) (Case 2-4)].

The answer of the court was obvious at this point, and it concluded that the contractor was liable.

In discussing negligence other topics relate to the contributory-negligence rule, the comparative-negligence rule, workmen's compensation, and various other legal considerations (Cases 2-5 and 2-6). These rules may lessen the eventual monetary loss, but in today's market if you were the sole or contributing cause, directly or indirectly, for the injury, prepare to accept liability.

CASE 2-1   Surveyor Liable in Tort

The Supreme Court of Illinois has held that a surveyor was liable, on the basis of tortious misrepresentation, for damages incurred by a person other than the one for whom the survey was prepared. The survey was found to be defective seven years after it was made.

The surveyor had prepared an inaccurate spot survey of a vacant lot in 1953 for a real estate development firm. Two years later a survey chart was issued by the surveyor to a builder who had purchased the land from the real estate developer. The new survey located a house on the originally inaccurate survey. It stated that "this chart carries our absolute guarantee for accuracy. . . ."

The builder had obtained a loan from an association that relied on the survey showing the house location. The plaintiff, then a prospective purchaser of the house and lot, was informed by the association that a construction loan existed and that he could purchase the property by assuming the mortgage. The property was then purchased by the plaintiff.

With the unknowingly inaccurate survey as a guide, boundary markers had previously been put on the land. In 1956, relying on the boundary markers, the plaintiff extended the existing driveway and built a garage. It was discovered in 1962 that portions of the existing driveway, the new driveway, and the garage encroached on the adjacent lot. The plaintiff started suit in 1964 for the cost of moving the house and garage and rehabilitating both.

The trial court returned a verdict in favor of the plaintiff. The appellate court reversed the decision. The action it said, was one of contract and the plaintiff had no contractual relationship with the surveyor on which to base its claim. The plaintiff appealed to the Illinois Supreme Court.

On appeal, the plaintiff argued that the surveyor could still be found liable without contractual relationship on various grounds, including strict liability, various implied and express warranties, and tortious misrepresentation.

The plaintiff's argument and the court's analysis centered on the surveyor's written statement that the survey carried an "absolute guarantee for accuracy."

The court rejected the argument of strict liability in tort since such liability is normally restricted to use against "sellers of products in defective condition unreasonably dangerous to the user or consumer." The inaccurate survey, the court said, did not constitute an unreasonably dangerous and defective product. The implied warranty argument, it added, did not have to be considered since, if any warranty existed, a basis for an express warranty could be asserted due to the surveyor's written guarantee.

In considering the basis for liability, the court disposed of the surveyor's defense that a contractual relationship must be present for any liability to exist. The court noted that the modern trend is to hold that liability exists by reason of a tort and not by contract. Liability in tort can be found without a contractual relationship, and the court stated, "We emphasize that lack of direct contractual relationship between the parties is not a defense in a tort action in this jurisdiction. Thus, tort liability will henceforth be measured by the scope of the duty owed rather than the artificial concepts of privity."

Although the requirement of contractual relationship no longer bars recovery, the court had to determine whether the surveyor was, in fact, liable for the wrong. The major question was whether the plaintiff had any right to protection. The plaintiff was not known at the time the survey was made, and the survey was not made directly for him. However, the court found that the plaintiff was a member of a foreseeable and known limited group of people who might reasonably rely on the accuracy of the inaccurate chart.

> As might reasonably have been foreseen by defendant [surveyor], who admitted he knew the plats were customarily used by lending agencies and others, that plat was subsequently relied on to his damage by a third party in connection with the financing and purchase of the surveyed property, [the court said]. Under these circumstances, it seems to us the fortuitous circumstance that the ultimate loss resulting from the faulty survey fell upon one other than the person for whom the survey was made should not absolve defendant from responding in damages.
>
> The situation is not one fraught with such an overwhelming potential liability as to dictate a contrary result, for the class of persons who might foreseeably use this plat is rather narrowly limited, if not exclusively so, to those who deal with the surveyed property as purchasers or lenders. Injury will ordinarily occur only once and to the one person then owning the lot [*Raymond A. Rozny, Jr. v. John Marnul*, 250 N.E.2d 656 (1969)].

In granting damages to the plaintiff, the court ruled that he had filed his suit within the five-year statute of limitations. The limitation did not begin to run, the court said, until the plaintiff knew or should have known about the defect.

CASE 2-2   Negligence Survives Acceptance

The New Jersey Supreme Court has ruled that acceptance of a building by the owner does not relieve the architect and contractor of liability for negligence in their work.

The case involved a low-income housing project for a city housing authority. The plaintiff claimed that the injuries for which he was suing were caused by the installation of an improperly designed heating system.

Defendants in the suit were the architect who had prepared the plans and specifications, the general contractor, the heating contractor who installed the system, and the housing authority.

Construction had been completed, and the housing authority had accepted the project. The housing authority then took over complete control and operation of the project as the owner-landlord.

Part of the heating system, as designed, built, and accepted, included exposed supply and return radiator pipes, which ran parallel to the floor and formed a ladderlike structure several inches from the base of the floor. The three-year-old son of one of the tenants in the project attempted to climb the pipes and was severely burned.

A lawsuit was commenced on behalf of the child. The plaintiff based its claim in negligence due to the alleged design and construction of a hazardous heating system because it included the exposed and uncovered piping.

The defendants, with the exception of the housing authority, argued that they were relieved of any liability to third persons when the project was completed and accepted by the owner. When the owner accepted the building, they were deprived of any control over the building, they said, and could no longer rectify any prior mistakes if any were found to exist. The conclusion of this argument by the architect, the general contractor, and the heating contractor was that the housing authority, as the owner, was now the responsible party for any existing defects.

The court noted that this argument, known as the *completed-and-accepted rule,* has been widely followed and accepted in the past. However, the majority view of today's courts is to hold that the rule no longer bars liability.

The court held that even after the work had been completed and accepted, the defendants were still held to the general standard of reasonable care for the protection and safeguarding of any third person who might foreseeably be endangered by their negligence. It concluded:

> They are not to be relieved from liability merely because their work had been completed and accepted by the owner. Such liability may rest on architects and engineers on the basis of improper design as well as on contractors for defective materials, equipment and workmanship [*Totten v. Gruzen,* 52 N.J. 202, 245 A.2d 1 (1968)].

CASE 2-3   Blasting Results In Absolute Liability

The Supreme Court of Pennsylvania has ruled, with one dissent, that public as well as private contractors are subject to the rule of strict liability for blasting damages. The dissenting judge said, however, that liability should not be imposed on government contractors in the absence of negligence [*Lobozzo v. Adam Eidemiller, Inc.,* 263 A.2d 432 (1970)].

The case involved highway construction under a state contract. The contractor on the project detonated a large number of explosives in preparing the roadbed. When the blasting occurred, the owner of a nearby grocery store felt the building tremble and saw the walls crack. He sued the contractor for damages.

The store owner based his claim on the theory of strict liability. He did not claim nor did he try to prove, that the contractor was negligent. He merely argued that the vibrations from the blasting damaged his property and that the contractor was absolutely liable for trespass damages that resulted from the blasting.

The contractor did not dispute the existence or validity of what is called the *rule of liability without fault for blasting damage* insofar as it applies to private contractors. However, he argued that the rule of a strict liability does not apply to blasting done under a public contract because public servants are exempt from the rule of absolute liability.

In rejecting the contractor's argument, the court said it is true that public servants often engage for the benefit of the public in ultrahazardous activities relating to explosives and are exempt from the rule of absolute liability. The reason, it said, is that the individual public servant can "neither control the degree of hazard he will create nor dictate the compensation he will receive for the performance of his required duties."

But this reasoning does not apply to an independent contractor working on a public contract, the court ruled. The contractor, it explained, "may balance the risk of loss from damage caused against the cost of insulating himself from such loss, and regulate his contract bid accordingly." For this reason, it said, an independent contractor on a public contract stands on the same footing as a contractor on a private contract, and is equally subject to absolute liability for blasting damages regardless of fault.

The court found that the store had suffered no permanent damage. It awarded the owner the costs of repair.

The dissenting judge said, that there is a well recognized exception to the rule of absolute liability, namely that

> neither the Government nor a Governmental Agency, nor a contractor performing for the Government or for a Governmental Agency in accordance with its plans and specifications, is liable for damages caused by his ultrahazardous activity in *the absence of negligence or a willful tortious action on his part.* [The principle of government or sovereign immunity has been] wisely extended [to public works contractors, the judge said, because otherwise] bidding on such jobs would be made more difficult and complicated and far more expensive than it already is.
>
> Since the Majority admit that no tortious or negligent blasting was proved, but merely damage without fault, I dissent, [the judge said].

CASE 2-4   Blasting Proved Costly

The New York Court of Appeals has held that a contractor was absolutely liable for the proximate damages caused to others by its blasting [*Spano v. Perini Corp.,* 25 N.Y.2d 11 (1969)].

The ruling came out of a lawsuit by a garage owner and the owner of an automobile in the garage, alleging damages to the garage and the car. It was undisputed that the contractor, engaged in the construction of a tunnel, had set off numerous sticks of dynamite on nearby property the day the damage occurred. However, during the trial the plaintiffs neither argued nor attempted to prove that the contractor failed to exercise reasonable care or failed to take necessary blasting precautions.

The court was faced with deciding the legal question of "whether a person who has sustained property damage caused by blasting on nearby property can maintain an action for damages without a showing that the blaster was negligent." Previously, unlike most states, New York still required, in the absence of rocks or other material from the blasting causing the damage, that negligence be proved.

In reviewing the fairness of the prior law, the court said, "The question . . . was not *whether* it was lawful or proper to engage in blasting but *who* should bear the cost of any resulting damage—the person who engaged in the dangerous activity or the innocent neighbor injured thereby." In answering this question, the court overruled prior decisions and held the contractor absolutely liable for its blasting damages. "Since blasting involves a substantial risk of harm no matter the degree of care exercised," it said, "we perceive no reason for ever permitting a person who engages in such an activity to impose this risk upon nearby persons or property without assuming responsibility therefor."

CASE 2-5 Contractor Incurs Dual Liability

A government contractor is potentially liable to the federal government for damages the government has to pay a contractor's employee as the result of injuries sustained on the job. Moreover, this liability may be in addition to the contractor's liability under the applicable state compensation law, the minority dissenting opinion in a recent U.S. Supreme Court decision noted [*United States v. Seckinger,* 90 S. Ct. 880 (1970)].

The contractor had entered into a contract with the federal government for plumbing work at a Marine base in South Carolina. A workman accidentally came in contact with a high-voltage electric wire while on the job and was seriously injured. He collected benefits under the South Carolina workmen's compensation law and then sued the federal government under the Federal Tort Claims Act in the Federal District Court. The District Court found the government liable to the employee for $45,000 as a result of its negligence. The federal government then sued the contractor to recover the $45,000. The government argued that the contractor was negligent and that the contract provided that the contractor "shall be responsible for all damages to persons or property that occur as a result of his fault or negligence in connection with the prosecution of the work."

The Supreme Court indicated that the case rested on the interpretation of the contract clause, federal law holding that "a contract should be construed most strongly against the drafter, which in this case was the United States," and that a person is not permitted to recover under a contract clause from the other contracting party indemnification for its own negligence "unless the court is firmly convinced that such an interpretation reflects the intention of the parties."

The court held that the contract clause did not clearly indicate a definite intent to allow the federal government to shift to the contractor the ultimate responsibility for the government's negligence. However, the court said the clause indicated that the contractor was liable for all damages which resulted from its negligence. The court concluded, "Seckinger [contractor] will be responsible for the damages caused by its negligence; similarly, responsibility will fall upon the United States to the extent that it was negligent."

The dissenting opinion raised an additional problem for federal contractors.

> When Seckinger entered into this contract, [the dissenters said,] it had every reason to expect that its liability for injuries to its employees would be limited to what is imposed by the South Carolina compensation law. That law relieved it of responsibility in tort in exchange for its guarantee that its employees would recover without regard to fault. . . . Now the Court heaps an unforeseen federal contractual burden atop the requirement the State has already imposed.

The resolution of this problem will depend upon the particular state workmen's compensation law.

CASE 2-6 Project Owner Not Responsible for Subcontractor's Negligence

The New York Court of Appeals has held that although an owner or general contractor has a legal duty to provide a subcontractor's employees with job safety, they are not responsible for a subcontractor's own negligent acts [*Rusin v. Jackson Heights Shopping Center, Inc.,* 27 N.Y.2d 103 (1970)].

The plaintiff in the case was the employee of an insulation subcontractor on a new shopping-center project, where in the course of installing roof insulation a scaffolding plank on which he was standing broke, causing the plaintiff to fall two stories and sustain injuries. The employee sued the shopping-center owner directly.

The court acknowledged that a duty rests on an owner or general contractor to provide a safe place to work that protects employees of subcontractors. The court also noted that in this case it was the subcontractor who supplied the scaffolding and who directed the specific place where the employee was working at the time of the accident.

In denying the employee's right to damages from the owner, the court held that it was the subcontractor who had been negligent.

THREE

Bids

Contract-awarding procedures can take various forms. Many private contracts result from direct negotiations between the construction parties and may include the designer, owner, contractor, financier, and others. In most instances private-contract bidding procedures are governed by the rules and regulations established by the party seeking bids, which usually is the owner. The private owner writes the rules, usually is permitted to change them when and as it deems appropriate, and has vast discretionary powers to alter the procedure. This right to waive, modify, or alter procedures is often found in the bid documents. There are very few legal contests challenging the propriety of the private owner's actions, whether the discretionary right is set forth in the bid documents or not. More will be required before a pattern can be established.

Public contracts are required to be let in accord with certain statutes. It is often hard to ascertain whether or not the particular contract in question is a private contract, subject to vast discretion, or a public contract, subject to statutory procedures. Many construction projects are financed with public monies. Mere financing does not necessarily bring the project within the statutory limitations. The real question depends upon the specific financing obligations and property interests of the owner. In many instances when public monies are used for financing the lender mandates that certain provisions be inserted in the bid documents and contract. These provisions often are required by statute, bringing the contract into the quasi-public realm and subjecting the bidding procedures to statutory procedures. The contractor should not automatically assume that a private owner means unlimited discretionary rights (he should check the funding commitments) or that public funding means that the contract procedures are automatically subject to regulatory and statutory mandates.

Generally a pure public contract, issued and funded by a public authority, will be bound by statutory regulations. These statutory provisions normally supersede and assume control over what the contract bid documents state. In most cases the issuing authority does not have the unilateral right to modify statutory provisions when seeking construction bids. Therefore, it is imperative that the contractor be aware of the statutory requirements for each and every public or quasi-public entity which has an interest in the project. All states have public bidding statutes. Their application depends upon the state law. Many states have separate statutes relating to boards of education, quasi-public authorities, cities, etc. In addition to being governed by state bidding statutes, many public authorities have statutory and administrative regulations which they have promulgated and which govern their operations. It is the contractor's right and obligation to know the law governing its bidding procedures.

Statutory requirements differ. Each state must be referred to for its particular scope. There are certain generalities, but like all rules, they are subject to exceptions. Normally, the owner is obligated to award the contract (if one is awarded) to the lowest responsible and responsive bidder (Case 3-1). It is often hard to ascertain compliance with this simple statement. The issuing authority must have prepared documents for bid in sufficient detail to permit the submission of competitive bids. If the documents are vague or uncertain or so restrictive that they unjustly restrict bidders, the bid documents are subject to legal attack. In one case the question hinged on the completeness and definiteness required of "suitable" plans and specifications for proper competitive public bidding. . . . The Delaware Supreme Court noted that the primary purpose of bidding statutes was to protect public funds. In determining what constituted "suitable" plans and specifications as required by the bidding statute, the court determined that this would be fulfilled by

> those which are sufficiently complete, definite, and explicit as to permit free, open and competitive bidding on a common basis. There is no statutory requirement, and the word "suitable" may not be stretched to create the requirement that plans and specifications be 100% complete. Plans and specifications issued under public bidding laws are not necessarily invalidated because they include flexible areas calling for responsive submissions. . . . Nor are public works plans and specifications necessarily invalidated because each and every prospective bidder may not be in a position to start out on an equal basis in responding to the invitation to bid. The bidding process itself is often an expensive and time-consuming undertaking which may eliminate busier or smaller prospective bidders [*Delaware Technical and Community College v. C & D Contractors, Inc.*, 338 A.2d 568 (Del. Sup. Ct. 1975)].

Public bidding rules are mandatory, and the failure to comply fully with the bidding statutes will invalidate a public contract.

> Generally, the object of statutory bidding requirements in connection with the letting of municipal contracts is to prevent fraud, collusion, favoritism, and improvidence in the administration of public business, as well as to insure that the munici-

pality receives high-quality labor and supplies at the most reasonable prices [*Village of Excelsior v. F. W. Pearce Corp.,* 226 N.W.2d 317 (Minn. Sup. Ct. 1975)].

It has been stated by numerous courts that the bidding statutes are for the public's benefit.

> Bidding statutes are for the benefit of the taxpayers and are construed as nearly as possible with sole reference to the public good. Their objects are to guard against favoritism, improvidence, extravagance and corruption; their aim is to secure for the public the benefits of unfettered competition. To achieve these purposes all bidding practices which are capable of being used to further corrupt ends or which are likely to affect adversely the bidding process are prohibited, and all awards made or contracts entered into where any such practice may have played a part, will be set aside. This is so even though it is evident that in fact there was no corruption or any actual adverse effect upon the bidding process [*Terminal Constr. Corp. v. Atlantic County Sewerage Authority,* 341 A.2d 327 (N.J. 1975)].

If the documents are not sufficient to secure competitive bidding, they are susceptible to being declared invalid. However, an owner "would not be precluded from considering alternative bids or circumscribed with respect to the business judgment involved in determining whether to accept one alternative as against another if the Authority included in its specifications, for comparative purposes only," sufficient information to ensure that each bidder could be compared by an objective standard and the lowest bidder could be determined for each alternative bid [*A & S Transp. Co. v. Bergen County Sewer Authority,* 342 A.2d 865 (N.J. App. Div. 1975)].

The next problem is determining who is a bidder. For a bid to be properly considered, most statutes mandate that the bid be submitted in a prescribed form and by a set preestablished time. Legal trends often take on the effect of a pendulum, swinging from one side to another. Case law used to be rather lax regarding late bids. If the late bid was not the fault of the bidder but the fault of some party over whom the bidder had no control, such as the mails or telegraph, tardiness was often deemed to be excused. As time passed, excuses became more restricted. Late telegrams are no longer an excuse when bidding pursuant to the Armed Services Procurement Regulations 2-303.4. Many public authorities have adopted the simple position that if it is not in the duly specified person's hands by the duly specified time, it is late and automatically, per se, unacceptable. This position, being the other end of the pendulum swing, has now come under legal attack.

The scope and extent of application of the statute depends upon the wording of the given statute or regulation and the judicial philosophy of the tribunal interpreting that particular statute. A bidder who believes that its bid should have been accepted or a bidder who believes that it has been denied a contract by the acceptance of a late bid has a right to bring suit. As recently stated by a United States District Court:

> a party denied a government contract as a result of alleged illegal activity on the part of a Federal Agency in letting the contract to another bidder, has standing . . . to

bring suit for declaratory and injunctive relief in order to determine the validity of the agency's action [*William F. Wilke, Inc. v. Dept. of the Army,* 357 F. Supp. 988 (D.C. Md. 1973), aff'd 485 F.2d 180 (1973) (see Case 3-2)].

In applying the restrictive and strict rule of exact time, this federal court declared the contract voidable when the bid was received only four minutes after the exact time specified in the bid documents. The court ruled that the exact-time requirement was mandatory and was "to provide a clear cut-off point after which bids will not be accepted." This was ruled even though bids had not been declared to be closed and no bids had been opened. This rule is apparently not enforced with such severity by most courts. The courts have held that technically late bids can be accepted provided there is no inference of fraud, or collusion, or other circumstances indicating that other bidders were disadvantaged competitively, or where the tardiness could be deemed a minor irregularity and be waived by the owner under its "inherent discretionary power ancillary to its duty" to obtain the best competitive price (Case 3-3). The courts have uniformly ruled that the public bidding statutes are for the public's benefit and not for the bidder's benefit. It is of utmost importance for the contractor, if it is late, to have its protest registered immediately with all appropriate authorities if they refuse to accept its bid. The contractor should insist upon the physical receipt of the bid and recording of the figures in some official document by the receiving authority. On the other hand, the low bidder before delivery of a late bid should be sure to register its protest with the authorities and note for the record all facts and circumstances surrounding the receipt of that alleged late bid.

The next determination is whether the bidder was "low," which is not as simplistic as it sounds. A single-line item or a one lump-sum bid presents few problems, but the problems become more complex when unit-price contracts are involved. What prevails, the bid unit dollar amount, the extended line item, or the totaled amount of all the line items? There is no clear answer (Case 3-4). The governing procedures are normally included as part of the bid documents and should be adhered to. Further complications exist when alternates are permitted. Most cases permit the owner to award the contract on the basis of the base bid plus alternates, but this should be specified in the bid documents. An unanswered question is the owner's right to select the base bid and, in lieu of selecting alternates in any prescribed order, to select unilaterally and haphazardly the alternates it desires. Care must be taken in preparation of the bid documents because if the solicitation is too ambiguous, it might then be open to attack for failing to present a document from which proper competitive bids could be obtained.

The next consideration relates to the responsiveness of the bidder. On public contracts it is generally recognized that if the bidder does not submit a bid in the specified manner, its bid may be deemed nonresponsive and therefore not be capable of being accepted. If there is a major mistake in form which would affect some substantive item of the bid, the bid will be deemed nonresponsive. If, however, the deviation is deemed to be a "minor informality or irregularity," the courts have generally recognized the owner's right to waive the minor informality or irregularity, accept the bid as being responsive, and award the contract based thereon. Although there is no set universal court rule for minor informalities, the best definition seems to be that in the Armed Services Procurement Regulations; it indicates that a minor informality is one which has no effect, or at least a negligible effect, on price, quantity, quality, or delivery. One recent state court decision indicated that "the test of whether or not an irregularity is material (and nonwaivable) is whether or not it gives a bidder a substantial advantage or benefit not enjoyed by other bidders" [*R. W. Rhine, Inc. v. City of Tacoma,* 536 P.2d 677 (Wash. 1975)] (Case 3-5). Owners have been permitted to waive, as minor defects and irregularities, the contractor's filing of a wrong bid bond, the filing of late bids, the furnishing of a bid bond in lieu of required certified check, etc. (Case 3-6).

> It is firmly established in New Jersey that material conditions contained in bidding specification may not be waived. . . . This rule, however, does not apply to minor or inconsequential conditions. Public contracting units may resolve problems arising from such conditions in a sensible or practical way. . . .
>
> Essentially this distinction between conditions that may or may not be waived stems from a recognition that there are certain requirements often incorporated in bidding specifications which by their nature may be relinquished without there being any possible frustration of the policies underlying competitive bidding. In sharp contrast, advertised conditions whose waiver is capable of becoming a vehicle for corruption or favoritism, or capable of encouraging improvidence or extravagance, or likely to affect the amount of any bid or to influence any protential bidder to refrain from bidding, or which are capable of affecting the ability of the contracting unit to make bid comparisons, are the kind of conditions which may not under any circumstances be waived. [*Terminal Constr. Corp. v. Atlantic County Sewerage Authority,* 341 A.2d 327 (1975).]

A condition of a public bidding specification requiring the apparently low and successful bidder to attend a preaward conference before execution of the contract is a condition that can be waived. However, the condition of prior federal approval of a contractor's "compliance position" before a formal unconditional contract award is not a condition that can be waived. This is especially true, ruled a New Jersey court, if the compliance position and approval thereof was a condition for the release of federal funds [*Terminal Constr. Corp. v. Atlantic County Sewerage Authority,* 341 A.2d 327 (N.J. Sup. Ct. 1975)]. Beware, "under federal or state law, unresponsive bids may not be corrected, after opening, in order to make them responsive" [*Rossetti Constr. Co., Inc., v. Brennan,* 508 F.2d 1039 (1975)] (Case 3-7). In other words, it is a matter of degree to be determined by the court in accordance with the applicable statute and regulation (Case 3-8).

Although the owner has had the right to waive minor informalities and irregularities, only recently have contractors started taking owners to court to force them to accept the bid and waive the minor informality. A recent decision stated:

> a minor technical defect or irregularity which does not affect the substance of a bid will not justify rejection of the lowest bid by a public body charged with awarding

the contract to the lowest bidder, because to do so would deny the people the benefit of the low bid [*Centric Corp. v. Barbarossa & Son, Inc.,* 521 P.2d 874 (Wyo. 1974) (Case 3-9)].

Although the owner normally has the right by statute to reject any and all bids, obviously it is not a nonreviewable unilateral right to reject "any" bid. The right to reject "all" bids is much more a discretionary right of the owner. However, even this discretionary right cannot be exercised arbitrarily or capriciously. Usually the language of the governing statute or bid document requires that the rejection be "in their [the owners'] best interests." The best interests are subject to judicial review (Case 3-10).

A New York lower court held that if there is an unequivocal statement that a bid is being withdrawn, an owner cannot award a public contract to that bidder, even though the bidder subsequently decides it wants to accept the award. However, in this case the contractor did not "withdraw" its bid; but before the expiration of the time its bid had to remain open, the contractor indicated that it did not wish to extend its bid. This, ruled the court, was not a withdrawal and the contractor still had the option, after the forty-five day period, "to let its bid stand or to withdraw it. As long as Hyland [contractor] let its bid stand and did not withdraw it, the county was empowered to accept that bid and award the contract . . ." [*Albert Elia Building Co., Inc. v. County of Monroe,* 88 Misc.2d 334 (1976)].

Whether a bidder is responsible is often determined by prequalification or selected bidders lists. In other instances this may be determined by prior conduct, criminal convictions, financial ability to post bonds, prior performance, and the like. These are all intangibles and subject to judicial review.

If the contractor believes it is the low responsive and responsible bidder and has not been awarded the contract, it should protect its rights and interests.

Customarily the procedure for protesting is specifically governed by legal procedural rules and regulations. Not only must the original protest be filed immediately but often specified steps must be taken immediately by the aggrieved bidder. The remedies available to the contractor run the gamut from a paper victory, whereby the court slaps the owner's hands but permits the contractor awarded the contract to proceed, up to a court direction declaring an alleged contract void and awarding a contract to the aggrieved party or directing that new bids be requested. Included among these recoveries might be the court's acknowledgement of the contractor's right, although denying injunctive or declaratory relief, allowing it to maintain the suit for lost anticipated profits or bidding damages. It is advisable for the aggrieved bidder and counsel to determine the extent of the possible recovery acknowledged in the legal jurisdiction where any trials will be held before proceeding with what might well be an expensive procedure of futility. However, without the immediate protest the contractor will probably not even have a choice of future decision.

The area of public negotiated design-and-build and turnkey projects has created a whole new area of concern and litigation. The courts seem to be scrutinizing the facts very carefully but upholding the resulting contract if it is within the public's best interests (Cases 3-11 to 3-13).

CASE 3-1   Nonreliable Low Bidder Denied Contract

The second low bidder was properly awarded a public contract when the low bidder was deemed not to be responsible and reliable by its past performance, held the New York Supreme Court Appellate Division [*J. N. Futia Co., Inc. v. Office of General Services of the State of New York*, 39 A.D.2d 136 (App. Div., 3d Dept., 1972)].

New York State's Office of General Services solicited bids for certain repair work. The state determined that the contractor that submitted the low bid was not responsible and reliable because of previous delays and lack of cooperation with state personnel on other contracts and because of a poor evaluation of the low bidder's previous work.

The statute governing the awarding of public contracts provides that construction "must be offered for public bidding and may be awarded to the lowest responsible and reliable bidder. . . ." The court said that the state had the right to review the performance of the contractor and that its decision that the low bidder was not responsible and reliable was proper.

CASE 3-2   Contract Valid Despite Late Bid

Although the U.S. District Court for Maryland ruled that a low bid accepted four minutes late was improper, it denied the on-time low bidder any right to the contract.

A U.S. Army Corps of Engineers' readvertisment for bids specified that proposals would be accepted until 3 P.M. on a certain date. At this time the bid officer opened the bid depository and while the proposals were being separated but before it was announced that the bid time had arrived, a final contractor submitted its bid. The last bid, which was the low bid, was delivered about four minutes after the scheduled opening time.

A contractor whose bid was the lowest of those submitted before the deadline protested the acceptance of the late bid, but the bid officer denied the protest. The late bid was then protested to the Corps' district engineer, who also rejected the protest.

The Corps awarded the contract to the late bidder and told it to begin work. The firm immediately entered into several major subcontracts for the project. The protesting contractor then obtained a temporary restraining order prohibiting further work. A question arose whether the protesting contractor could enjoin the entire contract.

The court said "a party denied a government contract as a result of alleged illegal activity on the part of a federal agency in letting the contract to another bidder has standing . . . to bring suit for declaratory and injunctive relief in order to determine the validity of the agency's action."

It also said regulations provided that late hand-carried bids or any other late bid not submitted by mail or telegram could not be considered for award and that the late bid should not have been considered. The fact that the bidding officer did not indicate it was bid-opening time until five minutes after the specified time was an insufficient basis to extend the time, the court said. The purpose of the time limit, the court explained, is to prevent fraud and to give all bidders an equal opportunity.

But even though the court said the low bid was late, it refused to grant the on-time low bidder the remedy of injunction. The court said the proper low bidder maintained only its right to seek compensation for damages incurred, such as bid-preparation cost, because of illegal government action.

The court concluded:

> Given the availability of alternative relief for the Plaintiff by way of a suit for damages in the Court of Claims and a judicial policy which counsels against interference with the executive procurement process, the Court finds no inconsistencies in its judgment which denied injunctive relief while granting a declaratory judgment in favor of the Plaintiff [*William F. Wilke, Inc. v. Dept. of the Army* 357 F. Supp. 988 (D.C. Md. 1973), *aff'd* 485 F.2d 180 (1973)].

CASE 3-3   Strict Adherence to Bid-opening Times Properly Waived

The New Jersey Appellate Court has upheld the authority of a public agency to waive strict adherence to bid-opening times and ruled that a bid received after the scheduled time was valid.

A public agency, advertising for bids on an urban renewal project, specified that all bids were to be received and opened by 2 P.M. on a certain day. The invitations for bids also provided that the agency had the right "to waive any informalities in the bidding."

On the specified day, inclement weather delayed one of the bidders who telephoned to say he would be a few minutes late. Over the objections of the other bidders the agency's director decided not to open any bids until this bidder arrived. At 2:02 P.M. the last bidder appeared, and when all bids were opened, his firm was the lowest and won the contract.

Another bidder brought suit against the agency claiming that it violated the state competitive bidding law by receiving bids after the time designated in the advertisment.

In reviewing the case the court noted that the law's purpose is

> to benefit taxpayers by securing competition and guarding against favoritism, improvidence, extravagance and corruption.
>
> Under the circumstances presented here, [the court said,] we view the delay as a minor irregularity which was properly waived by the Agency under its inherent discretionary power ancillary to its duty to secure, through competitive bidding, the lowest responsible offer [*William M. Young & Co. v. West Orange Redeveloping Agency,* 311 A.2d 390 (1973)].

CASE 3-4 Low Bidder Not Low Enough

A contractor's claim that it was low bidder, based on the extended unit price it submitted rather than its flat unit price, was rejected by the Commonwealth Court of Pennsylvania. [*H. J. Williams Co., Inc. v. Dept. of Transport.,* 371 A.2d 553 (1977)].

A bid proposal for the Pennsylvania Department of Transportation specifically required the bidders to furnish unit prices for each item of work and to extend the unit price by the approximated quantities set forth in the proposal for a final figure. However, it also indicated that "the extensions and totals will not be considered as part of this proposal."

After the bid opening, the apparent low bidder was announced on the basis of its final figure, but it was later discovered that another bidder had made a mathematical error by adding a unit item twice. The owner then awarded the contract to the new low bidder with the corrected price.

The original low bidder sued, asking that either it be awarded the contract or the owner be required to rebid the contract.

The court denied the claim, saying that the errors were in the extensions and addition, which the proposal form states are not part of the bidder's proposal.

The owner's verification of the bids and the awarding of the contract based on the unit price, and not the extended price, was deemed to be part of the owner's public duty and obligation to award the contract to the lowest responsible bidder, said the court.

CASE 3-5 Improper Bid Bond Judged
Minor Irregularity

A Washington state appeals court has ruled that the innocent submission of an improper bid bond was only an immaterial irregularity and that a public owner could waive it and accept the low bid [*R. W. Rhine, Inc. v. City of Tacoma,* 536 P.2d 677 (1975)].

The City of Tacoma solicited bids for the demolition of buildings in preparation for an urban renewal project. The bid documents provided that no bid would be considered unless it was accompanied by a proper bid bond. However, the documents also permitted the city "to waive informalities in bids received whenever such rejection or waiver is in its interest."

Several days after bids had been submitted and the apparent low bidder chosen, the winning contractor notified the city that it had mixed up two bid bonds and submitted the wrong bond with its bid. At the contractor's request, the city exchanged the bonds.

Claiming that this was a material irregularity in the bidding procedure, the second low bidder sued to halt the contract award.

The court noted that the low bidder had obtained the proper bond prior to the submission of its bid and that it had acted in good faith in its dealings with the city.

"The test of whether or not an irregularity is material," the court said, "is whether or not it gives a bidder a substantial advantage or benefit not enjoyed by other bidders."

After reviewing the facts in this case, the court determined that the low bidder did not gain any material advantage or benefit over the other bidders. Therefore, it concluded that the filing of the wrong bond was an immaterial irregularity that could properly be waived by the city.

CASE 3-6   Town Waives Bid Specification

The Superior Court of New Jersey's Law Division has ruled that a contractor's irregular submission of bid security is a minor informality that can be waived by the municipality that solicits the bids [*Township of River Vale v. R. J. Longo Constr. Co., Inc.*, 316 A.2d 737 (1974)].

In an advertisement for bids to construct a sewer system, the Township of River Vale reserved the right to waive any "informalities, irregularities or minor defects in bids received." But it clearly stated that all bidders must furnish certified checks equal to 10 percent of their bids to insure against default.

Although these instructions specifically precluded the submission of bid bonds, the low bidder furnished a bid bond for 10 percent of the bid in lieu of the required certified check.

After the second low bidder protested the municipality's intent to award the contract to the low bidder, the following day the low bidder substituted a check for the bond.

To find out whether or not it had the right to award the contract to the low bidder, the township brought the question before the court for a determination.

Noting that the purpose of bidding requirements on public contracts is to protect the public interest and not the individual interest of the bidders, the court stated, "While this policy dictates only bids which comply with the specifications and instructions are acceptable, it also dictates, lest the primary purpose of achieving economy be unnecessarily frustrated, that minor irregularities and immaterial variances in the form of the bid not be permitted to result in its invalidation."

The court said this principle is further strengthened in situations "where the municipality has, as here, expressly reserved the right to waive such defects and there is no suggestion of any fraud, bad faith or collusion surrounding the transaction."

In this case, the court concluded that the submission of a bid bond did not "deprive the municipality of its assurance that the contract will be entered into, performed and guaranteed according to its specified requirements." Also, it said the waiver of this defect would not upset competitive bidding or give one bidder an advantage.

As a result, the court ruled that the township could award the contract to the low bidder because the submission of the bond in lieu of the check was an insubstantial defect that could be waived and properly cured by the low bidder after the opening of the bids.

CASE 3-7 An Owner Can Refuse to Waive
Minority-Hiring-Plan Error

A U.S. Court of Appeals has upheld a public owner's refusal to waive irregularities in a minority-hiring plan submitted by a low bidder [*Rossetti Contracting Co., Inc., v. Brennan*, 508 F.2d 1039 (7th Cir. 1975)].

Bid advertisements for construction of a federally funded sewer project in Illinois included provisions requiring bidders to submit a special Appendix A outlining how they planned to comply with the Chicago Plan for minority hiring.

After the low bid was submitted, the bidder offered an amended Appendix A correcting defects in its original submission. However, the owner, an Illinois sanitary district, refused to accept this correction, and the contractor turned to the courts for relief.

A lower court found that the error in the original Appendix A was inadvertent and that the contractor was, in fact, in compliance with the Chicago Plan. Because the error was minor and it could be corrected without undermining the purpose of the minority hiring plan, the court relied on a law "permitting the waiver of minor irregularities and correction of bid defects which do not go to the price, quantity or quality of the goods or services to be performed." The district appealed.

The appellate court assumed the bidder had acted in good faith and was in compliance with minority-employment goals. It noted that the original error in Appendix A was apparently a typographical error that would have resulted in unacceptable minority use and noncompliance with the law. The Chicago Plan, the court said, specifically provides that bids that do not comply must be deemed unresponsive.

It said "that, while admittedly Appendix A does not go to matters of price or quality of work, it has been made a matter of bid responsiveness. Clearly, under either federal or state law, unresponsive bids may not be corrected, after open ing, in order to make them responsive."

CASE 3-8 A Bid Was Lost Because Of
Unacknowledged Addendum

A low bidder's failure to acknowledge in its bid an amendment to the invitation for bids was grounds for the rejection of the bid, the U.S. Comptroller General has ruled [*Comptroller General of the United States*, Dec. B-166333 (Apr. 8, 1969)].

The contractor had bid on the construction of bachelor officers' quarters in Norfolk, Virginia at the invitation of the Naval Facilities Engineering Command. Its bid of approximately $1.6 million was about $20,000 lower than the next highest bid. The government proposed to reject the bid because it did not contain an acknowledgment of addendum 2 to the invitation for bids.

The addendum added a requirement calling for wall hydrants and increasing the minimum hourly wage rates to be paid under the Davis-Bacon Act. The contractor claimed that its bid price included the additional costs for the addendum but that it had inadvertently omitted to acknowledge the addendum.

The contractor appealed to the comptroller general.

The comptroller general called attention to the Armed Services Procurement Regulations (ASPR), §2-405, which permits correction or waiver of minor informalities or irregularities in bids.

It was not disputed that unacknowledged amendments could constitute minor informalities and be waived. However, "In addition to having no effect or merely a trivial effect on price, the unacknowledged amendment must also have no effect on . . . quantity for the absence of acknowledgment to be considered an informality" under ASPR, the comptroller general said. Since the addendum changed the quantity of work included in the bid by requiring wall hydrants, a failure to acknowledge it was not a minor informality but was fatal to the bid, it concluded.

CASE 3-9   Failure to Submit a Hiring Plan Ruled a Minor Defect

The Supreme Court of Wyoming has ruled that a contractor's failure to include an affirmative-action plan in its low bid on a public contract was only a minor defect and that a city awarding agency could not reject the bid as a result of this flaw.

A bid package on a sewage-disposal plant in Wyoming, which was to be jointly funded by a city utility board and the federal Environmental Protection Agency (EPA), specifically required each bidder to submit an affirmative-action plan along with its bid. When the bids were submitted, however, the low bidder failed to present its minority-hiring plan. Although this oversight was corrected before the city reached its final decision on the contract award, the board passed over the low bid and selected the next lowest bidder. The contractor sued, claiming that the board's decision violated a bidding statute that required public contracts to "be let to lowest responsible bidder."

In court, the board acknowledged its obligation to award contracts to the lowest bidder but argued that in this case the contractor's failure to meet the specification for a hiring plan constituted a material departure from bid requirements and invalidated the bid.

Although the court confirmed the principle of law that the owner was relying on, it also stated:

> A minor technical defect or irregularity which does not affect the substance of a bid will not justify rejection of the lowest bid by a public body . . . because to do so would deny the people the benefit of the low bid. One of the considerations given to a determination as to whether a departure from bid specifications is material is whether or not a variation would give a bidder an advantage or benefit not allowed to other bidders so as to destroy the competitive character of the bidding process [*Centric Corp. v. Barbarossa & Sons, Inc.*, 521 P.2d 874 (1974)].

Noting that all the bids complied with EPA guidelines, which did not require the submission of hiring plans, and that the lack of the affirmative-action plan did not give the contractor an unfair advantage, the court said the board could not reject the bid for the reason it gave.

CASE 3-10 Rejection of Low Bidder Due to Labor Strike Held Improper

The Supreme Court of New York, Appellate Division, ruled as improper the rejection by the state of a low bid because a local labor union official warned the state that a labor dispute existed and that if the contract was awarded the project site would be picketed.

After the Office of General Services announced the low bidder for some demolition work on the $1 billion South Mall project in Albany, the business representative of the laborers' union told the state it was involved in a labor dispute with the low bidder. The state was told also that if the contract was awarded to the low bidder, picketing would spread to the South Mall project.

The state then notified the bidders that all bids were rejected "in the best interests of the State" and told one of the general contractors on the project to begin soliciting bids for the demolition work.

The low bidder filed suit to restrain the general contractor from soliciting bids and to compel the state to award the contract on the basis of the original bids. The low bidder claimed the state's actions were arbitrary and capricious, in violation of public policy, and not in the state's best interests.

The state argued the bidder could not satisfactorily complete the contract due to its labor problems and since all other bids were substantially higher, it was in the state's best interest to reject all bids.

The court, in a split decision said there was no proof of the nature and extent of the labor dispute, nor was there evidence that the state made any effort to investigate the facts. It concluded:

> In our view, it was an abuse of discretion to reject all bids on the facts that were before the awarding agency. If we permit a bid rejection based on less than well-established facts and sound judgment, we could be sanctioning the elimination of the lowest responsible bidder by an apparent threat of a third party [*Matter of Cristo, Inc. v. State of New York,* 42 App. Div.2d 481 (3d Dept. 1973)].

CASE 3-11 Negotiated Contract Valid Although It Violated Bidding Law

A suit seeking to set aside the award of a public contract because it violated a city's competitive bidding statute was denied by the Court of Appeals of Maryland due to the unusual nature of the contract [*Hylton vs. Mayor and City Council of Baltimore,* 300 A.2d 656 (1972)].

The city of Baltimore let a contract for construction of a resource-recovery solid-waste disposal system. The city did not call for competitive bids but awarded the contract on a negotiated basis. Baltimore residents filed suit alleging that the contract violated city-charter regulations requiring competitive bidding. They claimed that failure to comply renders the contract null and void.

Before awarding the contract, the city had prepared contract documents and solicited bids for the waste-disposal system, but all bids were rejected because none met specification requirements. The city then explored the possibility of obtaining a federal Environmental Protection Agency (EPA) demonstration grant to help fund the project.

EPA rules require that to be eligible for such a grant a city must submit only one proposal. And the system could not be a duplicate of a full-scale operating system nor could it be a fully untested one. The city investigated many system alternatives, but only one met its requirements. On the submission of this proposal to EPA, the agency awarded the city a $6 million grant.

The court stated that the purpose of the city's competitive bidding requirements is to obtain the best work at the lowest price and to safeguard public funds. It explained however, that there are occasions when those requirements cannot be complied with while safeguarding public funds at the same time. The court said that in this instance, where the service sought by "a municipality can by its nature be furnished by one and only one source, competition simply is not possible."

It is clear that public funds were not in jeopardy of being misapplied, the court said, and that the best price was obtained without competitive bids. It said that the city was not merely seeking a waste-disposal system from among a choice of alternatives. What the city required, the court said, "was a particular system, materially different from all others enabling it successfully to compete with other municipalities for a demonstration grant."

To apply for the grant, the court explains, the city had to preselect a particular process and persuade EPA that the process should be demonstrated so that if it worked on a full scale, other municipalities could adopt it without misgivings.

Basing its decision on the uniqueness of the system, the method by which EPA awards grants, and on evidence that the public interest was safeguarded, the court ruled that the contract was valid even though the competitive bidding requirements were not met.

CASE 3-12   No Contract For Low Bidder In Turnkey Housing Project

A contractor that was the low responsible bidder for a low-rent housing project was denied the contract despite the existence of a state statute stipulating that the low bidder shall be awarded the contract. The New Jersey Supreme Court held that the statute requiring competitive bidding and contract award to the low bidder was not applicable to federally assisted turnkey projects [*Lehigh Constr. Co. v. Housing Authority of the City of Orange*, 56 N.J. 447, 267 A.2d 41 (1970)].

A local municipal housing authority that had been created to administer a turnkey housing project which would be built with financial assistance from the Department of Housing and Urban Development (HUD) awarded the contract to other than the low bidder. The low-bidding contractor filed suit claiming that the authority's action was illegal since it was required by statute to give the contract to the low bidder.

The housing authority argued that the state statute was not applicable to federally assisted turnkey low-rent housing projects.

The court concluded that while the cost of construction on a turnkey housing project is of primary concern, the owner is equally, if not more concerned with design and overall construction quality of the entire housing project. The court held that the general need for competitive bidding was not applicable to this type of turnkey housing project.

The court noted that HUD required that its manual be adopted and used by local authorities for this type of federally assisted project and that the manual neither requires nor permits competitive bidding of the type specified by the statute. The court found that if the strictures of the state law were imposed by judicial interpretation, federal turnkey-project assistance might not be available for the state. The court held the municipality correct in disregarding the statute.

CASE 3-13   Bidding Laws Do Not Bar Turnkey Project

A contract for construction of federally assisted low-income housing on a turn-key basis did not violate the New York state competitive bidding law, according to the Supreme Court of New York, Rockland County.

The question arose in the town of Ramapo, where the town board had applied for federal assistance to enable its housing authority to contract for low-income and elderly housing. The housing authority subsequently advertised for construction proposals in compliance with the turnkey program of the Department of Housing and Urban Development (HUD). Six proposals were received, ranging in cost from $1 million to $6 million, with the acreage to be used ranging from 1 to 26 acres. One proposal was approved by the town board, the housing authority, and HUD, and a contract was awarded.

Various residents of the town then started legal proceedings to halt all work on the project, contending that the turnkey program violated the state's competitive-bidding and noncollusive-bidding-certification laws and that the resulting contract was null and void.

In ruling that the competitive bidding statutes do not apply to federally assisted low-income turnkey projects, the court stressed the difference between a turnkey contract and a contract awarded to the lowest responsible bidder for construction of a building according to a town's design and on town property.

> "Turnkey" operates only in those areas where the governing body of the community has certified a need for low-income housing, [the court said]. "Turnkey" permits a developer to submit proposals regarding property he owns or will own at the time of construction. The developer uses his own architects and presents an original design. This flexibility in design, and such entrepreneur participation, are factors often absent from usual public housing construction.

The state statutes, the court said, are intended to foster "honest competition in order to obtain the best work or supplies at the lowest possible price" and to deter fraud and corruption and are for the taxpayers' benefit. While conceding that a contract not let in accordance with the law is null and void, the court said,

"If 'turnkey' is to remain a viable concept, providing quality low-income housing expeditiously and at substantial savings, State bidding legislation must yield."

To hold otherwise, the court explained,

> "would lead to absurd results: that despite this State's overwhelming need for low-income housing, its public policy favoring participation of private enterprise in such construction, and the Legislature's specific direction to housing authorities to cooperate and to do all necessary to obtain Federal financing assistance, such projects must be frustrated in furtherance of a policy which bears no relationship to the evils it was designed to remedy."

Even if the state competitive bidding law and the federal turnkey program could not be deemed compatible, the court said,

> "where . . . compliance with both regulatory schemes would impair efforts to carry out the Federal interest, the State statutes are superseded to the extent both regulatory schemes are inconsistent [*Matter of Marino v. Town of Ramapo*, 68 Misc.2d 44 (1971)]."

FOUR

Mistaken Bid

On public bids and on many private bids the bidder is often obligated, by statute or bidding requirements, to furnish a bid bond, certified check, cash, or other security to assure the owner that the bidder will accept the contract if awarded. If the contractor does not accept the contract, as awarded, the security is subject to forfeit. Usually the security represents a percentage of the bid price and is to protect the owner against the default of a bidder refusing to accept the contract and to compensate the owner for the additional cost it may be forced to incur in going to the second bidder. As further security, the owner often requires, again either by statute or bidding requirements, that the bidder not be able to withdraw its bid for a given length of time. This allows the owner a time to review, analyze, and award the contract. On its face, most bidding documents seem to make it mandatory that the bidder stand behind its bid for any and all reasons, and if the bidder should attempt to withdraw its bid after opening, it would forfeit its security and possibly become liable for the difference between the low bidder and the second bidder. This conclusion is not per se legally mandated, however.

Often the low bidder, after bids are opened, realizes or believes that it has made a mistake in its bid sufficient to warrant its withdrawal of the bid. This withdrawal might be before or after the contract has been awarded. The contractor has rights regardless of what the bid documents appear to state. The courts have recognized that a contractor is entitled to withdraw its bid for major mistakes in bid under certain circumstances, without any liability or forfeiture on its part or on the part of its surety (Case 4-1).

The contractor's right to withdraw its bid is not an automatic right. The actions of the contractor are carefully reviewed by the court.

> The essential conditions to such relief by way of rescission for mistake are (1) the mistake must be of so great a consequence that to enforce the contract as actually made would be unconscionable; (2) the matter as to which the mistake was made relates to the material feature of the contract; (3) the mistake must have occurred notwithstanding the exercise of reasonable care by the party making the mistake; and (4) it must be able to get relief by way of rescission without serious prejudice to the other party, except for loss of his bargain [*Conduit & Foundation Corp. v. Atlantic City*, 64 A.2d 382 (1949)].

Although each court and jurisdiction will have modifications to this principle of law, the decision of the New Jersey court does outline the basic concepts of established case law. It should first be noted that the majority of decisions which allow the contractor relief for a mistake in bid grant to the contractor only the right to have its bid and award rescinded. This means that the contractor can have its bid treated as if it were nonexistent. The contractor normally does not have the right to come in, correct its mistake, and receive an award and contract based on a revised figure. Although this is not an absolute statement, it appears that a contractor will be awarded a contract at a higher price only if there has been a mistake which can be determined on the face of the bid and which the owner might treat as a minor informality or irregularity.

However, in one case, after going out for public bids for construction of a school, a public board of education released the low bidder due to a bid mistake. The contract was to be awarded to the second bidder, who then alleged a mistake. The mistake, apparently provable, was less than the difference in price between the second bidder and its bid. The bidder agreed to take the contract provided it either be given the increased price or an equal reduction in the amount of work by contract changes. The owner agreed to the latter, and the contract was awarded. During performance disputes arose, and eventually the contractor and owner came to a parting of the ways and a completing contractor was called in. During the ensuing lawsuit, a claim arose by the owner that the original contract was an illegal contract. In reviewing the validity of the contract, the court held:

> We do not mean to suggest that the Board, even acting in good faith, could avoid the obligation to solicit an additional round of bids if the changes involved were significant enough to involve a substantial possibility that another bidder might undercut Fabrizio [contractor] on the amended construction plans. The public is entitled under the statute to have the job done at the lowest cost. The possibility of achieving a bid lower than Fabrizio's on the plans as changed, however, does not appear to us substantial, considering the monetary value of the changes in light of the contract price and the amount by which other contractors' bids would have exceeded Fabrizio's price on the original plans. [Thus,] the Board did not violate the sanctity of the public bidding statutes and . . . the Board by its decision gave the public that which the statute was designed to give it—a contract based upon the lowest bid [*Fabrizio & Martin, Inc. v. Board of Education*, 523 F.2d 378 (2d Cir. 1975)].

Unless the bid is governed by a specific statute or regulation allowing the increase in price, the bidder should assume that a successful argument for mistaken bid will result in rescission and release of all liability between the respective parties and not a price increase.

Being granted rescission for mistake in bid is essentially an equitable relief and requires an honest unintentional mistake [*People v. John W. Rouse Constr. Corp.*, 274 N.Y.S.2d 981 (1966)]. Obviously, it is not purely a contractual remedy, as the contractual requirements would seem to call for the opposite decision. The equitable aspect is apparent from the first requirement for rescission. The trend is to hold that when something is so "unconscionable" as to be against the sense of justice and right, the courts will not enforce it. To become unconscionable, the mistake cannot be a minor one. The mistake must be of great consequence. Since relief for mistaken bid is founded in equity, the bidder must be continuously cognizant of the equity maxims that "he who seeks equity must do equity" and "he who seeks equity must have clean hands." The bidder must be prepared to bare its soul to prove how unconscionable it would be to have a contract forced upon it. It must prove its innocence.

The second requirement is that the mistake must relate to a material feature of the contract. Obviously, if the mistake relates to a minor aspect of the contract, it would probably not be of such great consequence that to enforce the contract would be unconscionable.

The hardest element to prove is what would seem to be the easiest: the contractor cannot just claim "I made a mistake." Such an unsupported exclamation does not further its cause. The contractor must *prove* where and how it made a mistake and that the mistake occurred "notwithstanding the exercise of reasonable care." All too often the contractor is denied rescission because it is unable to prove where or how it made its mistake. The documents upon which it prepared its estimates and takeoff have been thrown away. Disposal is a cardinal sin. The contractor should keep every single piece of paper used directly or indirectly in determining its estimates and bid prices. It should immediately open up a separate filing system for those documents. Do not throw them away, even after the bid is submitted. Often the basis for the contractor's price becomes of utmost importance during or even after the job, when another claim arises. If the piece of paper has a figure or quantity or related data on it, it should not be thrown away. Although an architect or engineer may recommend that the owner not award the contract to a low bidder because it alleges a mistake, unless you can prove the mistake, the owner's representative may be improperly exercising the owner's discretion and subjecting the owner to liability by consenting to the withdrawal. It must be remembered that on public works it is customarily mandated by the legislation that the lowest competitive price be accepted. Unless the contractor can prove its mistake, the owner is under a legal obligation to award the contract in accord with the low bid.

Even if the first three criteria are satisfied, the contractor still is not automatically entitled to rescission. To obtain relief, courts normally hold that the owner should be losing only the benefit of an inequitable bargain. The courts' rationale seems to be that the owner is not prejudiced by being able to accept the second bid promptly since, in fact, the second bid is a proper bid after the first bidder has proved its mistake. By accepting the second bid, the owner will be getting what it will pay for. However, if the bidder waits too long before protesting its mistake, or if the owner is seriously prejudiced by the low bidder's failure to protest properly, relief may not be granted. Prejudice may result if the second and third bidders' bids have been withdrawn with the passage of time or funding commitments have expired. Bidders with any suggestion of a mistaken bid should immediately go on record, in properly written form, and register their protest.

Although it is the bidder's obligation to protest, claim, and prove its mistake in bid, the owner is not totally void of responsibilities. In various jurisdictions, both by regulation and case law, the owner is under an obligation to call an apparent mistake to the contractor's attention. As stated by the Comptroller General of the United States,

> We have consistently held that the responsibility for preparation of a bid rests with the bidder. Therefore, a bidder who makes a mistake in a bid which has been accepted in good faith by the Government must bear the consequences *unless* the mistake was mutual or the contracting officer had either actual or constructive notice of the mistake prior to award. . . . It is equally well established, however, that if a material mistake is made by one party to a contract and the mistake is known by the other party, or because of accompanying circumstances the other party had reason to know of the mistake, the latter party has no right to take advantage of the mistake and the party making the mistake has the right to rescission and restitution [*Comptroller General of the United States*, B-165573 (1969)].

This obligation of federal contracting officers is governed by the Armed Services Procurement Regulations:

> After the opening of bids, contracting officers shall examine all bids for mistakes. In cases of apparent mistakes, and in cases where the contracting officer has reason to believe that a mistake may have been made, he shall request from the bidder a verification of the bid, calling attention to the suspected mistake [ASPR §2-406.1].

Although this obligation is a regulatory one, it has its basis on sound equitable principles. Similar rulings might arise and should be argued even in jurisdictions without such a regulation.

To avoid the inequitable consequences, and to avoid the argument that the owner knew or should have known of the mistakes, many owners when dealing with prime contractors and many prime contractors when dealing with subcontractors have the standard operating procedure of seeking verification of all bidders' prices. Courts have consistently ruled that an owner's actions after verification substantially if not totally reduce the owner's liability and satisfy its equitable responsibility; and that a contractor after verification, "cannot now be heard to say that the figure should be changed" [*Peter A. Camilli & Sons, Inc. v. State of New York*, 245 N.Y.S.2d 521 (1963)] (See Case 4-2). The act of verification should not be loosely performed, as knowledge of errors in the bid documents will preclude recovery of related claims (Case 4-3). Once verification is sought by the other party, the contractor should carefully and with sound cross-checking procedures review its bid. This may, and probably should, require the services of an estimator other than the one who prepared the original bid. Only after a verification has *in fact* been made should verification be issued. The consequences of improper verification are too drastic to be taken lightly.

The types of mistakes which are subject to rescission are not all-inclusive; they have been generally recognized as including mistakes in transposing figures, quantities, and interpretation of bid documents; however, relief has been denied when the mistake is one of judgment. To argue mistake need not require proof of fraud or inequitable conduct on the part of the other party. As stated in a New York case where the contractor was granted rescission for mistake resulting from its misinterpretation of the specifications,

> There is a difference between faulty judgment, such as underestimating the cost of labor and materials, and a mistake in the interpretation of the contract resulting in the omission of substantial items from the bid calculations. The first is a mistake in the estimate of value. "Practically never is this such a mistake as will justify rescission. The parties are conscious of the uncertainity of value. Value is one of the principal subjects of the agreement. Each party is consciously assuming the risk of error of judgment." The second is not a mistake as to value, but as to a material factor affecting value and for such a mistake relief will be given in a proper case . . . [*Balaban Gordon v. Brighton Sewer Dist.,* 323 N.Y.S.2d 724 (1971)]

If the bidder has made a mistake, it is advised to protest the award of any contract immediately, give notice of the mistake, and seek equitable relief with the issuing authority and in the courts if so mandated. The bidder is again advised to be aware of whether legislative or regulatory rules exist governing the procedure to be undertaken in case of mistakes in bids. These rules must be adhered to for relief. Mistakes may be overcome if properly pursued.

CASE 4-1   Bid Can Be Rescinded Because of Mistake in Cost Computation

The U.S. District Court for the Southern District of Iowa has held that a contractor should be permitted to have its bid rescinded due to a mistake in bid computation even though bid documents disallowed bid withdrawal [*M. J. McGough Co. v. Jane Lamb Memorial Hospital,* 302 F. Supp. 482 (D.C.S.D. Iowa (1969)].

A competitive bid had been submitted by the contractor for improvements to an Iowa hospital. A bid bond in the amount of $100,000 accompanied the bid. When bids were opened it was discovered that the contractor was low by more than 10 percent.

The contractor immediately requested that its bid be withdrawn. The hospital asked for bid-error verification and awarded the contract to the second lowest bidder, attempting to hold the low bidder liable for the difference in costs.

The cause of the bid mistake was attributed to a subcontractor's bid received at the last minute and erroneously recorded as $22,000 instead of $222,000.

In deliberating whether the contractor could get out from under the provisions of the bid, the court noted that the contractor gave immediate notice to the hospital that it made a mistake and intended to withdraw its bid. Noting that an opposing opinion exists, the court nevertheless stated that "by the overwhelming weight of authority, a contractor may be relieved from a unilateral mistake in his bid by rescission under the proper circumstances." Prerequisites cited by the court for such relief are (1) the mistake must be of such consequence that enforcement would be unconscionable; (2) the mistake must relate to the substance of the consideration; (3) the mistake must have occurred despite the exercise of ordinary care; and (4) it must be possible to place the other party in *status quo*.

Under these legal guidelines the court held that the contractor and the surety would be entitled to relief of rescission since the contractor had made every effort to explain its mistake to the hospital and that notice of the mistake had come before the hospital's acceptance of the bid. "The mere opening of the bids did not constitute the acceptance of the lowest bid," and furthermore, ruled the court, "it is generally held that acceptance prior to notification does not bar the right to equitable relief from a mistake in the bid."

The court found an honest mistake, and that to allow the hospital to take advantage of a clerical error would be clearly unconscionable, especially when the hospital was aware of the mistake before it tried to accept the bid.

With regard to the provision prohibiting bid withdrawal for forty-five days, the court noted, "it is sufficient to say that provisions such as these have been considered many times in similar cases and have never been held effective when equitable considerations dictate otherwise."

The court's ruling was that no contract existed between the hospital and contractor. The contractor's bid was deemed rescinded, and the surety was released from further liability.

**CASE 4-2   Bid Mistake After Verification
            Not Correctable**

A contractor who, at the government's request, corrected one mistake in its bid and verified the rest of the bid was not entitled to compensation for a second mistake found after the contract was awarded, the U.S. Comptroller General has ruled.

The case involved bidding on a reserve center maintenance shop in Wisconsin. After the bids were opened, it was learned that the low bidder's price of $817,043 was $80,000 less than the next low bid and $110,000 under estimate.

A government representative telephoned the contractor and requested a bid verification. The contractor found one mistake of $12,000, corrected it and verified the rest of the bid. It received a contract award after the bid had been adjusted to compensate for the mistake. Several months later the contractor discovered a second mistake involving a misplaced decimal point and requested additional compensation.

The comptroller general did not question the existence or the validity of the mistake because the contractor's records could substantiate the existence of the mistake. The question, however, was not whether there was a bid error, "but whether a valid and binding contract was consummated by the acceptance thereof." The contractor argued that since the government had its work sheets, which indicated the mistake, it was the government's duty to find the mistake and call it to the contractor's attention.

In denying the contractor's claim, the comptroller general held that there was no legal basis for the claim and stated,

> We do not believe that . . . the contracting officer had a further duty to minutely examine such worksheets for the purpose of discovering whether any other errors were made by the corporation in computing its bid prices for the entire job. After the error in the bid . . . was corrected, the contracting officer was not only justified in awarding the contract on the corporation's bid, as corrected, as the lowest received, but would have failed in his duty had he done otherwise.
>
> The acceptance, after confirmation, of the bid . . . was in good faith and under the circumstances consummated a valid and binding contract which fixed the rights and liabilities of the parties [*Comptroller General of the United States,* Dec. B-167864 (Oct. 10, 1969)].

CASE 4-3   Knowledge of Error
Barred Extra-Cost Claim

The U.S. Court of Claims has denied a contractor's claim for the increased costs of complying with a defective contract document because it found that the contractor had acknowledged and accepted the defect when it verified its erroneous bid.

A contract drawing detailing the replacement of an underground cable at a military installation in New Jersey contained two different scales. After a contractor estimated and bid the job using the wrong scale, it requested additional costs for performing the work in accordance with the correct scale.

The Armed Services Board of Contract Appeals found that the error was an obvious one that should have been discovered by the contractor during the bidding stage, and it denied the contractor's claim.

On appeal, the U.S. Court of Claims confirmed the board's ruling. It pointed out that on the date that the bids were opened, the government had requested a bid verification from the contractor. When none was forthcoming, the government official contacted the contractor. During a conversation, the contractor said that it realized that two different scales existed. At this point, the contractor was given a choice of either confirming the bid or withdrawing it.

The contractor later testified that it confirmed the bid without qualification because it feared possible repercussions on future government work.

As a result, the court concluded:

> If a contractor enters into a contract aware of the fact of defective specifications, it is not entitled to recover a claim based on these defective specifications.

At the time it was requested to verify its bid, the [contractor] was aware of the drawing scale error, and whatever duty the government may have had before to advise the [contractor] of the error faded. . . . If the [contractor] embarked on a "ruinous course of action," it was a journey it chose to take with its eyes wide open. It certainly did not act reasonably under the circumstances and the board rightly denied its claim [*Wickham, Inc., v. United States Ct. Cl.* 327-75 (Dec. 15, 1976)].

FIVE

Formation and Existence of a Contract

The performance of billions of dollars of construction work every year is done pursuant to contractual agreements. It is imperative that contractor and counsel have a good, practical, working knowledge of the basic legal requirements necessary for the formation and existence of a contract. Although there are untold number of types of contracts, variations in form, and subtleties, the contractor's obligation and initial concern is much more basic. With the proper understanding of the basic requirements for the formation of a legal contract, the contractor will be better able to avoid pitfalls, lawsuits, and liability. Three essential contractual requirements are (1) an offer, (2) an acceptance of that offer, and (3) consideration.

The first mandatory ingredient for a contract is the existence of an offer. There is no set format. It can take various forms. It may be written or oral, depending on local statutes and case law. It may be long or short. However, in all cases the offer must be *clear and definite*. It *cannot* be uncertain in terms and provisions.

Although generally the offer has no prerequisite form, many bidding requirements, whether they are public or private contracts, require that set formats be used. The failure to follow a specified procedure on a specified contract may result in the offer's being deemed nonresponsive and unacceptable.

The offer must be clear enough to be acceptable. The standard offer in the construction industry takes the form of a bid or a proposal. A public agency's invitation for bids, request for quotations, or requests for proposals are not offers which can be accepted to form a binding contract [*Kingston Bituminous Products Co. v. N. J. Turnpike Authority*, 192 A.2d 836 (1963)]; instead they are merely requests for offers so that the requesting authority can review such offers and, subject to guidelines, determine whether or not it wishes to accept them. If an offer lacks sufficient clarity, the court will deem it a nullity, and even if the offer was allegedly accepted, no contract will result as a proper offer was not present. The mere offer to build a structure for $10,000 does not have sufficient detail on which to establish a contract, especially when there are no preexisting plans, specifications, conceptual drawings, or other indications of the scope of the work. The contractor must carefully define the scope of work included in its offer.

Once a clear and definite offer has been established, the next question is how long that offer remains open for acceptance. Many bid documents and statutory requirements specify a length of time the offer must remain open and be subject to acceptance. The requirement that the offer be deemed nonwithdrawable for a length of time is usually deemed valid. Unless some legally excusable reason is proved, e.g., a mistake in bid, the offer must remain open for the specified time. If no time span is specified, the offer will remain alive according to case law and be subject to acceptance for a reasonable period of time. At the end of that reasonable period of time the offer will be legally dead. It is the judge who will determine what a reasonable period of time is. There is a large gray area in defining a reasonable and unreasonable time.

If there is no enforceable provision that the offer remain open for a specified time, the offer can be withdrawn any time before acceptance. Once the offer is withdrawn, it can no longer be the basis for a contract. There are a myriad of cases hinging on when the withdrawal of the offer becomes effective. This is especially true when the offer has been made by one means of communication and the acceptance is made by the same or another mode of communication, e.g., where the acceptance has not been received by the offeror when it withdraws its offer. There is no hard-and-fast rule, and the nuances differ from case to case.

A recent major area of dispute is whether or not the bidder incorporates as part of its bid certain standard or nonstandard general terms and conditions [*S. J. Groves & Son Co. v. L. M. Pike & Son, Inc.,* 340 N.Y.S.2d 230 (1973)]. Specifically, if a subcontractor is submitting a bid to a prime contractor for whom that subcontractor has done numerous projects before and with whom he has always signed the contractor's standard contract form without major alteration, is it presumed that the new bid of the subcontractor automatically includes the standard terms and conditions? Does the subcontractor have the right subsequently to refuse to accept the contractor's standard form of agreement? It would appear that if the parties had a standing procedure to use a set contract form without major modification from one project to another, the submission of an offer might well incorporate, by implication, the understanding that the final contract will be in the standard form. In order to avoid the potential dispute over what terms are included in the offer, several contractors now require that bids be made on their forms, which specifically acknowledge and bind the subcontractor to the general conditions and standard-form subcontract. These forms should be furnished to the bidder before submission of its bid or be indicated and available for review.

The acceptance part of the formation of a contract is often hard to discern in the daily construction activities. To be valid and create a contractual agreement the acceptance must be an acceptance of what was offered. Once an acceptance modifies any substantive part of the original offer, the acceptance becomes ineffective. It is generally recognized that an acceptance which changes a substantive aspect of the offer is, in fact, a counteroffer, and making a counteroffer terminates the original offer (Case 5-1). Thereafter, the original offer is no longer in existence and can no longer be accepted. Negotiations amount to a series of offers and counteroffers. There must be a mutual understanding (Case 5-2).

A subcontractor's submission of a bid for specified work (an offer) and the contractor's acknowledgment that the subcontractor has the job may constitute the contract. The contractor's subsequent forwarding to the subcontractor of its 50-page subcontract form and insistence upon its execution may well be deemed an improper act and constitute a breach of contract by the contractor: if no formal contract had come into existence, that standard form might be a counteroffer, relieving the subcontractor from any further obligations.

The acceptance must be within the time stipulated in the offer or within the period that the offer must remain open, or if no time is so stipulated within a reasonable time. Obviously, it must be before the legal withdrawal of the offer. If the time has expired for the duration of the offer, it is the offeror's alternative to extend the time [19 Comp. Gen. 356 (1939) and 46 Comp. Gen. 371 (1966)].

If no acceptance is in existence, no contract will be found. This may happen where a subcontractor submits an offer to the prime contractor, who then uses the subcontractor's price in preparation of its prime contract bid and possibly lists the subcontractor's name but gives the eventual subcontract to another. The subcontractor's remedy is in doubt (Case 5-3). There appear to be conflicting decisions, depending upon whether it was a contractual obligation of the prime contractor to specify the subcontractor's name.

The establishment of the offer and the acceptance leads the court to the third consideration, consideration. There must be some form of legal consideration for an offer and acceptance to constitute a valid contract. Consideration can take various forms. Usually it is financial compensation, but it may be a return promise, mutual obligations, or some other substantive, good, and valuable thing. A contract is said not to come into existence if the alleged consideration flowing from one party to the other is merely the performance of an act which that party was already legally obligated to perform. This legalism has come into play in various situations involving changes and extras, even when evidenced by signed change orders. If the party has been given a signed change order calling for additional compensation for doing what it was already under a legal and contractual obligation to perform, there has been no true change or consideration for additional compensation. It is strongly suggested that details of the consideration be clearly delineated in the offer, acceptance, and contract.

Contracts can be found to exist by deeds or other acts. The acceptance need not be in words; it can be implied (Cases 5-4 to 5-6). The owner is not entitled to withhold the performance of some ministerial act and thereby attempt to void an otherwise valid contract (Case 5-7).

Other principles of law and legal requirements come into play in formation of the contract, but they are basically variations on the theme already discussed. A common expression is that for a valid contract to exist there must be a "meeting of the minds" (Case 5-8). This is true. As recently stated, "In order for a valid contract to exist the parties must assent to the same thing in the same sense, and their minds must meet as to all the terms" [*Howel v. Allen*, 174 S.E.2d 55 (1970)]. There must be a mutuality of obligation between the parties. It is again strongly stressed that the contractor must take care in preparing the terms and conditions of its contract, since one "will not be subjected to a contractual obligation where the character of that obligation is so indefinite and uncertain as to its terms and requirements that it is impossible to state with reasonable certainty the obligation involved" [(*Dale's Service Co. v. Jones*, 534 P.2d 1102) (1975)].

Although a court will enforce an agreement although it represents a bad deal for one side (Case 5-9), even if the elements of an offer, acceptance, and consideration can be found, the court will not enforce any alleged agreement deemed to be against public policy or illegal. In fact, where criminal acts were committed in obtaining the contract and the contract has been performed, a contractor may be denied recovery of contract balances and be obligated to return all monies previously paid to it (Case 5-10). Numerous decisions have questioned the right of a party to be compensated for services when that party is not licensed to offer the services rendered (Cases 5-11 to 5-13).

CASE 5-1   Response to Readvertisement was Rescission of Earlier Contract

A contractor's submission of a bid in response to owner's readvertisement for proposals was ruled by the Supreme Court of Minnesota to be an acceptance of the owner's offer to rescind a previous contract which had been awarded the contractor on the basis of low bid [*Minnesota, Ltd., Inc. v. Public Utilities Commission of Hibbing*, 208 N.W.2d 284 (1973)].

The contractor was notified that it was awarded a municipal contract and that it would receive formal contract documents. Several days later, the owner requested the contractor's permission to cancel the contract. Despite the contractor's refusal, the owner advertised for new bids on slightly modified specifications. The contractor submitted a new bid but was not low bidder. It then sued the owner for breach of the first contract.

The court did not question the legality of the original contract, which it assumed was valid. The question was whether the first contract was rescinded. The court said "parties to a bilateral contract may rescind the contract by mutual consent. Mutual consent to rescind a contract . . . may be inferred from the attendant circumstances and conduct of the parties."

It ruled that the request for new bids by the owner constituted an offer to rescind the original agreement and the contractor's resubmission of a bid was reasonably interpreted as its acceptance of that offer. The court ruled that the contractor had no claim for damages since no contract had been breached.

CASE 5-2   Borrow Permit Not A Contract: No Mutuality of Obligation

A contractor was not liable for damages under a unilateral contract because mutuality of obligation did not exist, the Supreme Court of Idaho has ruled.

A contractor approached the plaintiff to inquire whether it could remove certain rock from the plaintiff's land for use in a flood-control project. The plaintiff agreed and a written document, called a *borrow permit*, was drawn up. The borrow permit granted the contractor permission to enter the plaintiff's property to quarry rock and to pay the plaintiff a set unit price for rock actually removed.

When the plaintiff discovered that the contractor was not quarrying the rock, it sued the contractor for failure to live up to the terms of the contract. The contractor argued that since there was no bilateral contract, there was no obligation to remove any rock.

The court held that

> A careful reading of the "Borrow Permit" indicates that it is nothing more than a unilateral offer which was to be accepted by performance. . . . The standard test for finding a bilateral contract between two parties is whether or not there is "mutuality of obligation" [*Green v. Beaver State Contractors, Inc.,* 93 Idaho 741, 472 P.2d 307 (1970)].

In this case the court ruled that the contractor was under no legal obligation to quarry rock from lands owned by the plaintiff and that the effect of the borrow permit was to give the contractor permission to quarry rock if it so desired and that if it did remove the rock to pay a set price.

CASE 5-3   Use of Subcontractor's Bid Not Enough To Create A Contract

The New York Supreme Court Appellate Division has rejected a subcontractor's claim for damages against a general contractor who used his bid and then selected another subcontractor. The inclusion of the subcontractor's bid and name in the prime contractor's bid to the owner did not by itself create a binding contract between the two contractors, the court said.

The prime contractor informed the subcontractor that it intended to submit a bid for certain work and requested the subcontractor to submit its bid for a portion of the work. It then used it in its own bid for the prime contract. And it named the subcontractor as the firm that would perform the work covered by the subcontractor's bid. After the prime contract was awarded, the subcontractor was told that another firm would get the subcontract. The subcontractor then sued the prime contractor for breach of contract.

The lower court upheld the subcontractor's claim that it had a valid contract. Although a valid contract cannot come into existence without an offer and an acceptance, the acceptance need not be by direct communication to the offeror, the court said. Here, the general contractor accepted the subcontractor's offer by its overt act and conduct in utilizing the subcontractor's bid and name, it ruled.

The lower court's decision was overruled on appeal. In holding that the subcontractor did not have a binding contract, the Appellate Division said:

> There is a certain equity in requiring the contractor to give the subcontractor the job where he has made use of the subcontractor's name and figures in securing a contract. On the other hand, under equally sound contract principles, an acceptance of a bilateral contract is not only a manifestation of assent to the proposition but is a giving of the return promise requested. In order to complete a bilateral contract, the offeree [prime contractor] must in fact make a promise to the offeror [subcontractor] and a promise, as the offeree should reasonably understand, is something which involves, if not communication, at least attempted communication. . . . Here there was certainly no return promise [by the prime contractor] communicated to the offeror [subcontractor] [*Cortland Asbestos Products, Inc. v. J. & K. Plumbing & Heating Co., Inc.*, 33 A.D.2d 11, 304 N.Y.S.2d 695 (1969)].

CASE 5-4   Deeds Made Contract

The actions between an owner and a subcontractor, after the general contractor had abandoned the project, created a direct contract between them, entitling the subcontractor to payment under the new contract, ruled the New York Court of Appeals [*Brown Bros. Electrical Contractors, Inc. v. Beam Constr. Corp.*, 41 N.Y.2d 397 (1977)].

The owner had hired a general contractor for the construction of a shopping center, and the general subcontracted the electrical work. Because of financial problems, the general fell behind in its payments to the subcontractor, who then threatened to sue.

To avoid a lawsuit, the owner began to issue joint payment checks to the general and the subcontractor. Eventually the general abandoned the project, but the subcontractor, with the owner's consent, continued to work.

When the subcontractor submitted an invoice for payment to the owner, the owner responded that it would make the payment after it received the necessary underwriters' certificate. After the certificate was furnished, the owner refused payment and the subcontractor sued for breach of contract.

The owner contended that no new agreement existed between itself and the subcontractor and that the subcontractor was merely completing its work under its original contract with the general.

In determining whether a contract existed the court said it would look to the "objective . . . intent of the parties as gathered by their expressed words and deeds."

The court commented that the subcontractor had not exercised its right to stop work after the general had defaulted but continued to work directly for the owner. It also noted that the owner paid other bills submitted by the subcontractor.

These acts, said the court, indicated a true intent to contract between the parties. The consideration for the new contract, it ruled, "can easily be found in the detriment to [the subcontractor] in continuing the work and the benefit to [the owner] in having it done."

**CASE 5-5   Implied Contract Allowed
                    Contractor to Recover**

A contractor is entitled to the reasonable value of its services although the contract fails to mention any terms of compensation, according to the Iowa Supreme Court. The ruling occurred in a case brought by a carpenter to foreclose a mechanic's lien [*Sitzler v. Peck et al.,* 162 N.W.2d 449 (1968)].

The carpenter was seeking to recover the balance due for the fair and reasonable value of labor and material furnished in the construction of a prefabricated house. It admitted that no written contract existed relating either to the work to be performed or to payment. Instead the carpenter alleged that it had performed the necessary labor and purchased and installed the required materials, pursuant to an oral contract. However, no mention of payment was made in the oral contract.

The court was faced with the question whether the carpenter would be allowed to recover the value of its services by showing their reasonable value even though the oral contract failed to mention any amount of compensation.

The court first noted that a contractor will not normally be permitted to recover the reasonable value of its services based on an implied contract when an express oral contract exists. However, the court held that "it is equally well settled that there may be an implied contract on a point not covered by an express one." The law further implies a promise to pay the reasonable value of services when no agreement on compensation has been made.

In this case the carpenter was permitted to prove the reasonable value of its services based on an implied contract. Although it had proved the existence of an express oral construction contract, the contract made no reference to compensation. Therefore, the implied promise to pay the reasonable value of the work performed could not be in conflict with the existing construction contract. The carpenter was allowed to foreclose the mechanic's lien for the balance due on the reasonable value of its services.

**CASE 5-6   Architect Paid for Work Done
                    Under an Implied Contract**

The Supreme Court of Minnesota has held that an architect that had worked on a project without a written contract was entitled to compensation that had been spelled out in a letter to the owner, even though the owner had never acknowledged the letter or signed any contract [*Bergstedt, Wahlber, Berquist Associates, Inc., v. Rothchild,* 225 N.W.2d 261 (1975)].

The owner of a seven-story parking garage in St. Paul had met with a principal in an architectural firm to discuss possible alterations to the building. Because no fee arrangement was discussed or entered into at this preliminary meeting, the architect wrote a letter to the owner explaining that the fee would be actual costs plus 25 percent. Although the letter contained a space for the owner's signature, he never signed it.

During the next several months, various meetings and conferences between representatives of both parties were held to discuss the design. Apparently, no mention was made of the fee at these meetings. Later, when the architect submitted a partial bill, it was paid.

Although the architect continued to work for the owner for a two-year period, with the exception of the initial payment, it received no compensation. Finally the architect claimed a breach of implied contract and sued the owner to collect the amount set forth in its letter.

In court, the owner said that because he had never entered into a written contract, he was not obligated to pay the fee.

Noting general principles of law, the court said, "Where the evidence fails to disclose an express agreement, the law may imply a contract from the circumstances or acts of the parties." Reviewing the facts, the court felt it was obvious that the two parties had worked very closely for two years and that "a normal architect-client relationship was maintained during this period."

In reaching its decision that the architect was entitled to its claim, the court said, "While it is a fact that Rothchild [the owner] never signed that letter, it does not follow that he did not acquiesce to its terms."

CASE 5-7   Lack of Formal Fund Certification Cannot Stop Contract

A contract that required a formal certification stating that appropriated but unexpended funds existed was found by the New York Court of Appeals to be binding even though the formal certification had not been issued [*Kooleraire Service and Installation Corp. v. Board of Education of the City of New York*, 28 N.Y.2d 101 (1971)].

The Board of Education for the City of New York had solicited bids for the heating and ventilating work in a school building and awarded the contract to the low bidder. The contract contained a clause that prevented a binding contract from coming into existence "unless the comptroller shall indorse hereon his certificate that there remains unexpended and unapplied . . . a balance of the appropriation . . . sufficient to pay the estimated expense of executing this contract as certified by the officers making the same."

While the contractor was performing the initial stages of his work, the Board of Education rescinded the contract, claiming that since the comptroller had never certified that sufficient unspent funds existed, even though those funds did exist, no enforceable contract existed. The contractor sued, contending that the Board of Education had breached the contract.

The court answered the question of whether the comptroller's failure to endorse the contract constituted a legal basis to deny the contract's enforceability by determining that the parties to the contract did not intend that the comptroller should have veto power but that the comptroller's duty was simply to certify the existence of proper funds, which, in fact, existed.

In upholding the existence of a valid, binding contract, the court held "the general rule is . . . that 'one may not take advantage of a condition precedent, the performance of which he has rendered impossible.' " The court concluded that the provision had one purpose and that was to show sufficiency of money available to cover the work.

CASE 5-8   Breach Of Contract Denied: No Meeting Of Minds

A subcontractor was denied recovery of breach-of-contract damages because it was unable to prove that a valid contract existed. A contract, to be valid, held the Court of Appeals of North Carolina, requires a meeting of the minds of the two contracting parties.

A contractor in the business of placing underground conduit lines was approached by a subcontractor that wanted certain concrete work. The subcontractor was told by one of the contractor's employees to submit its bid for the concrete work, as other subcontractors were doing. The subcontractor claims it submitted a written proposal and that the contractor accepted it. Subsequently, the subcontractor alleged, the contractor refused to allow it to do the concrete work. The subcontractor then filed suit charging breach of contract.

In reviewing the facts, the court noted that the subcontractor failed to show the court any written proposal and also failed to show that a price agreement with the contractor had been reached.

> In order for a valid contract to exist, the parties must assent to the same thing in the same sense, and their minds must meet as to all the terms.

The evidence, ruled the court, failed to prove a meeting of minds or the existence of a contract.

> The plaintiff's [subcontractor] evidence tends to show only that he negotiated with one of the defendant's [contractor] employees to do some concrete work. The evidence does not disclose with any certainty what the plaintiff agreed to do for the defendant, or what the defendant agreed to pay the plaintiff [*Bill Howell, T/A Bill Howell Constr. Co. v. C. M. Allen & Co.,* 174 S.E.2d 55 (1970)].

CASE 5-9   Contract May Be Worded to Deny Pay for Work

A Michigan court has ruled that a contractor who had agreed with an owner to perform repair work, subject to the repairs being approved by the Federal Housing Administration (FHA), was not entitled to payment since the FHA refused to approve and accept the repair work.

The case involved owners who wanted to sell their residence and obtain FHA financing on the property. The FHA issued a conditional commitment subject to certain repairs being made to the premises. The owners contracted with the contractor to perform the repair work. After the contractor allegedly completed its work, the dispute arose.

The owners contended that no money was due the contractor because their obligation to pay for work, labor and services was subject to FHA approval of the repairs. The owners also wanted a refund of the money given the contractor as an advance payment. The terms of the contract were apparently not in dispute, but the contractor still alleged that it was entitled to payment for the work performed.

The Court of Appeals of Michigan, in adopting the lower court's decision, found that since the contractor's work was not approved by the FHA, it was not entitled to any part of the contract price. Since FHA approval was a contract requirement, the contractor was obligated to meet this requirement to get his payment, the court said.

> The agreement in my opinion is one which is not particularly beneficial to you [contractor] and it may have been unwise for you to enter into such a type of agreement whereby you agreed that you would do work to the satisfaction of a particular governmental agency [the court said]. The parties are free to execute the agreements that they wish to, as I have indicated in the past, provided they are not illegal or contrary to public policy and this Court has no authority to change the terms of a contract simply because the Court might feel that it was an unwise contract for any party to enter into. I just do not have that authority nor does any judge in the state have that authority. [*Mullally v. Bey*, 166 N.W.2d 500 (1968), rehearing denied, (1969)].

CASE 5-10   Crime Does Not Pay

A New York appellate court has ruled as void a contract with a municipal official that was obtained by fraud. The court prevented the contractor from collecting an unpaid balance under the contract and ordered the contractor to return all funds already paid to it by the city [*S. T. Grand, Inc. v. City of New York*, N.Y.L.J. Apr. 19, 1972; 32 N.Y.2d 300 (1973)].

The contractor entered into an emergency contract with a city commissioner for cleaning a reservoir. Both contractor and official were subsequently indicted and convicted for conspiracy in obtaining a public contract without public bidding and on condition that the contractor would pay the commissioner and others 5 percent of the money received under the contract, to be divided in certain specified percentages.

The work was performed, and about $690,000 of the contract price had been paid, leaving a balance of about $150,000. The contractor started court action to recover the balance, and the city counterclaimed seeking the return of the previous payments.

A contract procured through such fraudulent and collusive bidding practices is against public policy and is therefore void, the court said. The question is whether such fraudulent acts prohibit the contractor from retaining any moneys received, in addition to collecting the unpaid balance, it added.

The court held: "To permit this respondent [contractor] to recover the balance allegedly due it on its void contract, or to deny the City recovery of its payments irrespective of when made, would effectively destroy the salutary policy underlying the applicable statutes and encourage their evasion."

In the light of the flagrant corruption permeating the contract and the total avoidance of any public bidding, to require the contractor to return the fruits of its criminal conduct should not offend conscience, the court explained.

CASE 5-11   Contract Valid in Spite of Unlicensed Party

The New York Supreme Court has ruled that a contract calling for architectural and engineering services was neither illegal nor unenforceable even though the party to the contract providing the design services was not itself licensed by the state.

The plaintiff in the case was an Austrian iron and steel company, the defendant a manufacturer of prefabricated modular-building systems. The two parties had entered into a contract whereby the overseas steel company was given exclusive license and use of the defendant's system for modular-building erection. Under this agreement, the modular-building manufacturer was to provide the Austrian firm with plans and specifications.

Following a disagreement, the plaintiff sought to have the contract declared void because the building manufacturer was not properly licensed (as required by New York law) to provide design services even though its pertinent employees were licensed.

While deciding the validity of the contract, the court noted that the purpose of the licensing statute was "to safeguard the life, health and property of residents of New York" and it inferentially acknowledged that performance of architectural and engineering services pursuant to a contract by an unlicensed person will result in an illegal and unenforceable contract. Nevertheless, the court, noting that the contract in question called for the manufacturer to provide design services, stressed that numerous other terms of the contract did not involve licensed skills. In addition, the court pointed out that the architectural and engineering services provided under the contract had in fact been performed by duly licensed professionals.

The court held:

> It cannot be . . . that an entire contract comprehending many services to be performed, including those calling for the services of licensed professionals, can be stricken because the party furnishing the services is not itself a licensed professional. To hold otherwise would mean that not only concept developers like defendants, but builders and general contractors would likewise be incapable of enforcing their contracts because architectural and engineering skills are incidentally involved. . . . The rights sought to be protected by the statute are adequately covered when the contractor, manufacturer or builder engages a properly licensed person to perform those

tasks which the law specifies call for certified skills. [*Eisen and Stahlwerke v. Modular Building and Development Corp.,* 64 Misc.2d 1050 (1970), modified 37 App. Div.2d 525 (1971).]

CASE 5-12   Unlicensed Consultant Denied Payment For Design Services

An architectural consultant had no right to payment for architectural services because he was not a licensed architect, held the Civil Court of the City of New York [*Wineman v. Blueprint 100, Inc.,* 75 Misc.2d 665 (1973)].

An owner signed a contract with, and paid an initial fee to, a person who called himself an architectural consultant for preparation of drawings and plans. During performance of the contract, a dispute arose, and the owner hired a licensed architectural firm to prepare drawings. The consultant sued for additional fees he said he had earned, and the owner counterclaimed for return of the initial fee.

The court noted that the architectural consultant was not a licensed architect and that this apparently was not known by the owner. It said also the architectural firm subsequently hired did not use any of the consultant's plans or drawings.

The court said that by state statute no person is permitted to practice architecture or use the title of architect unless he is properly certified. It granted the owner the right to a refund of the consultant's fee. The court said: "The plaintiff appears, from his testimony and letterhead, to be personally performing architectural services. Such activity is prohibited by Section 7302 [state statute]."

CASE 5-13   Architect Keeps Copyright

An architect did not divest itself of its common-law copyright when it filed plans with the building department, held the New York Supreme Court, Appellate Division [*Shaw v. Williamsville Manor, Inc.* 38 App. Div.2d 442 (4th Dept. 1972)].

The architect had prepared plans and specifications for the construction of an apartment building and had retained all rights to its plans under the contract. The owner of the property for which the plans and specifications were prepared filed the documents with the village clerk as required by a village ordinance.

After construction began and the building was more than 60 percent complete, the owner had financial problems and a foreclosure proceeding took place. The defendant purchased the property and completed the building without using the original architect. The architect claimed that the defendant used the plans to complete the building without its consent, and it brought suit for the reasonable value of its work, labor, and services.

The court acknowledged the general principle of law that "an architect has a common law copyright in plans prepared by him and may maintain an action against anyone using them without his consent until by publication they become the property of the general public." The court further acknowledged that a limited publication, one made under restrictions limiting the use of the plans and specifications, does not constitute a publication so as to make the plans and specifications property of the general public.

The question now posed was whether the filing of plans with the clerk constituted a general or limited publication. In following the current trend, the court concluded, "Such filing was a limited publication made for the definite purpose of securing a building permit and did not result in the surrender of any rights inconsistent with such limited purpose."

Since only a limited publication had taken place, the architect maintained its common-law copyright in its architectural plans and specifications, and it had the right to bring suit when the plans and specifications were used without its permission.

SIX

Contractual Relationship

The cry "sue for breach of contract" all too often fails to take into consideration the fact that the party you want to sue for breach of contract has no contract with you. Before one threatens another with a breach-of-contract lawsuit, alleges a breach of a contractual obligation, or even implies that a person owes you a contractual obligation, you must first determine that a contractual relationship exists. This contractual relationship has been call *privity*, but the term is better avoided because of the vast number of legal nuances clustering around the word. It is easier to indicate that unless a direct contractual relationship exists between two parties or some specific clause intends to create a contractual relationship, no contractual obligation exists and therefore no right of action for breach of contract exists.

A typical situation in which the lack of a contractual relationship becomes a defense is when one prime contractor alleges breach of contract against another prime contractor when no direct contract exists but each has an independent prime contract with the owner. A similar situation exists between subcontractors, between subcontractors and different prime contractors on the same project, between a prime contractor and the owner's architect or engineer, or between one prime and another prime's surety. In the normal situation no contract exists between these parties, and therefore without a contractual relationship no cause of action exists [see *Novak & Co., Inc. v. Travelers Indemnity Co.*, 85 Misc.2d 957 (1976), and *Lake County Tile Co. v. Root Enterprises, Inc.*, 339 N.E.2d 103 (1975)].

If that last statement ("no cause of action exists") is taken as gospel and an absolute, the reader has failed to read or appreciate what the author had said earlier. There are no absolutes in the law. There are always changing trends. There are always factual distinctions which can call for different conclusions. In fact, even the statement that there is "no cause of action" is legally incorrect. In the majority of cases there would be no *contractual* cause of action; however, liability might be found between parties where no contractual relationship exists on the basis of torts, statute, warranty, equity, or possibly criminal violation. To approach a given situation or contract with the belief that you may hide behind the wall of privity to avoid all liability is unwise, as the walls of privity have long since fallen.

The requirements for contractual relationships have come under tremendous attack in construction contracts in recent times. Actions have been popping up at a higher rate than ever before by contractors against owners' architects, primes against primes, and subcontractors against subcontractors. Liability is being found, sometimes without delineation for basis and other times on a contractual or quasi-contractual basis. Although apparently this is still true only in a minority of jurisdictions, the courts have started to apply the doctrine of third-party beneficiary to construction contracts so that direct contractual actions between two parties are permitted where they have a common contracting party. No third-party beneficiary relationship will be found unless the intent to establish this relationship is found in the contract.

In an action involving a mortgagor, mortgagee, general contractor, and subcontractor, the subcontractor claimed rights and entitlement under a building-loan agreement on the basis that the agreement was made for its benefit and that therefore it was a third-party beneficiary. However, the subcontractor could not point to any specific clause where either of the two parties to the building-loan agreement sought to confer a benefit to the subcontractor. In denying the subcontractor's right to claim under the building-loan agreement, the court held,

> It is not sufficient to show that one is only an incidental beneficiary under such an agreement or that one benefits through the mere operation of the contract. . . . The intention and purpose of the parties to a contract must be ascertained and determined primarily or largely from the terms, expressions and provisions of the parties to the contract. . . . The Building Loan Agreement contains the terms and conditions for the disbursement of mortgage proceeds from the lendor to the borrower and contains no assurance of payment to the general contractor, subcontractor or any other third party [*United States v. Chester Heights Associates,* 406 F. Supp. 600 (D.S.C. 1976)].

Several subcontractors and materialmen were denied the status of third-party beneficiaries to the prime contract and therefore were denied rights to enforce payment provisions ahead of a bank, which had filed security agreements. No third-party beneficiary relationship existed since the clear intent to establish such a relationship did not exist in the prime contract.

> In deriving intent, we must begin with the presumption that parties contract for themselves, and a contract will not be construed as having been made for the benefit of third parties unless it clearly appears that such was the intention of the contracting

parties [*Corpus Christi Bank and Trust v. Smith,* 525 S.W.2d 501 (Tex. Sup. Ct. 1975)].

A third-party beneficiary relationship has long been applied in the insurance field. The insurance company enters into a contract with the insured whereby the insured pays premiums and the other promises to pay benefits upon death. A beneficiary is named in the insurance policy but is not a signatory to the contract. On the death of the insured, if the insurance company refuses payment, the beneficiary of the insurance policy has a right to sue as third-party beneficiary. It was the intent of the insurance company and the insured to grant to the beneficiary the right, in case of a breach of an obligation of the insurance contract, to seek legal enforcement. The same theory has been argued in various construction cases. If the owner, for a multiple-prime-contract project, inserts contractual clauses in its prime contract with contractor A stating that A shall not interfere or cause any damage to prime contractor B, and if A should interfere or cause any damage to B, then A shall be directly liable to B; and if a similar clause appears in B's contract, and if it further states that B shall have a right of action against A in case of damage caused by A, then the basis for an action by B against A is probably present. Such third-party causes of action have been increasing. They have been commenced by contractors against architects under the theory that the contractor was a third-party beneficiary of the architect's contract with the owner. A major reason for the common party's trying to insert a third-party beneficiary-relationship clause into the independent contracts is that by the insertion of that clause the common party also tries to state that the injured party shall not have any right against the common party. This form of exculpatory clause attempts to protect the common party against liability. Although it is believed that the contractor has a right of action both against the owner and the other party, instances have arisen where the contractor has been precluded from suing the owner. The contractor's remedy and cause of action was limited to asserting its rights as a third-party beneficiary. It is noted that a party should not rely upon the third-party-beneficiary clause between its two contractors to preclude its own liability. The majority of courts will probably continue to hold the common contracting party potentially liable even though that party may have a direct third-party cause of action against the other party. On the other hand, the potential use and merit of the third-party-beneficiary clause as a deterrent to litigation should not be overlooked (Case 6-1).

CASE 6-1 Third-Party-Beneficiary Clause Upheld

A New York court ruled that one prime contractor could sue another prime in a dispute over contract obligations even though no contract existed between the two [*KEC Corp. v. New York State Environmental Facilities Corp.,* 76 Misc.2d 170 (1973)].

Both the plaintiff, an electrical contractor, and the defendant, a general contractor, held prime construction contracts with New York State, the owner. There were no direct contractual agreements between the two primes, but supplemental general conditions included in the prime contracts stated that the general contractor was obligated to coordinate the work of all prime contractors.

The electrical contractor claimed the general failed to coordinate the work properly, which delayed the electrical firm's performance and caused it to incur damages. The electrical company charged that this failure to coordinate was a breach of contract. The electrical contractor further argued it was the third-party beneficiary of the contract between the owner and the general and that it was permitted to sue the general contractor directly.

The electrical firm based its argument on a clause in its contract that

> The Contractor agrees that he has and will make no claim for damages against the Authority [state] by reason of any act or omission to act by any other contractor or in connection with the Engineer's or Authority's [state's] acts or omissions to act in connection with such other contractor, but the Contractor shall have the right to recover such damages from the other contractors. . . .

The contract said also that

> Should any other contractor . . . sustain any damage, during the progress of the work hereunder, through any act or omission of the Contractor, the Contractor agrees to reimburse such other contractor for all such damages. . . .

The court said that the general contractor is responsible for supervision and coordination of the work. It said also that one prime could bring legal action on a contract against another if, as in this case, the intent to confer a direct benefit on the third party is clearly shown.

SEVEN

Promissory Estoppel

Although a subcontractor may submit a specific bid for a prime contract and the prime contractor may incorporate the subcontractor's name and price in its bid to the owner, this may not create a subcontract or impose liability on the contractor; but the converse is not necessarily true. Even though no subcontract may exist, the subcontractor may be liable to the prime contractor and under a duty to stand behind its bid because of the doctrine of promissory estoppel. Promissory estoppel is an equitable doctrine which loosely translated means that a party is stopped from withdrawing its promise. The doctrine of promissory estoppel has been applied in principle to enjoin the subcontractor or supplier from withdrawing its offer even though the offer has not been accepted, no contract has been formed, and the subcontractor has attempted to withdraw its offer (48 A.L.R.2d 1069). Under the doctrine of promissory estoppel, the offeror can be liable for damages (the difference between its offer and the next highest offer) even though no contract exists.

The doctrine of promissory estoppel in construction contracts is a new theory and has not been fully recognized. In jurisdictions where it is recognized, it has generally been held that for the doctrine of promissory estoppel to be applied, four elements must be proved: (1) a clear and definite offer must exist; (2) the offeror must reasonably expect that the offeree, to whom the offer is made, will rely upon that offer; (3) the offeree must actually and reasonably rely upon the specific offer; and (4) withdrawal of the relied-upon offer must result in detriment or harm to the party relying thereon [*E. A. Coronis Associates v. M. Gor-*

don Constr. Co., 90 N.J. Super. 69, 216 A.2d 246 (1966); and *Drennan v. Star Paving Co.,* 51 Cal.2d 409, 333 P.2d 757 (1958).

> Originally the doctrine of promissory estoppel was invoked as a substitute for consideration rendering a gratuitous promise enforceable as a contract. . . . If promissory estoppel were to be limited to only those situations where the promise giving rise to the cause of action must be so definite with respect to all details that a contract would result were the promise supported by consideration, then the defendants' instant promises to Hoffman would not meet this test. However, sec. 90 of Restatement, 1 Contracts, does not impose the requirement that the promise giving rise to the cause of action must be so comprehensive in scope as to meet the requirements of an offer that would ripen into a contract if accepted by the promisee. Rather the conditions imposed are:
>
> 1. Was the promise one which the promisor should reasonably expect to induce action or forbearance of a definite and substantial character on the part of the promisee?
> 2. Did the promise induce such action or forbearance?
> 3. Can injustice be avoided only by enforcement of the promise?
>
> We deem it would be a mistake to regard an action grounded on promissory estoppel as the equivalent of a breach of contract action [*Janke Constr. Inc. v. Vulcan Materials Co.,* 386 F.Supp. 687, *aff'd.* 527 F.2d 772 (7th Cir. 1976) (see Cases 7-1 and 7-2)].

An oral bid was held to be enforceable on the basis of promissory estoppel even though no oral contract existed, and the requirements of the statute of frauds were not met. "The statute of frauds relates to the enforceability of *contracts;* promissory estoppel relates to *promises* which have no contractual basis and are enforced only when necessary to avoid injustice" (ibid). Therefore, the statute of frauds was held to be inapplicable in cases involving the doctrine of promissory estoppel. A material supplier was liable on the basis of promissory estoppel for the difference in price between its oral bid and the contractor's cost to purchase materials. The supplier failed to inform the prime contractor that its bid was based on an "or equal" submission, failed to have its materials accepted as "or equal" by the owner, and refused to supply the materials as specified. A supplier is liable and the doctrine of promissory estoppel will apply when

> A promise which the promisor [supplier] should reasonably expect to induce action or forbearance of a definite and substantial character on the part of the promisee [contractor] and which does induce such action or forbearance is binding if injustice can be avoided only by enforcement of the promise, [even though no formal contract exists (ibid)].

Although the principle of promissory estoppel is more often applied by a contractor against a subcontractor or a subcontractor against a supplier, it might well be argued by an owner against a prime contractor. In jurisdictions which apply this doctrine the effect is that the offeror is precluded from withdrawing its offer before a reasonable time has been given for the offeree's acceptance of the offer to form a contract.

The doctrine of promissory estoppel was used by a subcontractor's supplier against the prime contractor to cover payment for materials supplied to the subcontractor but not paid for. The prime contractor had promised to issue joint checks to the subcontractor and supplier and did so several times. In fact, the prime contractor eventually paid the full subcontract price either to the original subcontractor, its suppliers, or to the completing subcontractor after default. Under the doctrine of promissory estoppel, the court held that the prime contractor was liable for an amount even in excess of the original subcontract.

> All of the elements are present here. Olsen promised to issue joint checks for the purpose of inducing United to supply materials for the project. Olsen's promise did in fact induce United to supply the materials. Since United remains unpaid for a substantial amount of the materials it supplied, it will suffer injustice if the promise is not enforced. . . . Olsen's awareness that United was supplying materials to the project in reliance upon the joint check arrangement prevents Olsen from refusing payment to United now that the project is completed and Olsen has been paid in full by Rivers [owner]. While United was not vigilant in protecting its right to payment, Olsen was not justified in accepting United's performance without exercising some vigilance of its own to protect United as it had promised to do. If a loss is to fall on one of two innocent parties, equity dictates that it remain with him who is in the better position to have prevented it [*United Electric Corp. v. All Service Electric, Inc.,* 256 N.W.2d 92 (1977)].

Although the doctrine may appear one-sided on its face, the courts are not overliberal in its application. Before enforcement the courts will make a careful scrutiny of the facts to determine whether a contract ever came into existence. If no contract exists, has the party seeking the application of the doctrine of promissory estoppel fulfilled its prerequisites? The doctrines of equity require that the person who seeks the enforcement of this equitable doctrine prove that it has acted equitably and with clean hands in all instances. This has been effectively interpreted to preclude the enforcement of promissory estoppel where the contractor knew or should have known that a mistake existed in the offer; where the contractor waited an unreasonable length of time before notifying the offeror that its bid was accepted; where the contractor started further negotiations ("bid shopping") in order to get a better price; or where the offer was so qualified as to preclude the contractor's reasonable reliance.

The enforcement of the doctrine of promissory estoppel was denied on the basis that the contractor was unable to prove that its reliance upon the offer was reasonable and justifiable. This was based upon the great disparity in bids between the subcontractors who bid for the job.

> We hold that the trial court properly refused to apply the doctrine of promissory estoppel because Nielsen knew, or should have known, of the obviously mistaken bid by National. Consequently, such reliance as Nielsen claims it placed on National's bid was as a matter of law not reasonable [*S. N. Nielsen Co. v. National Heat & Power Co., Inc.,* 337 N.E.2d 387 (Ill. App. 1975)].

The doctrine of promissory estoppel is not automatic in its application. However, it cannot be overlooked. It is widely used as a negotiating tool to avoid litigation when the opposing party is properly educated as to its principle. It must be remembered that it is based on equity, justice, and fairness, and strict legal doctrines may not apply.

CASE 7-1 Subcontractor Bound by Bid Submitted to, and Used by, General Contractor

A California court has ruled that a subcontractor was liable on a telephoned bid submitted to a general contractor and relied on by the general contractor in its bid, even though no subcontract was ever signed or performed [*H. W. Stanfield Constr. Corp. v. Robert McMullen & Son, Inc.,* App., 92 Cal. Rptr. 669 (1971)]. The court, using the doctrine of promissory estoppel, said the contractor could recover the difference between the subcontractor's bid and the next lowest bid.

The general contractor, in preparing its bid for a Navy prime contract, had solicited bids from subcontractors, including a painting contractor whose first bid was about 50 percent of the next lowest painting bid. After being told about the discrepancy, the subcontractor phoned in a revised bid. The general contractor used the bid, telling the subcontractor that the bid had been relied on, that the prime bid was low, and that the subcontractor would receive a contract for signature if the prime contract was won. The subcontractor refused to sign a contract.

The lower court held that the general contractor had relied on a promise the subcontractor could not repudiate (promissory estoppel). It said the contractor had a right to rely on the subcontractor's bid, was unaware of any mistake in the last bid, accepted the bid within a reasonable time, had not made any counteroffers, and was damaged by the subcontractor's refusal to perform.

The appellate court affirmed the lower court's decision, noting that the doctrine of promissory estoppel is "not premised upon the existence of an enforceable contract." It rejected the argument that the contractor was not reasonable in relying on the bid, saying, "Once having alerted defendant to the possibility of an error in its bid, plaintiffs should not be held knowledgeable of or responsible for any subsequent mistake in the second bid."

The court also said the general contractor's actions did not defeat its continuing right to accept the subcontractor's offer.

CASE 7-2 Subcontractor Cannot Withdraw Bid Relied on by Prime Contractor

It is breach of contract for a subcontractor to withdraw a bid on which a general contractor has relied, the Court of Appeals of Ohio, Cuyahoga County, has ruled. [*Wargo Builders, Inc. v. Douglas L. Cox Plumbing & Heating, Inc.,* 268 N.E.2d 597 (1971)]. The subcontractor's bid must be held open for a reasonable period of time, the court said.

The subcontractor had made an oral offer to perform plumbing and heating work at a stated price. The general used the offer in its bid and received the prime contract. A week later, but before the general engaged the subcontractor, the subcontractor said it would not do the work for the price it quoted. The general subcontracted to another firm and sued the first subcontractor.

Applying the doctrine of promissory estoppel, the court said the subcontractor had made a clear and definite offer, hoping the general contractor would rely on it. The general did rely on it. "Under these circumstances, it would be unreasonable to permit defendant to withdraw or revoke its offer," the court explained.

EIGHT

Contract Documents

The *contract* is normally a massive and complex document. Contrary to many contractors' belief, it is normally not that single-page document entitled Agreement; instead it usually comprises and is intended to comprise hundreds, if not thousands, of pages, terms, conditions, and other documents. That short agreement must be read carefully because it usually contains a provision which states the intent that "incorporated herein and made a part hereof are the following documents." Such documents typically include the general conditions, special conditions, supplementary general conditions, technical provisions, specifications, information for bidders, advertisement for bids, agreement, proposal, addendum, plans, drawings, details, laws, rules and regulations, codes, etc., and the latest revisions thereof. When specifically referenced *and incorporated,* these documents become part and parcel of the contract. They are all to be interpreted together as a single contract. On the other hand, the contractor must not automatically assume that plans, specifications, or other documents are incorporated as part of the contract.

It is essential that if the contractor wants and believes that a specific document is part of the contract, the contractor should list that document in the contract in detail. All too often proposals by contractors, upon which the entire contract is founded, are not included as a contract document. Therefore, the original proposal and intent of the contractor may have little if any effect when the final contract is interpreted. In like fashion, owners often try to avoid liability by trying to exclude from inclusion as a contract document the boring data. The mere attempted exclusion does not mean total avoidance of the document, although it will definitely affect its relevance and weight. Plans and specifications which have been referenced in the "contract" and pursuant to which the contractor was to construct the project have been held to be not necessarily part of a contract, although referred to therein, since they were not specifically "incorporated" therein (Case 8-1). This resulted in their being guidelines, and had secondary importance in determining the contractor's contractual obligations. The extent to which documents are incorporated as part of the contract documents, merely by reference thereto, is a question of degree and is left to the discretion of the court. To avoid this possibility, all contract documents should be described (Case 8-2).

Substantial litigation has occurred over the question of whether or not or to what extent codes, laws, ordinances, and regulations are incorporated as part of the contract (whether referred to or not) and whether or not they take priority over statements and specific requirements of the contract documents (Case 8-3). It may generally be stated that contracts cannot alter legislative enactments. Therefore, applicable legislative enactments are incorporated as part of the contract, whether or not they are specifically referenced therein. Although conflicting decisions exist concerning the contractor's obligation to perform work in accordance with various codes, with or without additional compensation, it would seem that although the nondesigning contractor may be obligated to perform its specified work in accord with applicable regulations, it should not be required to perform nonspecified work because the design failed to incorporate the code requirements properly. In this situation it has been found that a contractor is entitled to additional compensation even though the code was incorporated by general terms although the code was not specified. The designer is responsible for incorporating the legislative requirements properly into the design whether the designer actually knew these requirements or should have known them.

> The city prepared the plans and specifications and asked for competitive bidding on the basis thereof. It could not be expected that the bidders would examine the various laws and building codes as to each item specified to see if the codes required some different method of construction. Such procedure would make the bidder's interpretation of the law rather than the specifications controlling. It would make the specifications so indefinite and uncertain as to destroy the validity of any contract awarded pursuant thereto. . . . We find that the provisions of the contract did not eliminate the right to extra charges if a change order was issued requiring more expensive construction, even though the change was due to some legal requirement overlooked in the specifications [*Green v. City of New York*, 128 N.Y.S.2d 715 (1954)].

It is strongly urged that each contracting party attempt to list, in detail, each and every document it intends to include as part of *its* contract. This means listing by date, description, title, and any other available designation.

CASE 8-1   Plans and Specifications Do Not
Broaden Contract Obligations

The Court of Appeals of Indiana has ruled that mere reference to plans and specifications does not make them contract documents and that they cannot enlarge obligations specifically set forth in a contract [*Oxford Development Corp. v. Rausauer Builders, Inc.*, 304 N.E.2d 211 (1973)].

A subcontract to furnish certain materials provided that work would be performed "according to the plans and specifications." When a dispute arose over whether specific work was within the scope of the agreement or should be deemed an extra, the subcontractor performed the work and sued the prime contractor to recover its additional costs.

In court, the prime contractor argued that the subcontract's reference to the plans and specifications incorporated them into the contract and specifically provided that the work in question would be done by the subcontractor.

Noting that the primary rule of contract interpretation "is to ascertain and give effect to the parties' intentions," the court recognized that parties can make plans and specifications part of their contract. In this event, these plans would have the same force as if they were actually contract documents. But in this particular case, the court said that "a reference to plans and specifications is not effective beyond the parties' agreement."

"Where qualifying words appear in the contract, such reference will be limited accordingly," the court explained. Without "express provision, the plans and specifications cannot operate to either restrict or extend the scope of the contract to subjects other than those covered by the contract."

Since the specific work was not included in the contract, the scope of the work required by the contract and the parties' expressed intent could not be enlarged by the plans and specifications, which were merely being referred to and not incorporated as part of the actual contract. Therefore, the subcontractor was entitled to recover extra compensation for this work.

CASE 8-2   Contractor's Liability Limited to
Work It Bid

A subcontractor who bids without knowing that the specifications have been changed by an addendum is entitled to the reasonable value of the additional work performed in accordance with the addendum, the Virginia Supreme Court of Appeals ruled [*Worley Brothers Co., Inc. v. Marcus Marble and Tile Co., Inc.*, 209 Va. 136, 161 S.E.2d 796 (1968)].

The general contract called for the construction of jail facilities in Richmond, Virginia. The subcontractor was to perform the tile work in accordance with plans and specifications. The architects, by addendum, changed and added additional requirements to the tile section of the specifications. The subcontractor neither received nor had knowledge of the addendum before submitting its bid.

After the subcontractor had completed a major portion of its work, one of the architects noticed that the work was not being performed as required by the addendum. Learning of the discrepancy, the general contractor directed the subcontractor to stop work.

Subsequently the general contractor directed the subcontractor to remove its existing work and replace it in the manner specified in the addendum. The subcontractor performed the work under protest and demanded the additional sum required to do the work.

The court determined that the subcontractor did not have knowledge of the addendum when its bid was accepted and that the addendum had materially changed the requirements.

The subcontractor was under no duty to compare the specifications furnished to it by the general contractor with the other specifications that were on file in the contractor's office. The court said that the subcontractor was required only to perform that work called for in the specifications shown at the time it bid. The subcontractor was not bound to any specification not shown to it at bidding time and which could not have been included in its estimate.

CASE 8-3   Safety-Code Requirements Part of Contract Obligations

The General Services Board of Contract Appeals denied a contractor's claim that work which was not directly specified but which was required under a contractually included safety code was beyond its contractual obligation [*Appeal of Baltimore Contractors, Inc.,* GSBCA 37A, 73-2 BCA 10,032 (Apr. 30, 1973)].

The contractor argued that it was not required to install handrails, drip pans, and concrete steps in elevator rooms at the FBI building in Washington, D.C., because, it said, neither the plans nor the specifications referred to them. The contractor claimed this was "an error of omission" and that it had a right to proceed on the assumption that the specifications were adequate and correct.

The owner, the United States government, denied liability based on a specification that "unless otherwise specified, all elevator material, design, clearances, construction, workmanship and tests shall conform to the requirements of the American Standard Safety Code for Elevators." The code, which the government said was part of the contract, called for installation of the work in question.

The board ruled that since the contractor was notified of and required to comply with the elevator-code requirements, it must install the disputed work as part of its contract.

NINE

Contract Interpretation

Once the legal existence of a contract is verified, the next major legal and practical consideration is determining what the contract says. Too often documents are subject to differing interpretations, differing claims about what they mean, and differing opinions. All this results in differing beliefs concerning what the contractual obligations are or are not. No guarantee could ever be given by an attorney that two judges or panels of arbitrators would come up with identical interpretations of a contract, but there are certain basic guidelines and rules of contract interpretation which are generally recognized by the judiciary throughout the United States. The application of these rules to given facts may call for contrary decisions in different cases, but the principles of law should be understood and known by every member of the firm involved, directly or indirectly, with the performance of the contract. Specific emphasis must be place on educating construction field personnel on the general principles of law since although they are not expected to be attorneys, their acts and omissions will be judged according to these principles.

It is not the court's function to rewrite the contract. The court's function is to interpret and enforce what exists. Courts have long stood for the proposition that their function is to divine the equitable and proper interpretation of the contract as the intentions of the parties are expressed in that contract.

> In construing a contract, the ultimate goal is to discern and give effect to the intent of the parties as that intent is expressed or is implied in fact in the contract taken as a whole. Since it is presumed that each provision of the Contract Documents was inserted deliberately and for a purpose, the intention of the parties will not be

determined from isolated provisions of the contract. . . . In construing the contract documents as a whole, provisions which seem to be in conflict should be reconciled if possible [*Roosevelt University v. Mayfair Constr. Co., Inc.,* 331 N.E.2d 835 (Ill. App. 1975)].

Their function is not to redraft the contract documents, which has been stated as being beyond their judicial powers (Case 5-9). However, the results of a court's interpretation might well be contrary to the written word.

In its role in our democratic society, the judiciary is bound to the dispensing of "justice" according to certain laws, rules, regulations, and statutes. The court is not only hesitant to enforce but it will not enforce contractual provisions which it rules are illegal, unlawful, unconscionable, or against public policy. In certain cases a court might refuse to recognize the existence of the entire agreement because it was void ab initio, was procured through unlawful or illegal means, involved an agreement wherein one of the alleged parties was legally incompetent to enter into an enforceable agreement, etc. More and more cases seem to be questioning the legal existence of a contract because of the failure to comply with bidding statutes properly. Such a situation may result in the entire contract's being void or declared invalid. The court is not bound by any general mandatory requirement that if it finds a specific provision which it cannot judicially recognize, it must strike the entire agreement. Often the court will pass judgment on several clauses or even a single clause of a contract, leaving the rest of the contract intact. To foster this result, many contracts specifically include a provision indicating that if a particular clause is found to be unenforceable, it should not affect the balance of the contract. Although the practical effect of the court's actions is to alter the contract by ruling certain provisions to be unenforceable, generally the court will not rewrite the provisions to make them legal. If a contracting party wants to write a bad deal or accept responsibility for damages it did not cause, the court will enforce it provided it does not reach the point of being against public policy or unconscionable (Case 9-1). The line of unconscionability and public policy is always changing and is subject to the times and equitable considerations.

To interpret a contract judicially requires the determination of the intent of the parties. There are many factors that a court will consider when determining the parties' intent. One of the first considerations is trying to determine how the parties interpreted the contract before the dispute arose:

The interpretation given to a contract by the parties themselves while engaged in the performance of it is one of the best indications of the true intent of the contract. Ordinarily, such a construction of the contract should be enforced. . . . This is a rule of justice and equity, and we apply it herein [*Omaha Public Power District v. Natkin & Co.,* 227 N.W.2d 864 (Neb. Sup. Ct. 1975)].

If a commonality of interpretation and intent can be shown to have existed before the dispute, the courts will often employ that interpretation as its decision (Case 9-2). It has been said that the interpretation of a contract by the parties before the contract becomes the subject of controversies is of great, if not controlling, weight and that the interpretation by the contracting parties of a contract during its performance is demonstrative of their contractual and legal intentions. The intent of the parties can be shown by various sorts of documentation, the conduct of the parties on this particular contract, or possibly the parties' actions, conduct, and interpretations on previous contracts employing similar language. It is wise for a contractor to document interpretations and intent even when there is no dispute at that moment.

The intent of the parties may become cloudy when one contracting party alleges that the written contract does not express what it believed to be the oral agreement. This creates litigation. To enjoin possible litigation say what you mean. All terms of the oral agreement should be set forth in total and complete detail. Otherwise there is a legal question whether the earlier oral statements can be introduced into evidence. The parol-evidence rule forbids the introduction into evidence of any earlier oral statements, terms, or provisions which are in direct conflict with the subsequently written contract.

A contractor was precluded by the parol-evidence rule from varying the payment terms of a written contract by introduction of an earlier oral agreement. Under the parol-evidence rule, evidence of prior or contemporaneous agreements which differs from or contradicts the terms of an unambiguous complete written contract is not admissible evidence in court in the absence of fraud, accident, or mistake [*South Side Plumbing Co. v. Tigges,* 525 S.W.2d 583 (Mo. Ct. App. 1975)].

However, if the prior oral understanding is used to clarify the written language, or if the prior oral agreement is not in conflict with a subsequent written agreement, such prior statements may be considered by the court in evolving its determination of the intent of the parties (Case 9-3).

Proof of prior oral agreements independent of the subsequent written contract neither contemplated by the parties in the written contract nor varying or contradicting the written terms is admissible and does not violate the parol-evidence rule [*Robert J. Gordon Constr. Co. v. Meredith Steel Constr.,* 537 P.2d 1199 (Nev. Sup. Ct. 1975)]. In a Louisiana case a subcontractor was allowed to introduce evidence of a subsequent oral agreement modifying the prior written contract. "Parol evidence is clearly admissible to prove a subsequent verbal agreement, modifying or even abrogating a written contract, if the contract is not one required *by law* to be in writing" [*Grossie v. Lafayette Constr. Co., Inc.,* 306 So.2d 453 (La. App. 1975)]. To avoid time-consuming and expensive litigation, it is wise to carefully set forth *all* oral understandings carefully in the written document, if one is being used.

When a court interprets a contract, the total contract is used. Most contracts specifically include and incorporate various other contract documents. The court's legal guidelines for interpretation require that the contract be read as a single unit inclusive of all contract documents. The basic principle of law is that a court will interpret the entire contract as if it were a single document, and the intent of the parties will be deduced from that document. One should not, as the court will not, segregate the contract documents so that one has no effect on the overall contract.

All too often a dispute will be based upon one party's stating that it has found a provision in the specification saying that the color shall be black whereas the other party states that it has found a provision in the contract saying the color shall be white. In effect, each party is stating that it has found a provision which substantiates its position and therefore the other provision is meaningless and of no importance. Although the argument of one of the parties may eventually be sustained by the court, the court does not approach the problem as if one provision were intended to be redundant or meaningless. Instead the court will specifically review the entire contract with the belief that no part of the contract was inserted as meaningless or meant to treat other parts of the contract as meaningless [Restatement of Contracts, §236 (a)] (see Case 9-4). It is the court's general philosophy that all provisions of a contract were initially intended to have meaning. It has been stated many times that

> an interpretation which gives a reasonable meaning to all parts of an instrument will be preferred to one which leaves a portion of it useless, inexplicable, inoperative, void, insignificant, meaningless or *superfluous;* nor should any provision be construed as being in conflict with another . . . [*Hol-Gar Mfg. Corp. v. United States,* 169 Ct. Cl. 384, 351 F.2d 972 (1965)].

The court will not

> reject nor treat as *redundant or meaningless,* any part of the contract if meaning reasonable and consistent with other parts may be given it or if the contract may be construed with the word or words left in [*Beagle-Chilcutt Painting Co.,* 60-2 BCA 2731 (1960)].

As a general rule, courts will make every reasonable and conceivable effort to give all provisions some force and effect.

Probably the single most important construction contracting principle of law (although sometimes considered secondary in evidentiary value) is the fact that a document will be interpreted against the person who drafted it. This principle of law applies to the party who drafted the contract, the change order, the letter, proposal, or any document. It is a universal rule with varying degrees of application. It has been applied even against the party who selected the use of the standard form. The rationale behind the rule is that

> Since one who speaks or writes can by exactness of expression more easily prevent mistakes in meaning than the one with whom he is dealing, doubts arising from ambiguity of language are resolved in favor of the latter [4 WILLISON, CONTRACT, 3d ed., §621, 1961].

If there is question about the interpretation of a written or oral statement, it will be interpreted against the party who selected the use of the words and who created the possibility and existence of the ambiguity [*Peter Kiewit Sons, Co. et al. v. United States,* 109 Ct. Cl. 390 (1974), and *Wood-Hopkins Contr. Co. v.*

North Carolina State Ports Authority, 202 S.E.2d 473 (1974)] (see Case 11-17 and also Cases 9-5 and 9-6).

The application of the principle of law is not automatic. The contractor cannot simply state that it disagrees with the interpretation of the party who drafted the document and thus conclude that it is entitled to win. The contractor must be able to prove that its interpretation was reasonable (see Cases 9-7 to 9-10). If the nondrafting party's interpretation is not within the "zone of reasonableness," its interpretation will have no effect on the court's decision (see Cases 9-11 and 9-12). The nondrafting party must act reasonably. On the other hand, where the drafting party's interpretation is also reasonable, this does not preclude the application of the rule of law. Where

> both plaintiff's and defendant's interpretations lie within the zone of reasonableness; neither appears to rest on an obvious error in drafting, a gross discrepancy, or an inadvertent but glaring gap; the arguments, rather, are quite closely in balance. It is precisely to this type of contract that this court has applied the rule that if some substantive provision of a government-drawn agreement is fairly susceptible of a certain construction and the contractor actually and reasonably so construes it, in the course of bidding or performance, that is the interpretation which will be adopted— unless the parties' intention is otherwise affirmatively revealed. . . . This rule is fair both to the drafters and to those who are required to accept or reject the contract as proffered, without haggling [*W.P.C. Enterprises Inc. v. United States,* 323 F.2d 874 (1963), *rehearing denied* (1964)].

The rule of law is applicable in all types of contracts, but it is more often given weight, if not greater weight, in situations where the nondrafting party has no real negotiating right to change the provisions in the document. It may be said that if the two parties truly negotiated each and every word, the application of the principle of law would be nonexistent.

The argument, which is too often heard from the owner's representative, is that its interpretation must control since it wrote the document and it knows what it intended to say. This argument has been put to rest by a United States Court of Claims decision. The court stated:

> A government contractor cannot properly be required to exercise clairvoyance in determining its contractual responsibilities. The crucial question is "what plaintiff would have understood as a reasonable construction contractor," not what the drafter of the contract terms subjectively intended [*Corbetta Constr. Co., Inc. v United States,* 461 F.2d 1330 (1970)].

In determining the intent of a contract, the court will look at the contractor's interpretation of the contract requirements to determine whether they were reasonable or not. The criterion for upholding the contractor's interpretation is it's reasonableness and not its correctness. With major or patent discrepancies or a drastic conflict in the provisions of the contract, the contractor is obligated to call such discrepancies to the owner's attention, but it is not normally required to seek clarification of any and all ambiguities or possible differences in interpretation. The government, as the drafter of the document,

> has to shoulder the task of seeing that within the zone of reasonableness the words of the contract communicate the proper notions as well as to assume the main risk of a failure to carry out that responsibility. [The contractor is] not expected to exercise clairvoyance in spotting hidden ambiguities in the bid documents and they are protected if they innocently construe in their own favor an ambiguity equally susceptible to another construction [*Appeal of T.G.C. Contracting Corp.*, ASBCA 19116, 75-1 BCA 11,346 (1975)].

Another consideration in the interpretation of a construction contract is whether or not trade custom and trade practice will be admissible evidence in proving the intentions of the parties, especially when the contract is not otherwise ambiguous. There seems to be a split of authority over whether trade practice will or will not be considered by the court (Cases 9-13 to 9-15). Obviously, when the contract says, "This contract shall be interpreted in accord with the best trade custom and trade practice," the court will use trade custom and practice in determining the parties' intent. If the written words are not clear on their face, the court usually will refer to trade usage. However, if the words are seemingly plain and clear on their face, in accordance with a lay nontrade interpretation, the courts have no uniform policy regarding the introduction of trade custom and trade practice. This is especially true if when trade usage and custom are allowed, an ambiguity will result [see *Calumet Constr. Co. v. Board of Education of City of Hoboken*, 76 Atl. 970 (1910); *Terminal Constr. Corp. v. Bergen County, etc.*, 112 A.2d 762 (1954); *Hostetter v. Park*, 137 U.S. 30 (1890); and *Bethlehem Steel Co. v. Turner Constr. Co.*, 2 N.Y.2d 456 (1957)].

The federal courts seem to be the most liberal in the acceptance of trade custom and trade practice. The Court of Claims has consistently permitted the introduction of trade interpretations

> notwithstanding that in its ordinary meaning it is unambiguous. That is to say that trade usage or custom may show that language which appears on its face to be perfectly clear and unambiguous has, in fact, a meaning different from its ordinary meaning [*Gholson, Byars and Holmes Constr. v. United States*, 351 F.2d 987 (1965)].

The parties are presumed to have knowledge of well-defined and obviously well-recognized trade customs and usages. If the nondrafting parties' reliance upon trade custom and trade practice creates an ambiguity and its interpretation is within the "zone of reasonableness," that document will be interpreted against the party who drafted it.

Many contractors have the belief that plans and specifications are to be interpreted differently from other parts of the contract. This is a misconception. Insofar as plans, specifications, and other technical items are normally incorporated as contract documents, their interpretation is subject to exactly the same rules of interpretation as is the rest of the contract. However, the contractor is forewarned that often there are specific contract provisions relating to the interpretation of plans and specifications which must be read carefully. In addition, many contracts provide an order of priority and preference between the various documents. Even if a contract clause says that the plan or the specifications shall govern, this does not automatically determine that one document will take precedence. Even when a contract clause stipulates that a specification shall take precedence over the contract plans, it is doubtful whether a general provision of the specification will take precedence over a full-scaled detail, dimension, etc., for that same point. Obviously there will be many instances where the contract clause specifying priorities will have a substantial effect on the final interpretation, but it should not be assumed to operate automatically.

Where no contract clause specifies a priority order (and even in many which do have such a listing) the courts will generally apply the rule of law that a specific statement shall have precedence over a general statement [*Barash v. State*, 154 N.Y.S.2d 317 (1956)]. This principle is based upon the parties' presumed intent that when they have specified something in detail on an exact item, it is intended to exercise control over a general statement which may apply to numerous other situations. Many factors must be considered in trying to determine which is the more specific document, e.g., (1) the title on the drawing, (2) the purpose of a given drawing or specification, (3) the date of the document, and (4) the scale or dimension on the document. Questions may arise whether the document was issued as an addendum or corrective document. Was it intended to be a clarification? The principle enforced by the courts is that when general terms and specific statements are included in the same contract and there is conflict, the general terms should give way to the specifics (Case 9-16 and 9-17), but even this principle of law and its application is not absolute. There are many contracts which provide that in case of discrepancies it is the contractor's obligation to call the discrepancy to the owner's attention before proceeding and that if the contractor fails to call the discrepancy to the owner's attention, the contractor will be deemed to have proceeded at his own risk and expense. This brings into consideration the question of responsibility for the accuracy of plans and specifications.

The general principle is that in a plan and specification contract, where the contractor is limited in implementing its own unilateral design changes, the owner warrants and represents that the plans and specifications are proper; that if the contractor builds in accord with the plans and specifications, the contractor is neither obligated nor responsible for the results, nor is the contractor liable if the results do not attain what the owner hoped for or required the contractor to guarantee or warrant in the general conditions (Case 9-18 and 9-19). An often cited case states:

> [If] the contractor is bound to build according to plans and specifications prepared by the owner, the contractor will *not* be responsible for the consequences of defects in the plans and specifications. . . . This responsibility of the owner is not overcome by the usual clauses requiring builders to visit the site, to check the plans, and to inform themselves of the requirements of the work. . . . [T]he contractor should be relieved, if he was misled by erroneous statements in the specifications.

[The] insertion of the articles prescribing the character, dimensions and location of the sewer imported a warranty that if the specifications were complied with, the sewer would be adequate. This implied warranty is not overcome by the general clauses requiring the contractor to examine the site, to check up the plans, and to assume responsibility for the work until completion and acceptance. The obligation to examine the site did not impose upon him the duty of making a diligent inquiry into the history of the locality with a view to determining, at his peril, whether the sewer specifically prescribed by the Government would prove adequate. The duty to check plans did not impose the obligation to pass upon their adequacy to accomplish the purpose in view. And the provision concerning the contractor's responsibility cannot be construed as abridging rights arising under a specific provision of the contract [*United States v. Spearin,* 248 U.S. 132 (1918)].

The reasoning of this and many other cases was succinctly set forth in a United States Court of Claims decision which stated:

[W]here a contractor is denied his own independent judgment as to the preparation and sufficiency of his own plans and specifications for the construction of prescribed structures by a provision in the contract which imposes upon him the duty of following the plans and specifications of the owner, and he does in a workmanlike manner follow such plans, he is not to be denied compensation therefor because it finally develops that the work done in accord with said plans does not develop the intended results [*Dayton-Wright Co. v. United States,* 64 Ct. Cl. 544 (1928)].

These rules of law seem to be adopted by most courts. In short, the owner is entitled to what it bargained for and the contractor is obligated only to perform that which is specifically set forth in the plans and specifications [*Drummond v Hughes,* 104 Atl. 137 (1918)].

However, the contractor cannot hide its head in the sand and rely solely upon the proposition of law that the owner warrants the accuracy of the plans and specifications and that if said plans and specifications are defective, the contractor has the automatic right to recovery. It is at this juncture that the contractor must call discrepancies to the owner's attention or proceed at its own risk (Case 9-20). Often the implied warranty of the owner and the expressed provisions in the contract which attempt to place the burden on the contractor's shoulders are in direct conflict with each other. Although the obligation of the contractor to call discrepancies to the owner might be more stringently applied when the clause exists than when it does not exist, equity and reason seem to require the contractor's calling apparent discrepancies to the owner's attention whether the clause exists or not. In several situations in federal contracts where clauses exist, the courts have placed the responsibility on the contractor to call all *patent and glaring discrepancies* to the owner's attention; otherwise the contractor will be deemed to have proceeded at its own risk and expense [*Beacon Constr. Co. v. United States,* 314 F.2d 501 (1963)]. This obligation to call patent and glaring discrepancies to the owner's attention, before opening the bids, places a great burden on the contractor to review the contract documents.

The rulings in the federal decisions swung from one extreme to the other until they reached a fair and equitable position. During the swinging of the pendulum the court noted that it is not a question of whether the contractor specifically knew of the discrepancy; the question was rather whether or not the discrepancy should have been known by a reasonably prudent contractor. If it should have been known, the contractor is presumed to have had knowledge of the discrepancy. This principle has been extended to a point where the court denied a contractor's reliance on the specifications even though the contractor relied on the contract provision which said that in case of differences the specifications shall govern [*Unicon Management Corp. v. United States,* 375 F.2d 804 (1967)]. The contractor still had the obligation to call a major discrepancy to the owner's attention.

During the swinging of the pendulum the court clarified the definition of *patent and glaring discrepancies* by making a distinction between the scope of the contractor's review of the contract documents during bidding stages, and during performance stages. If the contractor discovers the discrepancy during bidding (as distinguished from performance), it is still obligated to note the discrepancy. However, the contractor

> was under no contractual or legal obligation to inspect the drawings to determine their adequacy for construction prior to the contract award. Rather, its study of the contract documents was merely for purposes of estimating its bid, and it has not been shown that plaintiff [contractor] knew or should have known how defective the drawings actually were. Therefore, plaintiff's pre-bid examination of the drawings did not render the implied warranty [of the owner] inoperative through waiver or estoppel, and plaintiff may invoke such warranty as a basis for recovery [*John McShain, Inc. v. United States,* 412 F.2d 1218 (1969) (Case 9-18)].

Clearly the design responsibilities still rest with the drafting and designing party; however, equity and fair dealing require the contractor to call apparent, patent, and glaring discrepancies to the owner's attention before proceeding. Equity and good faith are presumed to exist between all parties and will be so enforced by the courts. Whether or not the contractor should have seen the contract discrepancy is not easy to ascertain. Various factors will have to be considered, e.g., the time the bidder had to bid the project, the location of the project, the size and complexity of the project and bid documents, the legibility of the documents, the number of addenda and their dates, and numerous other considerations (Cases 9-5, 9-7, 9-9, 9-10, and 9-20). The change in a simple fact and date from one case to another might call for a different conclusion.

The rules of contract interpretation apply in all situations. The rules cannot be minimized. Although facts may call for different conclusions, the same rules of law will apply. These rules of law will apply whether we are dealing with the interpretation of plans, the changes clause, delay clauses, or any other aspect of the contract. The contractor must always be aware that strict rules are tempered by justice and equity. Seldom will the courts enforce rules of law where a party has acted in bad faith or inequitably.

Exculpatory clauses present still another rule of contract interpretation. An exculpatory clause is one by which a party tries to eliminate, or at least limit, its liability where it would have otherwise have been subjected to liability if no clause existed. Typical examples of exculpatory clauses are indemnification and hold-harmless provisions, the no-damage-for-delay clause, and the denial of accuracy for subsurface or other data provisions. The enforcement of these clauses is not looked upon with favor. The courts have stated that one should not be allowed to eliminate liability for one's own wrongs (Case 9-21). On the other hand, the court is not permitted to rewrite the document (Case 9-22). Therefore, the question becomes one of degree. In many instances, the courts have held that where the attempted preclusion-of-liability clause is so hard or unconscionable, the clause is against public policy and therefore unenforceable. This is often the case when dealing with indemnification and hold-harmless clauses which attempt to eliminate liability when the damage was caused by that party's intentional acts. In several jurisdictions, either indemnification clauses have been voided by legislation unless the indemnification is a separate agreement with consideration flowing from one party to the other or all indemnification clauses within the normal construction contract have been voided.

When the clause is not deemed to be against public policy, the court has enunciated still another rule. Since the courts do not favor exculpatory clauses, the courts have held that they will interpret the exculpatory provisions strictly and not liberally. In other words, they will read the clause as narrowly as possible, so as to reduce and limit its applicability. If there is a way around the clause, so as not to avoid liability, that will be the interpretation most often followed by the court.

The no-damage-for-delay clause, by which a party denies liability when it is responsible for delays and merely grants an extension of time with no damages for delay, has been the subject of much litigation. The clauses have generally been ruled not to be against public policy and therefore enforceable (Case 9-23). They will be subject to strict interpretation, however, and by that interpretation have many times been deemed to be unenforceable to the given facts of the case. Decisions throughout the United States have resulted in a wealth of exceptions to the rule of enforceability of this clause. The exceptions vary from state to state, and *before a claim for delays is asserted* the contractor is advised to determine (1) whether there is a no-damage-for-delay clause in the contract, (2) which jurisdiction's laws the case will be governed by, (3) that jurisdiction's law and case precedent, (4) that jurisdiction's exceptions to rule, and (5) what other clauses might rightfully permit recovery of the damages; then the contractor should present its claim accordingly. The owner and its representatives are equally advised not to stand pat automatically behind such a clause, as the clauses are not total sanctuaries from liability. Each party should determine its respective rights and then sit down and negotiate.

The courts will not rewrite your contract; they will interpret your contract. Know your contract and make sure you say exactly what you intended.

The no-damage-for-delay clause has become a standard insertion in many prime contracts, subcontracts, and even material purchase orders. It may be said to represent a position opposite that of a suspension-of-work clause, which permits the contractor to recover damages incurred as a result of unreasonable suspensions and delays. The no-damage-for-delay clause attempts to avoid liability for delays, even when that party is responsible, in whole or part, for the delay or suspension. Every clause must be reviewed scrupulously to determine in what instances the clause allegedly applies. The enforceability, the scope, and the application of the no-damage-for-delay clause, as with all other contract provisions depends upon its exact wording.

As a general rule, the no-damage-for-delay clause is not against public policy. It is not, on its face, automatically deemed void or invalid by the courts. On the other hand, the clause is subject to the rule of strict interpretation, so that the scope of its application will be limited by the courts to as narrow an application as is reasonably possible.

The scope of enforcement seems to vary from jurisdiction to jurisdiction without any particular reasoning. In some jurisdictions, even where the clause is interpreted in accordance with strict construction principles, provisions have been ruled enforceable even when they have been broad and all-inclusive enough to cover any and all delays "from any cause in the progress of work whether such delays be avoidable or unavoidable" [*Psaty & Fuhrman, Inc. v. Housing Authority of City of Providence,* 68 A.2d 32 (1949); see also *Ericksen v. Edmonds School District,* 125 P.2d 275 (1942); *Siefford v. Housing Authority of City of Humboldt,* 223 N.W.2d 816 (Neb. (1974)]. This type of broad, general exculpatory clause has come under attack in other jurisdictions, to the point where enforcement is questioned [*Franklin Contracting Co. v. State,* 365 A.2d 952 (N.J. 1976)]. Several jurisdictions have denied the sanctuary effect of such clauses. Jurisdictions which seem to deny enforcement of broad shotgun no-damage-for-delay clauses have, as a general rule, enforced specific and precise clauses [*Peter Kiewit Sons, Co. v. Iowa Southern Utilities Co.,* 355 F. Supp. 376 (1973)] (see also Case 9-23). The reasoning appears to be that grandfather exculpatory clauses of total generality should not be enforced. However, when the clause specifies a particular cause or causes for the delay, the courts seem to enforce the clause on the basis that the specific delay contemplated by the clause was the actual delay encountered.

A contractor was denied additional compensation for delays which resulted when a separate prime contractor for a related project failed to complete the job on time. The court based its decision on the fact that the contractor was on clear notice by an unambiguous no-damage-for-delay-and-coordination contract clause that the owner would not be chargeable for damages for delay caused by the failure of third parties, on separate independent contracts, to complete on time [*Cooke Contracting Co. v. State of Michigan,* 223 N.W.2d 15 (Mich. Ct. App. 1974)].

If the delay was clearly within the contemplation of the parties at the time the contract was executed, the clause is effective. In at least one jurisdiction an owner's broad all-inclusive no-damage-for-delay clause was denied automatic effect, but instead of granting the contractor recovery the court remanded the case so that testimony could be taken to see whether the parties, at the time of executing the contract, did in fact have that specific delay in mind [*Ace Stone, Inc. v. Township of Wayne,* 221 A.2d 515 (N.J. 1966)].

It should be noted that there are many instances when contractors categorize their claims as delay claims and possibly terminate their rights of recovery due to a no-damage-for-delay clause. Often this suicidal approach is improper. Many contracts permit the contractor to recover additional costs which directly or indirectly arise from specific events under, and pursuant to, other contract clauses. Therefore, the contractor may have a right to collect what it has improperly classified as a delay claim in accordance with other specific provisions of the contract, e.g., the changed-conditions clause, changes clause, or owner-furnished-property clause.

Even when the no-damage-for-delay clause is present and effective within that jurisdiction, it is generally recognized not to be a total sanctuary because of various exceptions to its enforcement. There are no absolute exceptions, and each case must be taken on its own facts. One exception has been classified as *contractual abandonment.* This is difficult to prove in that it requires proof of the other party's intention not to proceed. A second exception has been categorized as *misrepresentation.* Fraud would clearly come within the scope of misrepresentation, as proof of fraud would require proof of an *intent* to deceive. It is not clear whether contractual misrepresentation requires proof of intent or not. Proof of inaccurate borings which were part of the contract documents have been held to be a misrepresentation and breach of warranty, even when no intent to deceive existed, and may be sufficient to also avoid the exculpatory nature of the no-damage-for-delay clause. A few jurisdictions have avoided the effect of the no-damage-for-delay clause by the exception in cases where there has been active interference on the part of the party seeking to hide behind the exculpatory provision. A clear definition of active interference has not been established. Although really an omission, it might be argued that an architect's failure to return shop drawings within a reasonable period of time is in fact legally and factually an act of active interference. The next exception is bad faith or tortious intent, which might include active interference.

Although the exceptions are numerous, the contractor should not hope that an exception will be the cause of a potential delay, or that the Judge will recognize the exception to the rule. Instead of relying on that type of thinking it is advisable to negotiate a more equitable nonexculpatory contract whenever possible.

CASE 9-1   Recovery Denied for Materials Destroyed by Fire

A subcontractor whose materials were destroyed by fire before installation could not recover from the general contractor, the Supreme Court of Nevada has ruled.

The materials belonged to an electrical subcontractor and were stored at the site. Neither the general contractor nor the subcontractor was responsible for the fire. The subcontract contained no provision covering the loss.

In holding that the subcontractor could not recover from the general contractor, the court said,

> The subcontract was for labor and materials to be incorporated into a building and was not a contract of sale. . . . One who contracts unqualifiedly to erect a structure for a stipulated price enters into an entire contract to complete such work and must bear the losses resulting from its accidental destruction before completion unless the contract stipulates that he will not be responsible . . . [*Mainland v. Alfred Brown Co.,* 461 P.2d 862 (1969)].

**CASE 9-2   Similar Contract Interpretations
            Precluded Recovery on a Delayed Claim**

The Armed Services Board of Contract Appeals has denied a contractor additional compensation for work it did under an ambiguous contract provision because at the time the work was performed the contractor interpreted this portion of the contract in the same fashion as the government.

The contract called for the construction of family housing units at an Air Force base in Arizona. During the performance of the work, the government required the contractor to do two hydrostatic tests on seamless pipe before encasing it in concrete and covering it with backfill. For five months the contractor performed these tests without complaint, but after the work was completed it protested the government's interpretation of the contract. Claiming that it was required to perform only a single test, the contractor asked for additional compensation to cover the cost of doing the second hydrostatic tests on the pipe.

Noting that up to the point of its protests the contractor had apparently interpreted the contract in the same fashion as the government, the board stated that both parties seemed to agree that two tests were required. Although the board concluded that the contract specifications could be considered ambiguous, it held that the contractor was not entitled to receive any additional compensation for the extra work in question.

Referring to a U.S. Court of Appeals decision on this subject, the board said,

> The interpretation of a contract by the parties to it, before the contract becomes the subject of controversy, is deemed by the court to be of great, if not controlling, weight. . . . It is a canon of contract construction that the interpretation placed by the parties on a contract during its performance is demonstrative of their intentions [*Appeal of Forsberg & Gregory, Inc.,* ASBCA 18069, 75-1 BCA 11,177 (Mar. 19, 1975)].

**CASE 9-3   Oral Testimony Permissible to
            Explain Contract Ambiguity**

The Supreme Court of North Dakota has ruled that a subcontractor could introduce evidence of oral discussions that took place before a contract was written in order to clarify its meaning [*Smith v. Michael Kurtz Constr. Co.,* 232 N.W.2d 35 (1975)].

A general contractor had submitted a bid for the general construction work, using a subcontractor's bid that was submitted in writing.

Apparently the total of all individual prime contractors' bids exceeded the amount of money the owner had available for the project.

The architect requested all contractors to reevaluate their prices and make suggestions to reduce the cost.

The general contractor met with the subcontractor and refigured the job. The subcontractor submitted a revised bid, which the general contractor accepted by written letter. The revised bid was ambiguous.

During the course of construction, a dispute arose over the height of the masonry walls.

The lower court permitted the subcontractor to introduce testimony intended to explain the meaning of the contract. The general contractor argued that testimony of oral discussions prior to a written contract is precluded by the parol evidence rule.

On appeal, the court acknowledged that the parol-evidence rule does preclude submission of oral testimony to vary the terms of a complete and unambiguous contract but said that the revised bid, which was part of the contract in this case, was ambiguous. "It is not error to permit parol-evidence to explain vague and ambiguous written contract provisions or to show representation made prior to the written contract which induced the party to sign the contract," the court said.

The oral testimony was accordingly permissible and the jury decision in favor of the subcontractor was affirmed. [*Smith v. Michael Kurtz Constr. Co.*, 232 N.W.2d 35 (1975)].

CASE 9-4 Interpretation Should Shun Conflict

The General Services Board of Contract Appeals has denied a contractor's claim for additional work it said was not required by the specifications. The two contract provisions that appeared to be at variance should be interpreted harmoniously rather than as conflicting, the board said [*Appeal of Piracci Constr. Co., Inc.* GSBCA 2740, 69-2 BCA 8040 (1969)].

The dispute related to stone supporting angles required in the construction of a Social Security Administration building. The contractor claimed that the specifications permitted the use of a manufacturer's standard shop-coat corrosion treatment for all angles. The use of this corrosion treatment was indicated in the contractor's shop drawings that were approved by the architects. However, the government later required the application of an additional corrosion treatment for certain angles. It was for this work that the contractor claimed extra compensation.

Behind the dispute were certain notations on two shop drawings. The notes indicated that some of the angles were to have a more costly corrosion treatment. The contractor claimed that the specifications and the extra corrosion requirements were in conflict. It argued that when there is a conflict between specifications and drawings, the specifications must prevail. As a result, it said, it was improperly required to undertake the more costly corrosion treatment.

The government argued that no conflict existed. It said the requirement contained in the specifications was a minimum requirement for all angles and that the special requirement in the drawings was an additional requirement for certain angles.

The board agreed with the government and held that the architect's approval of shop drawings did not permit a deviation from contractual requirements, which required the more costly treatment. "A contract should be interpreted so as to give a reasonable meaning to all of its parts, and contract provisions should not be construed as conflicting unless no other reasonable interpretation is possible."

CASE 9-5   Omitted Detail Created Contract Ambiguity

A contractor is entitled to be paid for additional services incurred as a result of an ambiguity that is not reasonably noticeable in the contract specifications, ruled the General Services Board of Contract Appeals.

A general contractor for the construction of a new U.S. Mint submitted a claim for additional labor and materials costs incurred while installing a fan. The government denied the claim, and the contractor appealed.

The government took the position that the contract required all facilities to be installed and put in proper working service and that inasmuch as the fan in question was indicated on a mechanical drawing, the contractor was obligated to install the fan and to supply electrical service to it. When the contractor argued that the fan was not indicated on the proper electric power drawing, the government contended that its omission was inadvertent. In addition, the government took the position that "the omission was so obvious that it should have been noticed at the bidding stage and that the appellant [contractor] should have sought clarification."

While noting an admitted deficiency in the specifications, the board considered the question of whether the admitted omission was so obvious as to constitute an apparent ambiguity, in which case the contractor might have been expected to have sought clarification.

The contractor's drawings prepared for the purpose of identifying fans and required wiring neither indicated the fan in question nor the wiring leading to it. Nevertheless, the board noted that the fan was shown on one mechanical drawing and on the motor-control electrical drawing but that these drawings were for purposes other than identification of fans and wiring.

In upholding the contractor's claim for additional payment, the board stated,

> We conclude that the specifications issued in this matter were defective and that the burden of that defect should not fall upon appellant. . . . The electrical installations were complex and extensive and the electrical subcontractor in estimating the electrical wiring component of the job could not be expected to cross-reference every piece of equipment, shown on hundreds of mechanical drawings, with the electrical wiring diagrams to be sure that circuits had been provided for every piece of equipment. That kind of responsibility lies with the designers of the project, not with those who

undertake to construct the project as designed. . . [*Appeal of McCloskey & Co., Inc.,* GSBCA 3070, 71-1 BCA 8628 (1970)].

CASE 9-6   Subcontractor Recovers from General Contractor for Failure to Clarify Contract

The Minnesota Supreme Court had ruled that a general contractor had to pay one of his subcontractors for extra work that the latter incurred because of ambiguities in the contract [*Paul W. Abbott, Inc. v. Alex Newman Heating and Plumbing Co., Inc.,* 166 N.W.2d 323 (1969)]. The reason it said, is that the owner and the general contractor had cleared up the ambiguities but the general contractor failed to inform the subcontractor.

The dispute related to plumbing work in new fire stations in St. Paul. A question arose whether some of the work covered in the subcontract was required by the specifications. The owner and the general contractor clarified the ambiguity. The subcontractor, who was not informed, did the work under protest and sued for the extra costs.

The court exonerated the owner but said the general contractor was liable for failure to pass on the clarification to the subcontractor.

CASE 9-7   Construction Deviations Allowed By Contract

The U.S. Court of Claims ruled that because a contractor's interpretation of contract specifications was reasonable, it was entitled to recover its extra costs in complying with the owner's directions which were excessive [*Kenneth Reed Constr. Corp. v. United States,* 475 F.2d 583 (1973)].

A contract with the U.S. Army Corps of Engineers called for the construction of concrete spillways for a Florida flood-control project. A dispute arose over the required tolerances for erecting the concrete formwork. The contract provided that "forms shall be true to line and grade." The government said this meant that no deviation in the formwork was permitted. The government's representative, believing that no tolerances were allowed, required the contractor to erect the forms with extreme accuracy.

The contractor argued that the formwork specification was not to be read literally. Instead, it said, the wording had to be read in conjunction with trade practice and in relation to all the specifications. The contractor pointed out that the contract permitted deviation in line and grade for the finished spillways and that its interpretation of the contract, which allowed the erection of forms within the tolerances allowed for the structure, was reasonable and should control.

The contractor based its bid upon these tolerances. It claimed that the government's insistence and continuous inspection and directions that all forms meet an exact standard was excessive and therefore compensable.

The question before the court was one of contract interpretation. The court concluded that the contractor's interpretation was reasonable and correct based on trade custom and usage. "The end product contemplated by the contract was a specified mass concrete structure with the wooden forms being but the means to be employed in achieving that end product." Because the specifications permitted deviations and spelled out allowable tolerances in the line and grade for the spillways, the court said "it would be unreasonable to assume that the parties intended to contract for a less than perfect end product but at the same time intended that the forms now be built with mathematical exactitude . . . ."

CASE 9-8 Contract Clause to Be Reasonably Interpreted

A plastering contractor on a government rehabilitation project has recovered as extra work the cost of patching plaster not included in the original contract [*Appeal of H. S. Kaiser Co.* VACAB 818, 69-2 BCA 7909 (1969)].

The dispute arose out of a contract for the rehabilitation of numerous buildings at a Veterans Administration hospital in Illinois. During the performance of its contract, the contractor noticed that large areas of existing ceiling and wall plaster had started to fall. The plaster was falling both around the areas where the contractor was working and in remote areas away from all work. The contractor notified the government of what was happening and was directed to replace these areas with new plaster. The government claimed that the replastering was a contract requirement. The contractor argued it was extra work. The contractor performed the replastering work under protest and then filed its claim for an equitable adjustment in the contract price.

The Veterans Administration Contract Appeals Board first determined that the cause for the falling plaster was not due to the contractor's working in the area. The plaster was falling because of its general deteriorated state. The board then had to decide whether the replastering was part of the contract work under the clause in the painting section of the specification which provided: "Plaster: Remove efflorescence. Fill all holes and cracks with patching plaster. Finish surface in manner to match surrounding plaster."

In interpreting the contract clause, the board concluded that the work required to remove efflorescence is totally different from the work required to replace fallen plaster. In fact, the patching plaster called for in the specification provision was not suitable for replastering large areas. The inclusion of the disputed contract clause under the painting section of the specification and not under a separate plastering section was considered to be further evidence that the replastering work was not required under the efflorescence clause.

On the basis of these facts the board held that it was not reasonable to hold the contractor obligated to replaster fallen deteriorated plaster under its contract. It said it was entitled to an equitable adjustment for performing this extra noncontract work.

CASE 9-9 Owner's Interpretation Loses

A contractor was entitled to an equitable adjustment in its contract price as a result of ambiguous and inconsistent contract terms and specifications, ruled the U.S. Court of Claims [*Leavell-Morrison-Knudsen-Hardeman v. United States,* 436 F.2d 451 (1971)].

Part of the contractor's contract for construction of one phase of the Houston Manned Spacecraft Center called for installation of air-conditioning systems. The contract stated that "ducts shall be insulated . . . ," and the contractor did not dispute this. The contractor did, however, question just what constituted a duct.

After the contractor had started insulation of what it considered to be ducts, the owner's (United States government) contracting officer, during a site inspection, noticed that certain flexible connectors for conveying air from the system's low-pressure metal ducts to ceiling diffusers were not insulated. The contractor contended that these flexible connectors were not ducts. The owner said they were.

At the owner's direction, but under protest, the contractor insulated the connectors. Upon completion, the contractor submitted a claim on the basis that the owner's requirement to insulate the connectors constituted a constructive change order since there was no contract requirement to insulate this work.

The Corps of Engineers Board of Contract Appeals denied the contractor's claim by ruling that anyone bidding on the job should have understood that the specification drafter considered the flexible connectors to be ducts and therefore they were to be insulated. The contractor appealed the ruling and the Court of Claims reversed the board's decision.

Reviewing the contract documents, the court noted that although the specifications referred several times to the equipment in question as "flexible ducts" they were also referred to as "flexible connections" and as "flexible hose." In another part of the specifications, noted the court, "ductwork" was required to be constructed out of steel or aluminum but the flexible connectors were to be constructed from a totally different material.

The court concluded that the contract was ambiguous as far as duct insulation was concerned and that the contractor was entitled to an equitable adjustment in its price.

**CASE 9-10   Incomplete Drawings Result in
An Extra to Contractor**

The Armed Forces Board of Contract Appeals ruled that a contractor on a school project was acting reasonably when it did not anticipate building several rooms as typical classrooms simply because of their juxtaposition to other typical classrooms when the working drawings did not so specify. The board granted the contractor the right to an equitable adjustment in its contract price to meet the construction requirements for a typical room.

During construction of the school, located at Fort Sam Houston, Texas, a dispute arose over whether the owner, the United States government, intended 10 rooms to be built as typical classrooms. The contractor claimed that since the working drawings did not specify that the 10 rooms in question were to be of typical classroom construction, as the plans specified for some other classrooms, it had not treated them as typical in preparing its bid.

The government argued that since the 10 classrooms were located in rows of rooms, the rest of which on the drawings were touched by a note calling for typical construction, it should have been obvious to the contractor that they, too, were to be treated as typical classrooms.

The contractor countered that it had been reasonable in relying on the information given by the typical classroom note on the architectural floor plan drawings to determine which rooms were to be typical classrooms. The contractor argued that since 10 rooms were not included, the owner meant that they were not to be typical.

The board ruled

> In view of the fact that there were several classrooms not noted for typical classroom treatment which the government did not intend should be given such treatment [twelve of a total of twenty-two which carried no notation]. We are not persuaded that a bidder should have been alerted to a contrary intention with respect to the [ten] rooms in dispute merely by the fact that seven of them were located in rows of similar type rooms in which the typical classroom note appeared on two or three other rooms in those rows.

The board said it did not agree that it should have been obvious to a bidder that a draftsman failed, or was unable, to stretch the typical classroom note by arrow or by line to include all rooms in the row which were to be typical, particularly because it would have been so simple for the draftsman to do.

It concluded that

> there were no indications on the architectural plans sufficient to alert a reasonably prudent bidder to the government's intention that the rooms in dispute were to be laid out as typical classrooms or to have occasioned an inquiry by such a bidder as to that intention [*Appeal of Browning Constr. Co.,* ASBCA 17708, 73-1 BCA 9913 (1973)].

CASE 9-11   Contract Ambiguity Denied, Specifications Clearly Written

To be considered ambiguous, a contract must be susceptible to more than one interpretation, and the contractor's interpretation must be reasonable if it is to be controlling, ruled the General Services Board of Contract Appeals [*Appeal of Robert E. McKee General Contractor, Inc.,* GSBCA 3175, 71-1 BCA 8625 (1970)].

One part of the painting specifications for the interior of a new federal building provided that "all surfaces above the lay-in [ceiling] panels shall have applied two coats of white gloss enamel to increase reflectance." Above the ceiling panels there were electrical conduit, fittings, and other metal work. The contractor said it was not responsible for painting these fixtures and because it was directed to, it was entitled to an additional fee.

Although the contractor argued that it was not required to paint the metal fittings because painting them would not increase reflectance, it failed to offer evidence and the government denied the contention. The contractor's second basis for its claim was that the specifications were ambiguous.

The board felt the contractor failed to prove that the specification was open to more than one reasonable interpretation. Denying the contractor's claim, the board held "the language of the specifications is clear, and sufficiently specific and directive as to lead to no ambiguity . . . . Accordingly, the board finds that the contractor was required to paint the electrical conduit, fittings and metal work. . . ."

CASE 9-12   Responsibility for Work Not Detailed in Drawings

The government has held a contractor responsible for doing certain electrical hookups even though the contract drawings did not detail the connections [*Appeal of Northeast Constr. Company of West Virginia*, DOTCAB 68-33 and 68-33A, 69-1 BCA 7556 (1969)].

The case involved a Coast Guard contract for construction of two barracks complete with all connections to the exterior utility services. After the work was started, the contractor requested the contracting officer to propose various changes because there was no contract drawing or provision requiring electrical hookup and connection of various items.

A change was issued for the work without a price, which was to be settled on future negotiations. However, the contracting officer subsequently determined that the work was part of the original contract and refused to allow any additional compensation. The contractor performed the work under protest and then sought payment for the work.

The sole issue before the Department of Transportation Contract Appeals Board was whether the contractor was required, by contract, to do the electrical connections despite the lack of electrical-hookup details in the drawings. In order to arrive at a decision, the board held that it was required to read all parts of the contract to establish its meaning and effect.

The specifications, the board noted, generally provided and anticipated that the contractor was responsible for a complete job, which included a fully operable electrical system. In light of the specifications, the board then considered whether the contractor's interpretation, based solely on the lack of detailed drawings was reasonable. It held:

> It is true that the electrical hookup details . . . were omitted from the contract. However, the omission of some detail does not relieve the contractor from the responsibility of performing a complete job otherwise required in the contract. The decisive test is whether the omission created such an ambiguity in the contract that the interpretation adopted and relied upon by the contractor was reasonable under the circumstances.

A reasonable interpretation of the contract as a whole obviously includes the necessary connections for the proper functioning of the equipment, the board said. It is not mandatory that every requirement be detailed in the drawings so long as "the contractor is given sufficiently clear notice of his requirements and obligations in the specifications," it explained.

In this case, even without detailed drawings, the contractor's contractual obligations were clear, the board said. The contractor's interpretation was found to be both strained and unreasonable, and its claim for additional compensation was denied.

CASE 9-13   Trade Custom Used to Settle Dispute

A Massachusetts state court has ruled that evidence of trade custom is admissible in cases where a contract is ambiguous [*Hardware Specialties, Inc., v. Mishara Constr. Company, Inc.,* 311 N.E.2d 564 (Mass. App., 1974)].

When a hardware subcontractor on a public housing project argued that it was not responsible for installing hardware under its contract, the general contractor disputed this interpretation and directed the installation. After installing the hardware, the subcontractor sued to recover the extra costs it incurred.

In court, the subcontractor argued that portions of the prime contract called for the installation of the finished hardware by another trade and that business custom did not call for it to perform the work.

Further, it claimed that the subcontract was ambiguous because although it required the subcontractor to perform and furnish all work, labor, and materials necessary for the completion of a particular portion of the specifications, it did not clearly specify whether the subcontractor should install the hardware. In fact, certain portions of the specifications indicated that a third party would install the hardware in question.

The court noted that the contract was, in fact, ambiguous and uncertain. Under these circumstances, it ruled that evidence of business custom "was admissable to resolve the ambiguity with respect to the duty of installation."

After reviewing the subcontract, current trade custom, and various portions of the specifications, the court upheld the subcontractor's claim for additional compensation.

CASE 9-14   Trade Practice Does Not Affect
Prime Contractor's Obligations

The General Services Board of Contract Appeals had held that a subcontractor undertaking a prime contract is responsible for all phases of that contract even though trade practice would assign certain portions of the work to another type of specialty contractor.

A contractor that was ordinarily a subcontractor won a prime contract on a federal project being supervised by a construction manager. Although the contract, which called for the completion of "all work of plastic, wall board and fireproofing," specifically required the installation of gypsum tile, the contractor argued that it was not its responsibility to install the tile. The basis of the contractor's argument was that it is trade practice that such work normally be performed by a masonry contractor.

Noting that in this instance the contractor was not a subcontractor but rather a prime contractor, the board ruled that it was the contractor's responsibility under the terms of the contract to furnish and install the disputed tiles.

In reaching its final conclusion that the contractor was not entitled to any extra compensation for the increased cost of installing the tile, the board stated that it was the contractor's obligation to coordinate its work with the other trades on the project. To fulfill this obligation, the board said that the contractor could hire its own masonry subcontractor to perform the specified work.

The board ruled

> In the light of our discussion, the contractor's argument that historically drywall contractors are not commonly required to install gypsum tile, while perhaps persuasive in determining work responsibility between two subcontractors, is irrelevant here. It is a well established principle of law that trade practices cannot override unambiguous contract provisions [*Appeal of William Armstrong & Sons, Inc.,* GSBCA 4032, 74-2 BCA 10,958 (1974)].

CASE 9-15   Clear Subcontract Cannot Be Changed by Trade Practice

A general contractor, claiming trade practice, cannot withhold final payment to a subcontractor on the ground that the general contractor had not received final payment from the owner, held a New York County Court [*Cable-Wiedemer, Inc. v. A. Friederich & Sons Co.,* 71 Misc, 2d 443 (1972)].

The subcontractor claimed that it was entitled to final payment because it had fully and satisfactorily completed its contract. The general contractor denied payment because, it said, it had not yet received final approval or compensation from the owner. The general contractor argued that "by trade custom and usage the general contractor always withholds moneys retained from a subcontractor pending final approval and acceptance of the total job."

The subcontract stated that "any balance due the subcontractor shall be paid within 30 days . . . after his work is finally approved and accepted by the Architect and/or Engineer." Included in the subcontractor's claim was a letter from the architect saying that a portion of the work had been approved and accepted. The architect added that payment for, and approval of, the total project did not relate to the fact that the subcontractor's work had been approved. But the general contractor denied the letter as sufficient proof of satisfactory completion of the subcontract.

In view of the clear subcontract provision, the court said, "there is no reason to resort to trade practices or evidence of custom for an interpretation when the contract is unambiguous." The meaning of the subcontract clause "may not be changed by an attempt to invoke trade custom," it said.

The general contractor's position, the court said, implies that even though a subcontractor's work was satisfactorily completed, it would have to wait because the work of another subcontractor was unsatisfactory or incomplete.

The court added that although the subcontractor had no control over the work of either the general contractor or other subcontractors, it is bound to be affected by their delay or incompetence. And if this was intended, the court said, it should have been spelled out in the contract.

The court concluded that final approval required in the subcontract need not be in any particular form nor given directly to the general contractor. "Final approval need only be given in a manner sufficient to clearly indicate the architect's approval," it said.

CASE 9-16   Specific Contract Provision Prevails

A specific provision in specifications takes precedence over a general floor plan, and a demand that the contractor furnish more expensive equipment than the specifications require amounts to a contract change, the Armed Services Board of Contract Appeals has ruled [*Appeal of Florida Builders, Inc.,* ASBCA 9013, 69-2 BCA 8014 (1969)].

The case involved the type of kitchen ranges a contractor was supposed to furnish. The specifications provided that the ranges "be similar and equal to the following brands" and then listed three manufacturers and models.

One of the models designated had only three burners. The contractor selected this model, but the government rejected it, claiming that the floor plan showing the location of the ranges had four circles on the range diagram. This, the government said, meant that the contract required four-burner ranges.

The board held that the three-burner ranges were permissible under the contract. The detailed specification provision, it said, determined what was contractually permissible. "The mere outline of four burners on the floor plans . . . cannot be considered a specific requirement for four burners."

CASE 9-17   The Meaning of "etc" Must Be
Related to Other Contract Words

The Armed Services Board of Contract Appeals has allowed a contractor extra compensation for doing work that was not included within the scope of "etc." as used in the contract [*Appeal of Apache Flooring Co.,* ASBCA 14355, 69-2 BCA 8011 (1969)].

Under the contract the contractor was to install new floor tile at Warren Air Force Base, Wyoming. The dispute was over whether the contractor had to disconnect, remove, and reinstall the toilets. The contractor had done this work under protest and then claimed additional compensation.

The contract's controversial provision stated, "Contractor shall remove by disconnecting plumbing, piping, vents, etc., from ranges, washers, dryers, refrigerators, etc., as necessary . . . . It shall be the contractor's responsibility to disconnect and remove any existing equipment and appliances necessary to install new floor tile."

The board held that the word "etc." did not include toilets, which are neither equipment nor appliances, and that the contractor was entitled to extra compensation in removing and reinstalling them.

"The word 'etc.' at the conclusion of that enumeration may broaden the listing to include items not specifically called out," it said. "However, where general words follow an enumeration of things, they are not to be construed in their widest extent but are held to apply only to things of the same general kind as those specifically mentioned." It granted the contractor's claim.

CASE 9-18   Owner Warrants the Adequacy of
Plans Contractor Uses

A contractor was entitled to damages for delays resulting from the government's breach of an implied warranty to furnish a set of drawings that were adequate for construction, the U.S. Court of Claims has ruled. The contractor, in reviewing the drawings during the bidding stage, was not required to analyze them to see if they were adequate and had a right to assume their adequacy, the court said.

The ruling was made in a suit filed against the United States by a general contractor to recover damages suffered by itself and its subcontractors during construction of an extension to the Department of State Building in Washington, D.C. The contractor based its action on a breach of warranty, claiming that the government had furnished illegible and inadequate plans and drawings.

The General Services Administration Board of Contract Appeals denied the contractor's claim on the ground that it lacked any jurisdiction to hear the appeal. The case then went to the U.S. Court of Claims.

Although plans furnished by the government need not be "perfect," they must be adequate for the intended purpose, the court said. In addition, when the government furnishes the contractor with detailed plans and specifications, there is an implied warranty that construction in accordance with the drawings and specifications will result in the satisfactory completion of the building, it said.

The court found that the government had failed to prepare the drawings with ordinary care and had issued them before performing necessary checking. In fact, the drawings "were not sufficiently legible or coordinated to permit satisfactory construction," the court said. Subsequently, the government, on its own determination, issued new drawings to eliminate the deficiencies.

In response to the government's argument that the drawing deficiencies were so obvious that the contractor should have recognized them and anticipated the delay, the court held:

> The true condition of the drawings was unknown to the plaintiff [contractor] at the time it bid the project. Seemingly, even the defendant [government] was unaware of the full extent of the inadequacies and lack of coordination in the drawings, particularly after the addenda were issued. There was no reason for the plaintiff to suspect that legible drawings could not be easily secured to replace those which were unreadable, or that the addenda drawings did not correct most, if not all, of the coordination errors apparent in the original drawings. Further, plaintiff was under no contractual or legal obligation to inspect the drawings to determine their adequacy for construction prior to the contract award. Rather, its study of the contract documents was merely for purposes of estimating its bid, and it has not been shown that plaintiff knew or should have known how defective the drawings actually were. Therefore, plaintiff's pre-bid examination of the drawings did not render the implied warranty inoperative through waiver or estoppel, and plaintiff may invoke such warranty as a basis for recovery [*John McShain, Inc. v. United States*, 412 F.2d 1218 (1969)].

> The court concluded that the government had breached its warranty, entitling the contractor and its subcontractors to reasonable compensation for the period of delay.

CASE 9-19   Prime Does Not Guarantee Design

In determining the legal effect of a standard construction contract guaranty clause, the Supreme Court of Washington has ruled on appeal that a prime contractor guaranteed his material and workmanship, and not the design.

The court concluded that the prime contractor was not liable for damages resulting from numerous defects and inadequacies in the curtain walls that its subcontractor had fabricated and installed.

The prime contractor had entered into a written contract to build a high-rise apartment building in Seattle, Washington. The project specifications had been prepared by the owner's architect. The specifications required use of a curtain wall of a specific trade name which, if used, would have been suitable for the building installation. However, the architect subsequently modified the specifications to require a lighter, less costly curtain wall. The specifications stated in the workmanship clause that the curtain walls were to be fabricated and installed in a first-class manner by a manufacturer regularly engaged in this kind of work, so as not to allow any weather infiltration.

The specifications also provided that the subcontractor was to notify the architect if he felt it necessary to modify the materials, workmanship or methods specified in order to meet contract requirements. Neither the prime contractor nor the subcontractor ever notified the architect that modifications were necessary.

After the building was completed and the architect accepted it, numerous defects were found in the curtain-wall units. They caused leaking exteriors. When the prime contractor refused to correct the defects, the owner claimed that the defects were the prime contractor's fault and that it was his responsibility to correct them. The owner based his argument on the terms of the standard guaranty clause in the general provisions of the prime contract. However, the court strictly construed the guaranty clause, which provided:

> Neither the final certificate nor payment nor any provision of the Contract Documents shall relieve the Contractor of responsibility for faulty materials or workmanship and, unless otherwise specified, he shall remedy any defects due thereto and pay for any damage to other work resulting therefrom which shall appear within . . . one year from the date of substantial completion [*Teufel v. Wienir*, 68 Wash. 2d 31, 411 P.2d 151 (1966)].
>
> The court held that it was the architect who specified by trade name the curtain wall to be used. The curtain wall specified in the modified specifications was not suitable for the purpose intended, the court said, and this was a design error. Since the leaks in the curtain wall were a result of a design defect and not due to faulty material or workmanship, the court concluded that the prime contractor was neither liable nor responsible for corrections under the standard guaranty clause.

CASE 9-20   Inaction on Discrepancy Can
Penalize Contractor

A contractor was entitled to an equitable adjustment for performing additional work even though it did not seek government clarification of a minor inconsistency in the contract, the U.S. Court of Claims has ruled. However, in two other instances, the court denied any recovery because the contractor failed to have obvious and patent contract discrepancies resolved by the government [*D & L Constr. Co. & Associates v. United States,* 402 F.2d 990 (1968)].

During the construction of a Capehart housing project, the contractor encountered various problems relating to work it was required to perform. Three separate claims were presented for review by the Court of Claims, each centering around the interpretation of Art. 2(c) of the General Provisions of the contract. This article provided, in part:

"In any case of discrepancy, either in the figures, in the Drawings, or in the Specifications, the matter shall promptly be submitted to the Contracting Officer, who shall promptly obtain a determination in writing from the Commissioner. Any adjustment by the eligible builder without such determination shall be at his own risk and expense."

The court was required, under separate factual situations, to determine whether a discrepancy existed, whether the contractor knew or should have known that a discrepancy existed, whether the discrepancy was of such a scope as to require the contractor to submit the facts to the contracting officer for clarification, and, finally, whether if the contractor was obligated to perform the disputed work as part of its contract without seeking clarification.

Discrepancies   The first claim involved determination of the method specified for constructing foundations, footings, and stem walls for 215 noncommissioned-officer units. The contractor claimed that, based on the plans and specifications, it planned to use standard forms for pouring uniform stem walls and foundations. However, after several foundations had been poured it was shown individual large-scale drawings for each house which indicated varying ground elevations around the perimeter of each house. The contractor was directed to abandon the use of standard forms and was required to construct individually tailored stem walls and foundations for each house. The contractor claimed that this constituted a change for which it was entitled to extra compensation.

The contractor alleged that there was no discrepancy in the contract documents requiring it to submit the problem to the government for clarification. Although it admitted that certain minor differences existed between the grading and drainage plans and the structural details, it claimed that no actual conflict existed when the documents were considered in the light of the general practice prevalent in the trade and past experience.

The government claimed that the contract required individually tailored foundations. It argued that since the contractor knew of the inconsistencies at the time it submitted its bid and had either failed to understand the meaning of the contour drawings or failed to seek clarification of the discrepancy, the contractor must bear the additional costs in changing from standard forms to individual forms. The government said that if the contractor had sought clarification as required, it would have been told that individual forms had to be used and the contractor could have bid on that expectation.

Before determining the actual meaning of the contract documents, the court established the guidelines for interpreting the contract. It was noted that the contractor had extensive experience in the construction of mass-produced houses of this kind. The court said, "This experience, under somewhat similar contracts, may be considered in determining the reasonableness of plaintiff's [contractor] interpretation of the contract documents."

The court found that the contractor had properly relied on the structural drawings, which were for the stated purpose of depicting the intended structure and foundation. The contractor's assumed error in the grading and drainage drawings for foundation purposes was further substantiated because these drawings were scaled so that 1 inch depicted 50 feet and therefore lacked any specific foundation details. Also, the balanced cut and fill of the dirt on the project would have been consistent with its interpretation and use of standard forms, whereas with tailored foundations it was required to remove a large surplus of earth.

The court then said, "Under the circumstances of this case, it is clear that the 'admitted inconsistencies' were not so gross and patent as to constitute adequate warning to plaintiff [contractor] that it was obliged to submit them to the contracting officer for his determination."

The court held that the contractor's interpretation was "within the zone of reasonableness" and therefore its interpretation, rather than that of the government, which had drafted the contract, should be adopted. The contractor was accordingly entitled to extra compensation under the changes provision that was written in the contract, the court said.

The two other claims involved the contractor's contention that it was required to plaster walls not so indicated in the contract and that it was required to construct larger roof overhangs than specified. In both these instances the court found the contract provisions were in direct conflict with each other. This required the contractor to submit the matter to the contracting officer for determination. The court stated that the contractor "cannot now bridge the crevasse in its favor; i.e., plaintiff cannot rely on the principle that ambiguities in contracts written by the government are construed against the drafter." The government's interpretation being reasonable, the contractor's claims were denied.

Access Road   The contractor was also entitled, the court said, to additional costs caused by the government's breach of its warranty that there would be suitable access to the site.

The contract drawings indicated that suitable access to the project site existed. In addition, the contract, as well as a letter written by the contracting officer, stated that the government would provide access during the construction period.

During the initial phases of construction all three of the principal access roads were open. However, when the government learned that the contractor's laborers were going to place pickets at the access-road gates, it directed and limited the contractor's access to a fourth and unsatisfactory road to allow the other contractors working on the site free access. The route designated for the contractor's use increased its traveling distance and its cost of performance.

The court held that the government had warranted that the contractor would have suitable access to the site. It said the government breached the warranty by limiting the contractor's access to one out-of-the-way and unsatisfactory road. Therefore the court ruled that the contractor was entitled to damages incurred by being limited to one specified road.

CASE 9-21   Contractor's Negligence Limits Subcontractor's Liability

The Supreme Court of Nebraska has ruled that a general contractor cannot hold its subcontractor liable for indemnification in cases where the contractor is negligent unless their contract's indemnification clause expressly covers the situation [*Peter Kiewit Sons, Co. v. O'Keefe Elevator Co., Inc.,* 213 N.W.2d 731 (1974)].

An employee of the subcontractor, injured on the job site, brought suit against the general contractor, claiming that his injuries were the result of the contractor's negligence. After hearing the evidence, a court found the contractor guilty of negligence and the subcontractor's employee guilty of contributory negligence. The general contractor paid the employee the damages awarded by the court and then sued its subcontractor for indemnification under a clause in their agreement that provided the subcontractor would "indemnify the Contractor against and save him harmless from any and all claims, suits, or liability for injuries to property, injuries to persons . . . and any other claims, suits or liability, on account of any act or omission of the Subcontractor, or any of his officers, agents, employees, or servants. . . ."

In its argument before the court, the contractor cited a number of cases in which other courts had held that a general contractor may be indemnified against its own negligence.

Although the court acknowledged these precedents, it concluded that this specific provision did not expressly permit the general contractor to seek indemnification from the subcontractor if the general contractor was negligent. Rather, the clause limited the contractor's right to recover from the subcontractor only to those situations where acts or omissions of the subcontractor were the specific cause of the loss. The court stated "that the parties are presumed to intend that the indemnitee shall not be indemnified for a loss occasioned by its own negligence unless the language of the contract affirmatively expresses an intent to indemnify for such loss."

CASE 9-22   Subcontractor Liable when Prime Is Negligent

A subcontractor was held liable to the prime contractor under an indemnification clause of a contract even though the prime was negligent as a point of law. The Supreme Court of Alabama held the subcontractor liable since it was the party primarily responsible for an injury [*Walter L. Couse & Co. v. Hardy Corp.,* 274 So.2d 322 (1973)].

The dispute involved liability for a pedestrian who allegedly was injured on a public sidewalk that was torn up and made unsafe by the subcontractor in the performance of its work. The pedestrian sued the owner, the prime, and the subcontractor. The prime then filed a claim against the subcontractor based on the indemnity provision of the subcontract: "The Subcontractor will protect, defend, indemnify and hold harmless [prime contractor] from any damages, claims, liabilities, or expenses whatsoever . . . arising out of or connected with the performance of this order."

The question before the court was whether the prime could collect from the subcontractor under this clause when the prime was negligent as a matter of law. The court said that for any indemnity provision to prevail it must clearly provide that the subcontractor agrees to indemnify the prime contractor against claims even though the contractor might be guilty as a matter of law since it was responsible for its subcontractor's acts.

The court said that in construing the indemnity provision, the word negligence does not have to appear. The wording was clear, it said, that the subcontractor would be responsible for damages even though the contractor might be guilty of negligence where the injury arose from the subcontractor's performance and where the subcontractor was the cause of the negligence. But, the court said, the contractor had the right only since it was not guilty of the primary negligent act that caused the injury out of which the liability arose.

CASE 9-23   Contract No-Damage-for-Delay Clause Bars Claim

A contract clause which barred a contractor's claim for delays arising from a specific event is valid and enforceable, and the contractor is not entitled to any increased costs resulting from the delay, a New York court has ruled.

The contract called for reconstruction of a portion of a New York state highway and the construction of a new highway segment. The new highway was to run through two parcels of private property, which were occupied by the owners when the contract with the state was executed.

The contractor claimed that the state breached the contract because it delayed in acquiring the property and allowing the contractor to perform its work on the property. The delay, claimed the contractor, hindered its progress and caused it to incur excess costs even though it finished work on time. The state denied that it delayed obtaining possession of the property or that the contractor was damaged by the nonavailability of the property. In addition, the state argued that the contractor was barred from claiming damages for this delay because a special note in the contract forbid such a claim. The note stated:

> The Contractor should understand that immediate possession of all buildings within the highway limits is not now available. Negotiations for possession are now in process and such buildings, with their surrounding premises, will be available to the Contractor as soon as they have been vacated.

The state appealed the lower court's decision that granted the contractor's claim on the basis of the state's unreasonable and unwarranted delay in acquiring the property. A primary question on appeal to the New York Supreme Court, Appellate Division, was whether a contract provision barring a claim is valid and enforceable and if so, under what conditions it will be construed as a bar.

In reaching its final decision that the contract clause was valid and enforceable to preclude the contractor's claim, the court held:

> If the delay or obstruction is within the contemplation of the parties at the time the contract is entered into the "no damage" clause will be valid and enforceable unless the delay was caused by conduct constituting active interference with performance.
>
> In the instant case it becomes clear that the alleged delay of which claimant complains is the precise delay provided for in the Special Note provision of the contract.
>
> The delays complained of, and which the state sought to protect itself against, were within the contemplation of the parties at the time the contract was entered into and . . . the delay was not brought about by the active interference of the state. [*Peckham Road Co. v. State of New York,* 300 N.Y.S.2d 174 (1969) aff'd 321 N.Y.S.2d 117 (1971)].

TEN

Breach of Contract

Not all breaches are created equal, nor do the contracting parties necessarily have the same rights and remedies for the different breaches. Although the breach can take various forms, there is a dividing line between a *material*, or substantial, *breach* and an *immaterial*, or minor, *breach*. A material breach will give rise to certain remedies, whereas an immaterial breach may well have other remedies. The distinction between the two is a matter of degree, often left to the judge's discretion. Many contracts specifically provide and list various forms of breach which may be deemed material. One cannot assume that a material breach in one contract will automatically be a material breach in another contract. The distinction and awareness that a difference exists is of utmost importance because if the contractor should employ the remedies for the material breach, e.g., throwing a subcontractor off the job, when in fact only an immaterial breach exists, the contractor might find out the hard way that it reacted unreasonably and used unreasonable force and remedies, and *it* might be declared the one in default.

In a recent case, a contractor's termination of a subcontract was deemed to be premature and a default of its subcontract obligations because the subcontractor could still reasonably complete its work on time. Since the subcontractor was not in default, the contractor was held to be in default [*Rimmer & Garrett, Inc. v. Donnell & Fussell*, 306 So.2d 74 (La. App. 1975)].

The question of default is all-important to the breach-of-contract concept. The mere allegation that you have been damaged does not prove a breach. The mere allegation that the other party did something you did not anticipate does not mean there has been a breach. For a breach to exist, one party must be able to *prove* the existence of a default by the other party (Cases 10-1 and 10-2). For a default to exist, one party must be able to prove that the other party was under a contractual or legal obligation to do or not to do a given act (Case 5-8). On the face of it, it appears to be a simple procedure. However, too often contractors are damaged, scream breach, and create animosity and adverse feelings when in fact no default ever occurred. Find the obligation, prove it, and then be prepared to prove the default before alleging a breach. Finding the contractual obligation is not a simple procedure. The contract should be reviewed by the attorney. The obligation and breach of that obligation must be proved before any breach of contract is established.

A breach can occur even before the performance date. Legally this is called an *anticipatory breach.* More often than not it occurs in a moment of passion. Suppose a contractor and subcontractor have two independent subcontracts for two totally separate and distinct projects. On project A the subcontractor, say a sheet-metal worker, is awaiting final retainage. On project B the contract has been entered into, the subcontractor has taken dimensions and submitted drawings which have been approved, is now fabricating, but is not scheduled to deliver for several months. Let us also assume that it takes 2 months to fabricate the materials after final approval of submittals for project B. During the negotiation of the final retainage on project A, the contractor backcharges the subcontractor and after a fiery battle the subcontractor takes the check, less the backcharge, storms out of the office, and swears that it will never perform or complete any other contract or project for the prime, whether in existence now or in the future.

Does the prime contractor have to wait until the date of scheduled delivery before it holds the subcontractor in breach of contract? Understand that the prime contractor will possibly be in default if it waits until scheduled performance to find out that the subcontractor meant what it said, since it would take many months before a new subcontractor could fabricate materials. Only the lawyer would make money. The answer is "no." The law states that where words, acts, or conduct indicate a clear intent not to perform, the injured party need not wait until the performance date to declare the other party in default. The default can be declared now, and the contract can be deemed to have been anticipatorily breached. In the heat of passion one should watch one's words lest one be deemed to be teetering on the verge of an anticipatory breach. It is also suggested that when such a statement has been made by another, an immediate letter be written setting forth the true facts and asking for an immediate return response which should indicate whether the intention to default was properly interpreted. Often the letter can avoid great anxiety and large legal bills.

Since the contractual obligations differ from contract to contract, no book can state what instance or event is a breach or whether that breach is a material or an immaterial breach. Remember, however, that a breach can be waived [*Page v. H.B. White & Son, Inc.,* 277 So.2d 725 (La. 1973)] (Case 10-14). Your right to collect damages for a breach can be waived. The breach might be legally forgotten unless the injured party protects its rights (Case 10-3). When the event occurs, the contractor must immediately go on record indicating at the very least that it is reserving its rights. The breach must be protested.

Breaches might involve cardinal changes, excessive changes, or bad estimates (Cases 10-4 and 10-5), failure to give proper access, unreasonable delays, or implied and express warranties (Case 10-6), failure to properly coordinate, misrepresentations (Case 10-7), excessive force, improper testing (Case 10-8), defective workmanship (Case 10-9), irrational acts (Case 10-10), or a myriad of different possibilities. In one case the architect and owner had agreed that the cost of the project should not exceed a certain amount; unfortunately, the actual cost as bid was 100 percent higher than estimated, and the court ruled the architect could be denied its compensation [*Stanley Consultants, Inc. v. H. Kalicak Constr. Co.,* 383 F. Supp. 315 (D.E.D. Mo. 1974)].

One of the most usual breach claims relates to progress payments. The fundamental concept is still the same: find the *obligation and duty* and prove that the other party is in default of that obligation. You must also be able to prove you have fulfilled all conditions and obligations on your part that were to be performed to date (Case 10-12).

It is generally acknowledged that on construction contracts there is *no* implied right to receive periodic progress payments. The right to progress payments is a contractual right, and unless a clause exists granting the right, there is no right to receive payment until completion of the work. Many alleged breaches relating to progress payments are unfounded, as the complaining party is truly unable to find a default. The contractual right to progress payments is normally conditioned upon the requisitioning person's fulfilling of legal conditions precedent and filing various prerequisite documents. If these documents are not filed, the right to receive payments may not arise. The question whether a contractor is entitled to stop work because it has not been paid its progress payment, in strict accord with the contract, is again a question of degree. If there had been a *substantial* failure, a material breach exists. If the failure, although it does exist, is not of a substantive nature, it appears that the contractor has no right to stop work. The leading case is one wherein the court held

> in a building or construction contract like the one in question, calling for the performing of labor and furnishing of materials covering a long period of time and involving large expenditures, a stipulation for payments on account to be made from time to time during the progress of the work must be deemed so *material* that a substantial failure to pay would justify the contractor in declining to proceed. . . . As is usually the case with building contracts, it evidently was in the contemplation of the parties that the contractor could not be expected to finance the operation to completion without receiving the stipulated payments on account as the work progressed. In such cases a substantial compliance as to advance payments is a condition precedent to the contractor's obligation to proceed [*Guerini Stone Co. v. P. J. Carlin Constr. Co.,* 248 U.S 334 (1919)].

Note, however, that this decision talks about a substantial failure to pay in the first part, and in the latter part it talks about substantial compliance. The trend seems to be that there must be a substantial compliance and that a failure to substantially comply with payment obligations is a breach and would justify abandonment of further performance. A second-tier subcontractor who was to receive payment by monthly installments properly viewed the subcontractor's failure to make monthly installments as a material breach of contract entitling it to suspend work until payment was received [*Watson v. Auburn Iron Works, Inc.*, 318 N.E.2d 508 (Ill. App. Ct. 1974); see also *Ringelberg v. Kawka*, 219 N.W. 593 (Mich. 1928)]. The added costs to perform the work, assuming the contractor refuses to continue, rest with the owner, and the owner cannot seek recoupment from the contractor. Substantial compliance depends on facts and is not subject to absolute guidelines. The right of a subcontractor to receive final payment, even before the prime contractor's receipt of payment, seems to be the trend (Case 10-13).

Another major area of dispute relates to the owner's implied obligation to coordinate the work of the various prime contractors. The word "implied" must be used since actually most contracts with multiple primes specify that the contractors shall coordinate between themselves and usually specify that one particular contractor has ultimate responsibility. However, a line of decisions has held that the owner cannot totally void itself of the responsibility. From a practical point of view, the general construction prime contractor has little power over the electrical prime contractor. There is only one person with the right to terminate the electrical prime contractor; there is only one person who holds the purse strings; that is the owner. Contractors are obligated to make all reasonable attempts in trying to coordinate the work; they must notify the owner when another prime fails in its obligation, and then the owner may be liable for breach of contract if it fails to take *reasonable* steps in trying to coordinate performance. The obligation placed upon the owner does not appear to be an absolute one, but it is an obligation to take reasonable steps.

As the contract is drawing to a close, parties often find themselves at each other's throats screaming "breach" for failing to comply in strict and exact accord with the contract. Payment is refused, and lawsuits are commenced. Completion is often a question of degree. The fact that the contractor has failed in some respect to adhere fully to strict performance should not be a basis for denying recovery of substantial monies. The contractor is never permitted to deviate from the contract, with an intent to deceive, and still recover full payment. On the other hand, where its error was neither fraudulent nor willful and it has *substantially* performed its work, it will not be denied compensation (Case 10-9). The question of substantial performance was posed to the court in a New York case. Judge Cardozo ruled:

> an omission, both trivial and innocent, will sometimes be atoned for by allowance of the resulting damage, and will not always be the breach of a condition to be followed by a forfeiture. . . . Nowhere will change be tolerated, however, if it is so dominant or pervasive as in any real or substantial measure to frustrate the purpose of the contract . . . . There is no general license to install whatever, in the builder's judg-

ment, may be regarded as "just as good" . . . . The question is one of degree, to be answered, if there is doubt, by the triers of the facts [jury] . . . and, if the inferences are certain, by the judges of the law . . . . *[Jacob & Youngs v. Kent,* 230 N.Y. 239 (1921)].

Probably the most important aspect of the decision is found in its equitable considerations when the judge said,

The transgressor whose default is unintentional and trivial may hope for mercy if he will offer atonement for his wrong . . . .[ibid.].

The doctrine of substantial performance is based upon the equitable belief that the party who has acted in good faith but has in some minor respect failed to comply fully should still be entitled to the specified compensation less some amount of "atonement" [*Jardine Estates v. Donna Brook Corp.,* 126 A.2d 372 (N.J. 1956)]. For substantial performance to exist the essentials necessary for the use of the project must be present. A contractor should be entitled to the reasonable value of its work, subject to contract limitations, even though it has not *fully* complied with *strict* performance.

Remedies for contractual breaches take various forms. In some instances, where the owner is in default, the contractor might be entitled to the contract price for that portion of the work performed, and in other instances it might be entitled to the reasonable value [*Hayeck Building & Realty Co., Inc. v. Turcotte,* 282 N.E.2d 907 (Mass. 1972)]. The reasonable value might exceed the contract price, especially when the contract price was originally taken at a loss and the owner precluded completion. Some courts, however, note that the reasonable value should not exceed the contract price. The innocent party is generally said to be entitled to recover its damages which flowed from the breach. Damages can be difficult to itemize. The party who has defaulted must shoulder the added costs and burdens to remedy the breach [*Appeal of N. MacFarland Builders, Inc.,* 75-2 BCA 11,608 (1975)].

In other instances the collection of dollars might not be sufficient relief, and the contractor might seek some form of equitable relief. This might involve the court's directing a party specifically to perform an act, or as an alternative the court might enjoin the performance of various acts. Rescission is a possible relief, although not a common one in construction. For a contract to be rescinded, the facts must show that there was a substantial breach, or that the injury caused by the breach was irreparable, or that damages would be inadequate, difficult, or impossible to assess [*Kole v. Parker Yale Development Company,* 536 P.2d 848, *cert. denied* (Colo. C. App., Div. II, 1975)].

The law is complex, but, simply put, the courts try to place the injured party back in the same position it would have been had the breach not occurred. It is up to the innocent party to prove the breach and the costs. It must assert the breach when it occurs, as it may be precluded from raising the breach later (Case 10-14).

CASE 10-1   Must Prove Fault in
Breach-of-Contract Claim

A contractor has been denied breach-of-contract damages allegedly incurred as a result of having been furnished defective plans prepared by the government. The United States Court of Claims held that the government did not breach its implied obligation to furnish plans, specifications, and rock-boring data, which, if followed, would result in satisfactory performance, even though satisfactory performance could not have been so obtained [*Jefferson Constr. Co. v. United States*, 392 F.2d 1006 (1968), *cert. denied* 393 U.S. 842 (1968)].

The contractor had been awarded a contract by the General Services Administration. The plans and specifications were prepared and furnished by the government. In the preparation of the contract documents, the government had taken fifteen core-boring test samples of the subsoil adjacent to the area of the proposed foundation pads. The plans represented the foundation-termination depths at the elevation where the core drillings had indicated refusal. Though the actual core-boring samples were made available for examination, the contractor never examined them. From these plans the contractor unilaterally concluded that it would hit rock ledge at the elevation points of refusal.

The contractor started excavation for the first of the thirty-six foundation pads to the depth indicated on the plans as the refusal point. However, clay was encountered regularly, rather than rock ledge.

The contractor was then directed to excavate to proper depths by the government engineer pursuant to the changed-conditions clause of the contract. Excavation of thirty-four of the thirty-six footings terminated at elevations different from the refusal point.

The fact that the contractor was required to continue performance in the absence of known foundation depths totally disrupted its progress. The disruption delayed the work and forced the contractor to complete it under unanticipated weather conditions. The additional direct costs incurred in changing the excavation termination points were paid for under the changed-conditions clause. The resulting delay damages were the basis for this case.

The Board of Contract Appeals dismissed the request for delay damages, stating that claims for delay damages were breach of contract claims not within the board's jurisdiction. The contractor appealed this decision, alleging that the government warrants the adequacy of its plans and specifications so that compliance therewith will result in acceptable performance. The government breached the contract by furnishing defective plans, it claimed.

The court said that if the problem had arisen from the government's failure to be reasonably careful in its preparation of the plans, the basis for a breach of contract claim would exist. But the fact that the specifications or plans were wrong does not establish a breach. The court noted that the contractor must prove that the elements of negligence and fault were present.

Here, the contractor had proved only that for some unknown reason the government plans were wrong but not why. If the delay was the result of a changed condition without the fault of the government the contractor would be limited to its contractual relief under the changed-conditions clause, the court said. Therefore, as in this case, where the site conditions differed materially from those indicated on the plans and no fault in the preparation of the plans or borings was proved, there can be no breach of contract. The contractor's breach-of-contract claim was denied, and its remedy was limited to that provided by the contract.

CASE 10-2 Contractor Fails to Prove Contract Assertions

The Supreme Court of Alabama has denied a contractor's claim for the cost of bringing additional subsurface material to a jobsite because the contractor failed to show that the owner had made any positive contractual assertions that enough on-site material existed [*Burgess Mining & Constr. Corp., v. City of Bessemer, Alabama*, 312 So. 2d 24 (1975)].

An airport-construction contract provided that "the Contractor may secure topsoil and subbase material from within the project limits." After the contractor was forced to bring additional subbase material to the site, it sued the owner for its extra costs, claiming the owner had warranted sufficient on-site material existed. The owner cited contract provisions requiring bidders to inspect the site and disclaiming responsibility for "actual soil or material conditions" differing from those indicated in the contract.

The contractor relied on decisions of other courts that contractors have the right to rely on owner's statements.

The court said that before these other rulings were applicable the contractor must prove that the contract contained "positive assertions that the material in the project site met the specifications as to quality and quantity."

Holding that the contractor did not prove this, the court denied the contractor's claim.

CASE 10-3 Subcontractor Does Not Have to Insure Against Owner's Error

The Nebraska Supreme Court has ruled that a subcontractor did not breach its contract when it failed to provide the necessary insurance coverage to indemnify an owner-contractor against its own negligence [*Omaha Public Power District v. Natkin & Co.*, 227 N.W. 2d 864 (1975)]. An owner, acting as its own prime contractor for the construction of a power-plant addition, subcontracted part of its mechanical work. The subcontract, which was drawn up by the owner, required the mechanical subcontractor to furnish various insurance certificates. The agreement specifically provided that the subcontractor was not allowed to start work until the insurance had been obtained and approved by the owner.

During construction, one of the subcontractor's employees fell through an unguarded hole in the floor and was injured. The injured employee sued the subcontractor, the owner, and an architect. Although a court found that the subcontractor had not been negligent, it ruled against the owner and its architect.

The owner then brought suit against the subcontractor, seeking indemnification under a hold-harmless clause in the subcontract. When the court refused to permit this action on the ground that the subcontractor had not been negligent, the owner sued the subcontractor for the amount of money it was forced to pay its employee. In this suit, the owner claimed that the subcontractor had breached its contract by not furnishing the necessary insurance to indemnify the owner-contractor against its own negligence.

After finding that the subcontract did not expressly state that the subcontractor would furnish this type of insurance, the court then considered whether the subcontract indicated a clear intention of the parties that such insurance should be provided.

The court noted that the owner did not question the insurance coverage provided by the subcontractor during the initial stages of the project, even though it had the expressed right to stop all work if it did not approve of the coverage. Instead, it permitted the subcontractor to start work. This failure, said the court, indicated that the owner-contractor felt that the insurance coverage complied with the contract. Therefore, the court ruled that the subcontractor had provided adequate insurance coverage and was not obligated to indemnify the owner.

CASE 10-4   Inaccurate Cost Estimate
Is Breach of Contract

The Supreme Court of Michigan has upheld a lower court's decision that an architect's gross underestimation of probable construction costs constituted a breach of contract that could cost the architect his fee and make him liable for the damages of the owner [*Kostohryz v. McGuire,* 212 N.W.2d 850 (1973)].

An architect and an owner entered into a standard architectural contract for the design of a building that required the architect to submit a statement of probable construction cost based on area, volume, and unit costs.

Relying on the architect's estimate that the building would cost approximately $40,000, the owner, who was also the general contractor, went ahead with the project. Four years later and after more than $60,000 had been spent, the building was only partially completed and an additional $20,000 would be required to finish the job.

The owner brought a suit against the architect to recover damages for the architect's malpractice, claiming that the architect's error had breached a contract that required an accurate estimate of probable construction costs.

The architect countered that the estimate was not prepared as a guaranteed or firm figure but was merely an opinion. He cited the contract that provided "The Architect cannot and does not guarantee that bids will not vary from any Statement of Probable Construction Cost or other cost estimate prepared by him."

A lower court had rejected the architect's arguments and found that he had breached the contract and was liable for the damages sustained by the owner. The question before the supreme court was whether sufficient evidence had been submitted to warrant the lower court's decision.

In its review, the supreme court noted that the lower court had ruled on the spirit and purpose of the agreement rather than the specific language. And it had stated, "The fact that the costs exceeded the estimate substantially was sufficient, without the aid of an expert to prove a breach of the architect's contractual duty to render a reasonably accurate statement of probable construction costs."

In regard to the damages, the court went on to say, "An architect who substantially underestimates through lack of skill or care the cost of a proposed structure . . . may not only forfeit his right to compensation but may become liable to his employer for damages."

After hearing all the evidence, the supreme court concluded that the case had been properly presented and sustained the lower court's decision that the contract had been breached.

**CASE 10-5 Estimated Maximum Cost Is Not
a Guaranteed Maximum Price**

A contract that included an estimated maximum cost did not preclude a contractor from recovering a sum in excess of that estimate, held the Supreme Court of Missouri [*J. E. Hathman, Inc. v. Sigma Alpha Epsilon Club,* 491 S.W.2d 261 (1973)].

The contractor was hired to perform demolition work on a building that had been damaged by fire. While the work was under way, the owner prepared plans and specifications for rebuilding the structure. Without taking bids, the owner contracted with the demolition contractor for the reconstruction. A contract was signed before final plans were issued.

The contract, a standard American Institute of Architects form, provided a fee to the contractor of 6 percent of construction costs and an "estimated maximum cost" of $300,000. However, the contractor claimed it was entitled to a sum, including its 6 percent fee, of over $400,000. The owner argued the contractor was entitled to a maximum of $318,000 and the contractor sued for the difference.

Initially, the court said that the contract was not ambiguous and that the parties had clearly entered into a cost-plus-fee arrangement and specified the types of costs which were covered. The court said the owner could not introduce extrinsic evidence to try to prove that the $300,000 was really a guaranteed upset price. But examining the phrase "estimated maximum cost," the court said "estimated" could be defined as approximate. In fact, it said, the word indicates a lack of accuracy.

Concluding that the contractor was entitled to recover the difference, the court said,

> The fact that the word "estimated" was used in conjunction with "maximum cost" does not change the meaning of "estimated" or make the phrase ambiguous. Together they simply indicated an approximation . . . of the maximum cost of labor, material and other construction costs. The phrase is not an expression of a guaranteed maximum, as (the owner) contends.

CASE 10-6   Builder Liable on Its
Implied Warranty

A Kentucky court has held a contractor-seller liable to the purchaser for breach of an implied warranty when water collected in the basement of a new dwelling [*Crawley v. Terhune*, 437 S.W.2d 743 (1969)].

The contractor, after constructing the house, sold it through a real estate broker. Several months after the purchaser moved into the house, rainwater came through the walls, collected in the basement, and would not drain out. The purchaser instituted suit against the contractor, claiming that it had breached an implied warranty. After the lower court entered judgment in favor of the purchaser, the contractor appealed.

The Court of Appeals of Kentucky was required to determine whether an implied warranty could arise out of the sale of a new building and whether the contractor could be held liable for the purchaser's damages under the implied warranty. The court noted that the majority court rule is that no implied warranty exists as to fitness, condition, or quality in the sale of a new dwelling. However, the court refused to accept the majority rule. It stated:

> Because the caveat emptor rule [let the buyer beware] is completely unrealistic and inequitable as applied in the case of the ordinarily inexperienced buyer of a new house from the professional builder-seller, and because a contract by the builder to sell a new house is not much distinguishable from a contract to build a house for another, we are disposed to adopt the minority view to the extent of holding that in the sale of a new dwelling by the builder there is an implied warranty that in its major structural features the dwelling was constructed in a workmanlike manner and using suitable materials.

CASE 10-7   Owner Liable
for Misrepresentation

A contractor can recover extra costs it incurs because the owner misrepresents items specified in the contract, according to the New York Supreme Court, Appellate Division. And the owner is precluded from shifting responsibility for discovering the incorrectly specified conditions to the contractor when the period between bid advertising and opening is too short [*County Asphalt, Inc. v. State of New York*, 40 App. Div.2d 26 (3d Dept. 1972)].

The contractor sued the owner, New York State, for breach of a highway construction contract. The contractor claimed compensation for the cost of certain excavation work which, it said, was misrepresented and omitted in the contract. The state denied the claim for the extra work alleging "there were no misrepresentations as to the subsurface condition of the soil and that . . . [contractor's] failure to make any independent subsurface investigation or analysis of soil conditions estops it from asserting any claim for damages." But the court said that the contractor was not obligated to make its own subsurface investigation because "there was insufficient time to conduct an independent subsurface exploration."

During the design stage the state estimated that excavation would total 1,550,-000 cubic yards of unclassified material and estimated select borrow at 40,000 cubic yards. But the state's contract estimate for excavation was 900,000 cubic yards and borrow was eliminated completely.

In its review and analysis of the original design, the state anticipated encountering more than 250,000 cubic yards of unsuitable material. But the state's proposal form showed this item at less than 90,000 cubic yards. In fact about 225,000 cubic yards of unsuitable material was excavated, and more than 500,000 cubic yards of select borrow was used.

The actual quantity of excavation and borrow exceeded the contract amount by more than 450,000 cubic yards. The state said it did not know why borrow was eliminated from the contract, and it paid the contractor for supplying this material. The state also said that it did not know why the contract estimate for excavation was so low compared with the preliminary estimate.

In deciding that the contractor was entitled to damages, the court said that the actual jobsite inspection did not indicate any difficulties with location and extent of unsuitable material. And, it said, any inspection of subsurface conditions during the three-week period could not be expected to prevail over the misleading information supplied by the state which had been compiled over a three-year period.

The court held that the state had incorrectly set quantities and locations of unsuitable material to be excavated. And, it said, the state, by omitting the borrow provision, implied that after the unsuitable material was removed, the remainder would form a good surface on which common borrow could be used as backfill. The court concluded that the state knew or should have known the existence of the conditions that were not reflected in the information given to prospective bidders.

CASE 10-8   Testing Procedures Improper

A subcontractor that supplied concrete for testing procedures at a flood-control project was allowed to recover the cost of replacing the concrete when it failed performance tests, held the New York Supreme Court's Appellate Division in a memorandum decision.

The prime contractor was to construct a county flood-control project, and the concrete specified was to be subjected to certain compressive strength tests. Testing was to be in accordance with set ASTM procedures.

The subcontractor supplied the concrete in accordance with the contract requirements. One batch of concrete tested after the twenty-eight-day curing period failed the individual compressive test and caused the average of five tests to fall below the minimum designated strength. The prime contractor was then directed to remove the failed concrete and replace it with a new batch. The subcontractor was ordered to furnish additional concrete at no cost.

In an action to foreclose a mechanic's lien, the subcontractor filed suit against both the prime contractor and the county for the costs of supplying additional concrete. The prime contractor argued that it had either been supplied defective concrete by the subcontractor or, in the alternative, that it had, in fact, substantially complied with the county's contract requirements.

The court stated that

> Where a contract contains certain specified tests of performance and provides that
> the passing of such tests shall be deemed conclusive proof of performance, the
> contract is conclusively presumed to have been performed upon the completion or
> fulfillment of the conditions constituting such tests. . . . Where the work, in fact, has
> been substantially performed in accordance with the provisions of a contract, the
> failure to take or pass stipulated tests, due to the fault or neglect of the party for
> whose benefit they were to be accomplished, should not bar recovery . . . [*McIntosh
> Ready Mix Concrete Corp. v. R. D. Battaglini Corp. and the County of Broome,* 36
> App. Div.2d 561 (3d Dept. 1971)].

In its memorandum, the court noted that there was substantial evidence to
indicate that the concrete that failed the tests was, in fact, in accordance with
specifications and requirements. In addition, held the court, persons vested with
control of testing procedures and test samples had, "violated in different respects,
the testing requirements of ASTM C-31 and, therefore . . . the county was not
justified in rejecting the questioned concrete on the compression tests taken."
The subcontractor was found entitled to recover its additional costs from the
county.

CASE 10-9   Contractor Pays for Defective Workmanship

The Superior Court of Delaware has allowed a contractor to recover for its work
even though workmanship proved defective. The work on the job was substantially completed [*Trader v. Grampp Builders Inc.,* Del. Super., 263 A.2d 304
(1970)].

The case involved a contractor who installed a new roof, but when the work
was complete, the owner refused to pay the balance due the contractor because
of alleged defects in the roof. The contractor filed suit to recover the money owed
him, and the owner counterclaimed for the cost of materials supplied and the
cost of removing the roof.

The contractor stated that the owner provided neither plans nor specifications
for the job but had been present at the job site inspecting the work and giving
instructions.

"The issue in this case," said the court, "is whether a builder whose product
contains defects in workmanship is barred from recovery under a construction
contract when the owner has participated in inspection, and supervision of the
construction, and where the builder's product has been used for more than a
year without repairs."

The court concluded that the contractor had substantially completed its work
and, despite certain defects, was entitled to the reasonable value of the work
performed. Nevertheless, in determining the amount of recovery the court placed
a value on the damages caused by faulty workmanship and credited the owner
who deducted it from the balance due the contractor.

**CASE 10-10   Contractor's Irrational Acts
Constitute Breach of Contract**

The Supreme Court of Minnesota has held that a subcontractor was entitled to walk off a job and yet collect the reasonable value of its services from a general contractor with whom it had a dispute [*Dunkley Surfacing Co., Inc. v. Geo. Madsen Constr. Co.,* 173 N.W.2d 420 (1970)].

The case involved a subcontractor who had agreed to perform specific excavation work for a stated price, but who was delayed by unusually severe rains. Attempting to accelerate the job, the general contractor directed the subcontractor to get additional equipment on the job, but while he was doing this, the general contractor rented additional equipment from another contractor. The subcontractor was then told that it was going to be backcharged for the additional equipment as well as any other equipment the general contractor might bring to the jobsite. When the subcontractor protested, it was advised that if it did not agree with the way the general contractor ran the job, it could leave the job, which it did. The subcontractor then initiated suit to recover the reasonable value of its work.

The court ruled in favor of the subcontractor and held a breach of contract by the general contractor in exerting unreasonable force and unanticipated control over the subcontractor's performance.

**CASE 10-11   Harmony Clause Does Not Bar
Nonunion Subcontractor**

The Court of Appeals of North Carolina has ruled that a subcontractor does not have the right to bar a second-tier subcontractor from the continued performance of a job simply because the second-tier subcontractor is nonunion.

On a large hospital project in North Carolina, which is a right-to-work-law state, an agreement between a subcontractor and a second-tier subcontractor provided:

> All labor used throughout the work shall be acceptable to the Contractor and of a standing or affiliation that will permit the work to be carried on harmoniously and without delay, and that will in no case or under any circumstances cause any disturbance or delay to the progress of the building, structure or facilities or any other work being carried on by the Contractor, Owner and/or General Contractor.

During construction, a dispute arose between a union and the second-tier subcontractor, which employed nonunion workers. After union pickets appeared at the site, employees of both the subcontractor and the general contractor refused to work until the second-tier subcontractor either negotiated a collective-bargaining agreement with the union or stopped employing nonunion labor.

To get the project back on schedule, the subcontractor hired another firm to complete the job and sued the original second-tier subcontractor for breach of contract.

In its suit, the subcontractor claimed that the second-tier subcontractor violated its agreement by employing labor that was not acceptable and that prohibited the work from being carried out "harmoniously and without delay."

After reviewing the evidence, the court noted that under state law it is policy not to deny work "on account of membership or nonmembership in any labor union." Moreover, it said, statutes provide that union membership not be a condition of employment.

Stressing that the subcontractor had not proved that the employees of the second-tier subcontractor lacked the skill or supervision needed to produce satisfactory work, the court stated that all the evidence did not show that the employees were not acceptable because they were not union members.

The court ruled,

> The question presented is whether, under these circumstances, the harmony clause may be lawfully invoked by plaintiff to establish a breach of contract sufficient to justify the plaintiff's actions in removing defendant from the project and canceling the contract between them. We hold that under the laws of this State it may not [*Toole & Kent Corp. v. C. E. Thurston & Sons, Inc.* 203 S.E.2d 74 (1974), aff'd 209 S.E.2d 450 (1974)].

**CASE 10-12   Subcontractor Liable for
Walking off the Job without Reason**

A subcontractor that walked off the job after the contractual completion date but before its work was completed terminated its subcontract unjustifiably, the U.S. Court of Appeals, First Circuit, has ruled [*Drew Brown Limited v. Joseph Rugo, Inc.*, 436 F.2d 632 (1st Cir. 1971)].

The subcontractor was under contract to deliver and erect reinforcing steel for six college buildings in Bangor, Maine. It walked off the job just before finishing its work, on a date after the prime contract's set completion date. The subcontractor claimed that the general contractor failed to make progress payments and to coordinate job progress.

The court denied the subcontractor's claim of improper payments, noting that the contract called for payments based upon the amount of reinforcing steel "delivered and erected." The subcontractor was trying to bill on the basis of delivery only, the court said, and found that the general contractor was not delinquent in making payments for delivered and erected steel.

In denying the claim that the general contractor violated its duty to coordinate the work, the court pointed out that the subcontract did not require advance scheduling by the general contractor. Furthermore, the court said, the subcontract did not make time of the essence.

The court ruled that the subcontractor breached the subcontract and was liable for the general contractor's damages.

**CASE 10-13   Subcontractor Entitled to Payment
after Reasonable Time**

The North Carolina Court of Appeals held that a subcontractor was entitled to receive its final payment from the general contractor even though the subcontract stated that final payment was not due until the owner made its final payment, which the owner had not done [*Howard-Green Electrical Co., Inc. v. Chaney & James Constr. Co., Inc.,* 182 S.E.2d 601 (1971)].

The plaintiff, an electrical subcontractor, had completed its work and had been paid the contract price less retainage. The question was whether the subcontractor could demand final payment before the general contractor had received its final payment. The competency of the work was not questioned.

A dispute, not involving electrical work, between the general contractor and the owner delayed the payment. Citing a provision in the subcontract that "final payment will be paid within 15 days of acceptance and payment for the entire contract by the owner," the general contractor argued that final payment should be postponed until the owner made its final payment.

In concluding that the subcontractor was entitled to its final payment, the court held that the plaintiff contracted solely with the general contractor and did not contract with, or extend credit to, the owner, nor did the plaintiff accept responsibility for any part of the building project other than the electrical work. Further, no contract provision conditioned the plaintiff's receiving full payment from the owner. Rather, the provision postponed payment only until final settlement of accounts between the general contractor and the owner could reasonably be expected.

In reaching its decision, the court stated that the reasonable period of time for final settlement had passed and that the subcontractor's work had not been questioned.

CASE 10-14   Owner, Aware of Unspecified Work, Denied Cost of Changes

The Court of Appeal of Louisiana, Fourth District, denied a home owner repair costs spent to have completed work corrected to be in accord with the contract because the owner was aware, during construction, that the work was not being done properly.

Before final acceptance of construction of his house, the owner gave a contractor a punch list spelling out certain items to be completed. The work was performed and accepted.

Several years later the owner filed suit against the contractor alleging that it failed to abide by the contract and demanded damages. The owner claimed, among other things, that the specifications required underground electrical service installation while the contractor installed overhead wires. The contractor claimed, however, that this deviation from the contract was with the knowledge and consent of the owner. This item was not on the punch list.

The court granted the owner a credit for the difference in cost of installing the two systems but not the cost of repair. It concluded that the owner

> cannot now, after completion and acceptance, be heard to complain about the type of electrical wiring that was used. The plaintiff and the examining architect did not complain about this item until asked by the attorney preparatory to suit, to examine the plans, specifications, etc., to make sure he included all possible claims [*Page v. H. B. White & Son, Inc.,* 277 So.2d 725 (1973)].

ELEVEN

Changes

The laws relating to changes, extras, and additional work are a world of rules and more rules, exceptions, and exceptions to the exceptions. It is the single area of construction law where contractors repeatedly fail to adhere to legal advice. However, although the legal advice is proper and correct, no project would ever be completed if the rules were followed to the word. It is for this practical reason that the courts have so many exceptions and varying themes on the law relating to changes. The contractor must be fully aware that it faces substantial risk by not following its attorney's advice and hoping that an exception will be recognized and applied to its given facts. Zones of legal safety exist when the contractor acts in accordance with the rules; its burden of proof enlarges and its chances of success diminish with each step it takes outside that safety zone. The obvious business consideration has always been whether or not the contractor stops work on a $1 million job waiting for the $500 change order. In this instance, the legal advice and business decisions are often in opposition.

As a starting point, the broad rule is that the owner has no inherent *implied* right to make unilateral changes to the contract, whereby the contractor is *obligated* to perform. The right to make changes and the right to compel performance of the change is a contractual right.

> In order to recover for items as "extras," they must be shown to be items not required to be furnished under plaintiff's [contractor] original promise as stated in the contract including the items that the plans and specifications reasonably implied even though not mentioned. A promise to do or furnish that which the promisor is already bound to do or furnish, is not consideration for even an implied promise to

pay additional for such performance or the furnishing of materials [*Watson Lumber Co. v. Guennewig*, 226 N.E.2d 270 (Ill. 1967)].

The all-important question is: What does the contract state? In that rights and obligations are contractually determined, each decision will depend upon the specific words involved, and it is therefore extremely difficult to generalize.

A typical changes clause provides that the owner has the right to make changes within the general scope of the work; that the contractor is obligated to perform the change; that the change must be in signed written form; and that the price must either be predetermined or subject to computation and further review. The "basic" law is that such a clause is valid and enforceable (Case 11-1). The contractor is precluded from recovery if it does not comply with the contract terms (see 1 ALR3d 1273 and 2 ALR3d 620).

When dealing with changes, for the best legal *and* practical approach the following questions should be carefully reviewed, analyzed, and answered:

1. What does the contract state?
2. Does the changes clause apply in this instance?
3. Assuming that it does apply, have you complied with it?
4. Assuming it does apply and you have not complied, what are the exceptions to the enforcement of the clause?
5. Have you complied with an exception?
6. Assuming that you have not complied with an exception, do you have an equitable basis on which to argue for the establishment of still another exception?

CARDINAL CHANGES

The right to make changes is not an unlimited right. Most clauses specifically provide that the right to make changes is limited to changes "within the general scope" of the work. If the change is not within the general scope of the work, it might be deemed a *cardinal change*. A cardinal change is one which is beyond the scope of the contract and therefore is not proper.

> It is difficult, probably impossible, to draw in advance a precise line between what is authorized by such a reservation [changes clause] and what is not. It authorized such changes as frequently occur in the process of constructing buildings, in matters of taste, arrangements and details; but it does not authorize a change in the general character of the building [*McMaster v. State of New York*, 108 N.Y. 542 (1888)].

Compelling a contractor to perform a cardinal change might, in fact, be a breach of contract [*Luria Brothers and Co., Inc v. United States*, 369 F.2d 701 (1966)]. More important is the fact that the performance of a cardinal change is the performance of work not within the general scope of the contract, and if the work is outside the general scope of a public contract, it might not be compensable. The results can be drastic. A cardinal change has been found to exist when the essential identity of the thing contracted for is altered or when the method or manner or anticipated performance is so drastically and unforeseeably changed that essentially a new agreement is created [*National Contr. Co. v. Hudson River Water Power Co.,* 192 N.Y. 209 (1908); *Westcott v. State,* 36 N.Y.S.2d 23 (1942)].

A contractor may not want to perform major changes because of such factors as cost limitations in the contract, prolongation of time, bondability, other jobs coming on, or other reasons. The contractor that does perform the work should do it under protest so that it may have an argument that it is not limited to the rights expressed in the changes clause. It may have a chance to collect damages for breach of contract.

Many public contracts are bound by statutory enactments. These enactments often contain provisions limiting the extent and scope of changes and are valid whether they are included in the contract or not. Even if the contractor proceeds in accord with a fully executed change order, if the change order is an abuse of authority beyond the scope of the original contract, the contractor may find that it is not entitled to payment (Case 11-2). The extent of the change order may have exceeded the permissible percentage limitation of the applicable bidding statute (Case 11-3). The change may have been so major that the owner was obligated to put it out to public bid. There are no defined boundaries for a cardinal change (Case 11-4).

A statutory requirement permitting the increase of contract quantities up to 25 percent was held to be valid,

> where a unit price contract is advertised and bid for, and subsequent additions are made in volume only, it cannot be unjust to merely amend the contract. The variable in the contract is the total estimated number of units and the constant is the unit price. Therefore, no harm results from amending a factor which is necessarily subject to change under many different circumstances [*Village of Excelsior v. F. W. Pearce Corp.,* 226 N.W.2d 316 (Minn. Sup. Ct. 1975)].

The contractor and owner are advised to take scrupulous care in determining whether the change is proper or not. Even though the contractor has acted in good faith, recovery may still be denied. Know your legal limitations before proceeding, and know when *not* to proceed. With cardinal changes, there is no room for debate between the practical decision and legal decision. The law controls.

DOES THE CLAUSE APPLY?

All too often disputes center around the allegation that the contractor is not entitled to be paid for changed work since the required formal written executed document did not exist. However, the following question must first be answered: Was the changed work the type which mandated a written change order? If the changes clause does not classify the specific work in question, then arguably payment might be had even when the formal contractual requirements are not met. For example, if the contract prohibits payment for "changes in the plans or specifications" unless pursuant to a signed written change order and the owner's representative directs the contractor to discontinue operations on the first floor and to shift its forces to the third floor and then to jump to the sixteenth floor and then back to the first and third floors, the contractor may still be entitled to payment. This is so even if we assume that the particular judge accepts no exceptions to the rule which requires a formal change-order document. The court might still award the contractor payment. The reason for possible success is that the clause, in the hypothetical question, precludes payment when the plans or specifications are changed. However, in the example, the plans and specifications were not changed; only the method and manner of performance were changed. Therefore, the judge who wants to decide for the contractor could very justifiably rule that way, since it is not necessary to look into the application of the rule or the exceptions because the contract clause in question was inapplicable to the factual situation. The federal standard contract changes clause itemizes changes in both the plans and in the method and manner of performance. This would seem to add some credit to the distinction in the hypothetical argument and court decision.

In a different situation, assume that the contract prohibits any payment "for extra work unless done pursuant to a written change order." In this instance, while performing work, the contractor encounters a field problem relating to the location of ducts and structural steel. The owner's representative orally directs the contractor to change work. Work is performed, and payment is denied. Again, assume that this is in a jurisdiction which does not recognize any exceptions to the requirement for the formal change order; can the contractor recover? Assuming the court's desire to compensate the contractor, the court might well say that the clause in question related specifically to "extra" work and did not apply to "additional" work. Although a minority of decisions makes a distinction between extra and additional work, there have been and will continue to be cases making a distinction. A court's definitional distinction is as follows:

> The distinction between extra work and additional work being that the former is work arising outside and entirely independent of the contract—something not required in its performance, the latter being something necessarily required in the performance of the contract and without which it could not be carried out. The necessity for this additional work might arise from conditions which could not be anticipated and which were not open to observation and could not be discovered until the specified work under the contract was actually undertaken [*Shield v. City of New York*, 84 App. Div. 502 (1st Dept. 1903)].

The result of this argument is that the requirements of the changes clause did not apply to a given situation, and therefore the technicalities of the clause were inapplicable. Thus, the first-line approach must be the careful consideration of whether or not the particular and exact language of your changes clause covers your legal and factual problem. Does the clause apply to you?

HAS THE CONTRACTOR COMPLIED?

The next consideration, assuming that the clause does apply, is to determine whether or not the contractor has complied. Too often the contractor will throw up its hands in defeat or immediately look for an exception to the rule before considering the possibility that it has legally complied with the clause. Many situations involve the use of certain preprinted forms for change orders. These specific forms seldom exist in a fully executed proper state before the work was performed. *The question is whether that format was specified and required by the contract.* More often than not, it is not.

Normally, the three essential requirements of the changes clause are a *signed written order.* The contractor is advised to have that formal form before work. But assuming it does not exist when the work was performed, the first investigation should be to determine whether a writing exists. Since most contracts do not specify the format for the writing, *various* documents might, in the judge's discretion, constitute the writing so as to fulfill the "written" portion of the clause requirement. That writing might be found in letters, transmittal notices, revised plans and specifications, notations on shop drawings, job minutes, field records, daily reports, signed time and material slips, internal memoranda, or other documents. Even though such documentation may not be in the possession of the contractor, it may be in the owner's possession, and pretrial discovery procedures often turn up valuable "writings."

The next consideration is to determine whether the words *written order* require a "written order" or a "written" "order". If they are read together as a single phrase (which they are not), the owner's furnishing a sketch, revised drawing, or new plan, along with the oral directive to perform the work "or else," would not fulfill the technical requirements. However, if the words are interpreted to mean that both a writing and an order must exist, the sketch and oral directive would suffice. For this reason alone the contractor is urged to keep and file every single written note, document, sketch, etc., it receives. It is recommended that the contractor annex to that document, if it is not self-explanatory, a full history of oral orders relating thereto. Confirm all oral orders in writing. If no written order is furnished, as required by the contract, it seems that the case law permits the refusal to proceed [*John W. Johnson, Inc. v. Basic Constr. Co., Inc.,* 292 F. Supp. 300 (D.C. 1968), aff'd 429 F.2d 764 (1970)] (Case 11-5).

The third consideration relates to the word "signed." The same procedure must be adopted as in the analysis of the "written order." Will a rubber stamp suffice? Is the architect's or engineer's seal a signature? Are the initials appearing on the transmittal sheet sufficient? Must the signature actually be on the order which is in written form, or can the signature appear on some other document which clearly relates and refers to the facts in question? Must a signature exist, or can a name be typed? Can the signature be implied by the failure to object? This might be the case when there is forwarded to the party who directed the change a confirming letter in which a request for a response exists but to which there was no response. Must the signature be furnished to the contractor, or may the signature of the owner on some document it submitted to the lending institution seeking funds for this particular item of work be sufficient? The questions are numerous provided the approach to the problem is open. Lack of compliance should not be assumed. Careful scrutiny of the contract clause and the existing facts must again be performed. It must be remembered that recovery, when based on a right, is more readily accomplished when you have complied with the clause than when you are arguing an exception.

AUTHORITY?

The next major consideration, assuming compliance, is the authority of the person who issued the change order. The existence of an executed written change order does not mean that it is proper. A major legal and contractual question is presented when one questions the authority of the person issuing the specific change order. Many times the contract specifies the name of the person who allegedly has sole authority to issue the change order. However, is that person the exclusive person? The contract must be read carefully. That designated person or position more often than not is defined elsewhere in the contract. For example, if the changes clause requires it to be executed by the "commissioner," the contractor should then go to the specification section which defines commissioner. That definition might include "his duly authorized representative." Obviously the next problem is finding proper documentation indicating who that duly authorized person is, and if no such documentation exists, seeing whether that person can be pinpointed by implication or inference from prior acts. Too many contractors have been misinformed and believe that the architect or engineer is almighty during performance. After all, they are the ones who normally approve the payment requisitions, disapprove bad work, try to interpret the contract documents, and act with unlimited power. This belief in the totalitarian authority of the architect is not only many times unfounded but can also lead the contractor into a dangerous trap, i.e., the belief that the architect has the automatic and unlimited authority to issue changes to the work. This authority can only be delegated by contract. In fact, most contracts, and specifically the American Institute of Architects Agreements, forbid the architect from being the sole authorizing and issuing authority for change orders which would effect an increase in the price. The architect, by contract, normally does not have the authority. Many contract forms go so far as to say that if the architect does order a change, even in writing, the contractor has the right to see the architect's written permission from the owner to order that change and that if the architect fails to show such permission, the contractor need not and better not perform. The right to delegate authority on public contracts is often limited by statutory enactment.

EXCEPTIONS?

Assuming that the contract-changes clause applies and that the contractor has not complied, the question is then raised whether or not there are any ways around the rule so that the contractor can get paid. The answer is "possibly yes." It must be understood at the very outset that even though numerous exceptions exist, the burden is on the *contractor* to prove the existence of an exception and its compliance with the exception. If no exception exists, the contractor must prove that the facts warrant the application of a new exception. The burden is on the contractor. Courts which have previously upheld the general rule have, depending upon the equitable considerations, held that where words, acts, or conduct amount to a waiver modification, rescission, or abrogation of the changes clause, the technical requirements of the clause may not be applied. Payment may not have to be keyed to the written change order (Case 11-6).

The first cry of the contractor is normally that the other side *waived* the requirement of the formal contract clause. Waiver is an exception [*T. Lippin and Son, Inc. v. Jorson,* 342 A.2d 910 (Conn. 1975); *Howard J. White, Inc. v. Varian Associates,* 2 Cal. Rptr. 871 (1960)]. Simply by crying exception, the contractor creates a major stumbling block, i.e., whether the person who allegedly waived the requirement of the contract had the authority to do so. Does an architect have the right to waive provisions of the owner's contract? Does an engineer have the authority to waive the requirements of a public contract? Does anyone have the right to waive mandatory provisions of public contracts? The cases cover the entire spectrum of the authority and the right to waiver. Many cases have allowed recovery even though the owner neither affirmatively waived the contract clause nor affirmatively granted the architect the power to issue changes. Recovery was allowed on the basis of acquiescence. The owner was deemed to have waived the contract requirements. A typical example is the owner's continued payment of requisitions which include, on the face of them, numerous changes which were neither authorized nor issued by the owner in accordance with the provisions of the contract. However, by the continuous payment, the owner may have acquiesced in the architect's authority and waived the formal contract requirements. Other possibilities may arise when the owner is present at job meetings, hears the oral directive being issued by a nonauthorized person, and has the obvious ability to void the directive but does nothing. Here again is a situation for arguing waiver. The same argument can be made against the prime-contract provision by the subcontractor (Case 11-7).

A subcontractor was entitled to recover for extras ordered by a general contractor even though the contract permitted recovery for extras only if ordered in writing.

> It has been held that such a contract does not preclude oral modification if the party who could thereafter insist on limiting changes only as evidenced in writing, does not do so . . . . Further, oral modifications in written building contracts are permitted, and recovery may be obtained on substantial performance under the contract as modified [*Mayer Paving and Asphalt Co. v. Carl A. Morse, Inc.,* 365 N.E.2d 360 (Ill. 1977)].

When a contract writing is required, the owner's oral directive has by various courts been deemed to be a waiver [*Kenison v. Baldwin,* 351 P.2d 307 (Okla. 1960)]. Since the contract clause was for the owner's benefit, the owner has the right to waive its enforcement. By giving an oral directive with expected reliance, the owner may well be deemed to have waived the formalities of the change-order provision. The whole theory of the waiver exception is more difficult for public contracts [*Progressive Clay Co. v. Springfield Township, Union County,* 168 Atl. 652 (N.J. 1933)].

A subcontractor was entitled to collect for changed work done pursuant to an oral agreement, even though a prior subcontract required the existence of written change orders. The parties' subsequent oral agreements and actions were held to have modified the prior written contract, which called for written change orders [*Grossie v. Lafayette Constr. Co., Inc.,* 306 So.2d 453 (La. App. 1975)].

An alternative argument is the fact that the owner's oral directive is an offer, the contractor's response is an acceptance, and a new oral contract came into existence for this work. This would be a separate and distinct contract from the other contract, which required the written change. It is generally acknowledged that where a party's conduct indicates authorization and approval for work to proceed,

> under these circumstances the defendant cannot now contend that the plaintiff [contractor] is not entitled to compensation because he failed to obtain prior approval of a quotation for additional work [*Griffin v. Geneva Industries,* 228 N.W.2d 880 (Neb. 1975)] (Case 11-6).

The entire argument and presentation of exceptions is guided by principles of equity and

> the effectiveness of a non-written modification in spite of a contract condition that modifications must be written depends upon whether enforcement of the condition is or is not barred by equitable consideration, not upon technicality of whether the condition was or was not expressly and separately waived before the non-written modification [*Universal Builders, Inc. v. Moon Motor Lodge, Inc.* 244 A.2d 10 (1968)].

The contractor's burden can be substantial, but do not overlook the argument.

One of the equitable considerations is whether the person who issued the directive was aware that the contractor intended to be paid for the work. Contractors often proceed with work without specifically indicating that they intend to be compensated for that work. It may not be necessary to list a dollar amount, but the fact that compensation is expected must be made known. If the contractor proceeds without protesting the directive or without clearly stating the fact that it anticipates to be paid, it has been classified as a *volunteer* (Case 11-8). Volunteers normally do not get paid. In a Texas case the court ruled that the fact that extra work was performed when the owner "required" the contractor and subcontractor to do the extra work was an implied agreement by the owner to pay reasonable compensation. "Accordingly, there was no reason for Union [subcontractor] and MPD [prime contractor] to notify Black Lake they expected it to pay for the work" [*Black Lake Pipe Line Co. v. Union Constr. Co.* 520 S.W.2d 486 (Tex. App. 1975)].

Once a directive is given, confirm it in writing. Set forth all the facts and indicate that you are proceeding in accord therewith. If the work must be done under protest, do it under protest. The oral directive not only creates tremendous obstacles regarding the requirements of the changes clause, but often proof is a greater obstacle. Memories disintegrate, and memories alter the past course of events.

In a limited number of jurisdictions the doctrine of *constructive change order* has emerged. In many respects, this formal doctrine is an overlap of the waiver situation. The constructive-change-order doctrine is applicable in the federal contracts, but this doctrine is extremely difficult to win because it is an exception to the written public contract. The constructive-change-order concept was stated in a Board of Contract Appeals decision which indicated that

> a contracting officer can and sometimes does delegate his authority to technical representatives . . . . And in these circumstances, the Government is bound by the directives given by the representative. Thus, in numerous cases it has been held that a Government inspector authorized to inspect contract work has "constructively changed" the contract work by his inspection activities. Similarly, an engineer or some other kind of technical advisor whose function is the giving of technical guidance to a contractor may also order a change in work. Thus, it seems clear to us that what is at issue here are the actual functions of the Government's engineer, and appellant's engineer as well, as measured by what was said and done. On the other hand, we also disagree with the appellant's general position, which seems to regard every oral exchange between the Bureau's engineer and a company employee as a constructive change order if it resulted in altering the course of the work in any respect however insignificant or whatever the surrounding circumstances.
>
> As we see it, the constructive change doctrine is made up of two elements—the "change" element and the "order" element. To find the change element we must examine the actual performance to see whether it went beyond the minimum standards demanded by the terms of the contract. But, this is not the end of the matter.
>
> The "order" element also is a necessary ingredient in the constructive change concept. To be compensable under the changes clause, the change must be one that the Government ordered the contractor to make. The Government's representative, by his words or deeds, must require the contractor to perform work which is not a necessary part of the contract. This is something which differs from advice, comments, suggestions, or opinions which Government engineering or technical personnel frequently offer to a contractor's employees [*Appeal of Industrial Research Associates, Inc.,* 68-1 BCA 7069 (1968)].

In a case where the contractor was given a constructive change order, the court stated:

> It is pertinent to note at this point that where a contract contains the standard "changes" provision and the contracting officer without issuing a formal change order, requires the contractor to perform work or to utilize materials which the contractor regards as being beyond the requirements of the pertinent specifications or drawings, the contractor may elect to treat the contracting officer's directive as a constructive change order and prosecute a claim for an equitable adjustment under the "changes" provision of the contract [*Ets-Hokin Corp. and Bank of America National Trust and Savings Association, Third Party Plaintiff v. United States,* 190 Ct. Cl. 668, 420 F.2d 716 (1970)].

Although the constructive-change-order doctrine might not be specifically recognized, the concepts and elements are essentially the same for arguing the exceptions to any changes clause. In all cases, the two elements, the change and the order, must be proved and that burden must be assumed by the contractor.

Changes to the contract have been found to exist in an untold number of different factual situations. Contractors have been allowed to receive changes, extras, and additions to their contract as a result of excessive inspection requirements [*Kenneth Reed Constr. Corp. v. United States,* 475 F.2d 583 (1973)] (Case 9-7): inadequate specified construction methods (Case 11-9); improper directives to dismiss subcontractors (Case 11-10); performance of nonspecified work; performance of work in accordance with codes but which differed from the contract documents; design deficiencies (Cases 11-11 and 9-10); furnishing overtime—the list goes on and on.

The contractors' practical question is: *Do I perform, and if I perform, will I get paid?* Know your contract before you work, not after. Many arguments alleging changes fall by the wayside because the contracting party has failed to read and comprehend its set contractual obligations fully (Case 11-12). The obligation for proper shop drawings rests with the contractor (Cases 11-13 to 11-15). The contractor should not be entitled to collect for its own inadequacies (Case 11-16) or for the owner's *reasonable* rejection of proposed changes (Case 11-17).

In determining whether a change exists, what work is contractual or a basis for more compensation, the court will apply the standard rules of contract interpretation (Cases 11-18 and 11-19). Know your contract. Know what it says.

CASE 11-1   Extra Work Claim Must Comply with Contract

The Supreme Court of Mississippi has denied a contractor's claim for extra work because the work was performed without a written directive from the owner. The terms of the contract were clear, the court said, and precluded the owner's representative from giving directives for extra work.

Involved in the dispute was the demolition and removal of a building and a contract for the construction of a new bank on the same site. The foundations of the old building were not removed during the demolition. Although the contractor anticipated their presence, it did not know their exact location until it hit them in testing the site to place the piles.

The structural engineer, an employee of the owner's architect, told the contractor it could not use the old foundations for the new building and told it to remove them. The contractor considered their removal extra work and so informed the architect. The lower court allowed the contractor to recover the reasonable value of the work even though the owner had not indicated that the work was an extra and had not waived any of the contract terms.

The contract, in limiting the architect's authority, said,

> The Architect shall have authority to make minor changes in the work, not involving extra cost, and not inconsistent with the purposes of the building, but otherwise, except in an emergency endangering life or property, no extra work or change shall be made unless in pursuance of a written order from the Owner, signed or countersigned by the Architect, or a written order from the Architect stating that the Owner

has authorized the extra work or charge, and no claim for an addition to the Contract Sum shall be valid unless so ordered.

Elsewhere, the contract stated that the architect had authority to act for the owner only to the extent expressly provided in the contract or in writing.

In reversing the lower court, the supreme court rejected the contractor's argument that the structural engineer was the owner's representative and that it is a custom of the trade for the contractor to comply with a request of the owner's representative. A written contract that is clear will prevail over custom, the high court said.

> We can only conclude in comparing these plain terms to the vague assumption of the contractor that custom of the trade would implement the written document in his behalf, that the former prevails [the court explained]. The written contract anticipated every contingency upon which this suit is based. Its very purpose was to forestall imposition of vague claims derivative of custom within the trade with which laymen are often unfamiliar. The owner, being desirous of limiting its financial obligation, should not have its pocketbook exposed to the custom of architects and contractors unless it agrees thereto.
>
> In this instance the owner agreed to pay for extra work only if it was authorized in writing prior to its execution. Having contracted directly upon the point, there was no leeway for an award on a *quantum meruit* basis [*Citizens National Bank of Meridian v. L. L. Glascock, Inc.,* 243 So.2d 67 (1971)].

CASE 11-2   Renegotiated Public-Contract Change Order Voided

A New York appellate court has ruled that a major public-contract change order, which was negotiated, was illegal and that the negotiated price must be redetermined by the court [*Albert Elia Building Co., Inc. v. New York State Urban Development Corp.,* 54 A.D.2d 227 (1976)].

The court stated that the owner's "contractual power to modify by change order is not a grant of authority to make a different or new contract without complying with the competitive bidding statutes."

A New York contractor started an action against a public authority claiming that a change order for the construction of a connecting tunnel was illegally given to the contractor performing the prime contract on the site. During the subsequent litigation, the work was completed and paid for under the change order.

The prime contract for the construction of a convention center in Niagara Falls, New York, was awarded in 1971 for $16,864,000. One year later, the owner decided to build a plaza on another site to be connected to the convention center by a tunnel. In 1973, the public authority issued change orders for the tunnel to the same contractor at a negotiated price of $428,100.

The contesting contractor claimed that the public-bidding statutes required the authority to bid the tunnel project and that "by illegal official action he had been denied the award of the contract."

The court agreed that the convention-center contract was governed by the public-bidding statutes and that the contractor had a right to court review of its claim. It noted, however, that the competitive-bidding statutes do not forbid change orders which are "merely incidental to the original contract."

This right, it added, is still subject to certain limitations.

Deciding whether the change order for the tunnel exceeded the limitation, the court stated that "no important general change may be made which so varies from the original plan or is of such importance as to constitute a new undertaking."

The owner, it said, could modify the work required by the contract so long as it did not "alter the essential identity or the main purpose of the contract."

The court concluded that the tunnel was beyond the scope of the originally contemplated contract and therefore was an illegal change order.

As to the money already paid for the tunnel work, since no claim of wrongdoing was alleged against the contractor, the court refused to apply the rule of "complete forfeiture."

Instead, it concluded, the contractor must refund the owner the difference between the contract price and the price which could have been obtained through competitive bidding. This measure would be determined at a hearing from expert testimony.

The court said the contesting contractor was entitled to counsel fees as its compensation.

CASE 11-3   Contractor's Recovery Limited by Bidding-Law Violation

A contractor that performed a substantial amount of extra work for a city under the direction of the mayor and members of the city council and under an amendment to a valid contract was not entitled to recover the contract price because the amendment violated the statutory competitive bidding requirements, the Supreme Court of Wisconsin has ruled.

The court, however, did allow the contractor to recover the value of the benefits the city received on the theory the city should not be unjustly enriched.

The basic contract ($50,000) related to work on a city lake and dam in Hillsboro and complied with bidding requirements. The amendment, covering $100,000 of additional work, involved extra lake excavation. It was initiated by the mayor and members of the city council, but it was not put out to competitive bidding.

Apparently the public-bidding statute permitted the contract to be increased by changes, but only up to a maximum of 15 percent of the cost of the original contract. The law, the court said, protects the public against "fraud, collusion, favoritism, and improvidence in the administration of public business" and assures the best buy for the money. It renders contracts made in violation of the law void and unenforceable. For this reason, the court ruled, the contractor could not recover the $100,000 it claimed under the amendment either on the basis of contract price or under the theories of equitable estoppel or promissory estoppel, either of which would prevent the city from denying the validity of the contract.

However, there is a growing body of authority to the effect that to permit recovery on the theory of unjust enrichment would not lead to the evils once imagined [the court said].

We here conclude that when work has been performed for a municipality under a contract which is *malum prohibitum* and not *malum in se*, which contract is entered into in good faith and is devoid of any bad faith, fraud or collusion, and where the statute imposes no penalty, a cause of action based upon the equitable doctrine of unjust enrichment can be maintained . . . . When a municipality has received the benefits of work performed, or materials furnished in good faith, it is not just to permit the municipality to retain those benefits without paying the reasonable value thereof [*Blum v. City of Hillsboro,* 183 N.W.2d 47 (1971)].

The court said the contractor could not recover any profit, nor could the final amount be greater than the unit price in the original contract. Subject to these limitations, the court said it could recover "the value of the actual benefit conferred as distinguished from the reasonable value of the work performed and materials furnished."

CASE 11-4   Numerous Minor Changes Are Not a Cardinal Change

Although the Postal Service Board of Contract Appeals denied a contractor's claim that the number of changes ordered by the government constituted a cardinal change and a breach of contract, the board allowed the contractor to recover for the impact that the changes had on the overall completion of the project.

The contract called for construction of a post office in an office tower. During construction, the government issued 162 bulletins, requiring a number of changes. Although the contract's changes clause anticipated changes of up to $950,000, the contractor performed work in excess of that amount.

In an attempt to recover all its additional costs, the contractor argued that the government had issued an unreasonable number of changes, that these changes amounted to a breach of contract and that they directly affected the overall completion of the project. A board investigation showed that the bulletins required 200 changes.

To determine whether these changes amounted to a breach of contract, the board looked at the definition of a cardinal change. It noted that

a cardinal change is one which thoroughly modifies the nature of the structure to be erected under the contract by a particular change or a series of changes. To find a cardinal change requires consideration of the quality and magnitude or cumulative effect of the changes ordered . . . . There exists, therefore, no rule which makes the number of change orders issued by a contracting officer by itself the measure of unreasonable changes or abuse of authority by the contracting officer [*Coley Properties Corp.,* PSBCA 291, 75-2 BCA 11,514 (1975)].

In this case, the board found that the number of changes taken collectively amounted to about 10 percent of the estimated cost of the post office.

On its face [the board said] such a changed cost does not appear abusive or outrageous in its magnitude, and the total sum of the change work did not alter the basic fabric, utility or quality of the structure which the contractor agreed to build.

As a result, the board ruled that the bulletins did not constitute a cardinal change.

Although it disallowed the contractor's damage claim, the board permitted the contractor to recover the extra costs of the changed work and added that the contractor could recover additional direct costs that it had incurred in completing the unchanged work.

Noting that the changed work required the contractor to complete a large portion of the post office out of sequence and in a manner that reduced normal efficiency, the board said the contractor "is entitled to recover increased performance costs due to the impact of the changes ordered by the government."

CASE 11-5   Subcontractor Wins Suit over Extras

A subcontractor was entitled to stop work, abandon its entire contract, and collect damages when the general contractor refused to give its written authorization assuring payment for extra work it ordered, a federal court has ruled.

The ruling was handed down in a suit by a painting subcontractor against a general contractor for breach of contract, negligence, and interference with its contract rights. The construction project involved erection of a group of buildings for the State University of New York in Albany, New York.

The subcontract provided that the general contractor had the right to order changes in the work during the course of performance and that the subcontractor's contract price would be adjusted accordingly. However, the subcontract specifically stated that no additional compensation would be allowed unless the general contractor's extra work order to the subcontractor was in writing.

After the subcontractor had started painting, the paint on the ceilings began to peel. The architect investigated the cause of the problem and ascertained that the general contractor, in removing forms, had failed to remove all the stearic acid used in the removal of temporary molds or forms, which caused the peeling. Although the specifications required only two coats of paint, the general contractor was directed to apply a third coat to cure the peeling problem.

The instruction to apply a third coat of paint was passed along orally to the subcontractor. In accordance with the contract provisions, the subcontractor refused to do the extra work unless it was given either a formal written change order or some other document assuring that it would be paid for this work. When the general contractor refused to give any written assurances of payment, the subcontractor stopped work and abandoned the project. The general contractor then confiscated the subcontractor's equipment on the site and hired another subcontractor to finish the work.

The U. S. District Court for the District of Columbia, in the light of the provisions in the subcontract regarding extra work, held that the subcontractor had a legal right to stop work in view of the fact that the contractor insisted that the plaintiff [subcontractor] do the required extra work without giving it any assurance of payment. The attitude of the contractor in this respect was wrong and the subcontractor was entitled to stop work and abandon the contract [*John W. Johnson, Inc. v. Basic Constr. Co., Inc.*, 292 F. Supp. 300 (D.C.D.C. 1968), aff'd 429 F.2d 764 (1970)].

In determining what damages the subcontractor would be entitled to recover, the court awarded to it the contract balance due on the work actually performed, as well as the value of the material and equipment confiscated by the general contractor.

However, the court declined to allow any recovery for the profit the subcontractor would have earned had it completed its work, because the subcontractor had abandoned the work instead of insisting upon continuing and finishing its subcontract.

CASE 11-6   Pay for Extras Not Keyed To Written Authorization

A contractor was entitled to additional costs for performing extra and changed work even though the required written authorization for the extra work did not exist.

The contractor had entered a written contract for the construction of a motel and restaurant in Pennsylvania. The contract specifically provided that all change orders had to be in writing and signed by either the owner or the architect.

During the course of construction, the owner's agent made numerous verbal requests to the contractor for changes in the work. The contractor proceeded with the changed work only after having informed the agent that additional costs would be incurred and having received the agent's promise to pay for the additional work. However, nothing was put in writing in regard to these many requests, and the contractor was not paid.

The owner, in refusing to make payments, argued that the contract stated that no extras would be allowed unless performed pursuant to a signed written change order.

In considering the contractor's claim, the Pennsylvania Supreme Court noted that the lack of a written change order does not automatically preclude the contractor's claim. The owner, it said, could still be found liable for extra work performed under oral direction. It explained that liability could be imposed on the owner under the theory that the extra work was performed under an oral contract separate and distinct from the written contract or under the theory that the condition requiring a written authorization for extra work had been waived.

In this case the court held the owner liable under either principle of law. Not only did the owner's agent request the changes and promise to make payment, but he was often at the site and saw the contractor perform the extra work, the court said. It noted that the agent knew that the extra work was being performed without proper authorization and, rather than protesting, he watched the work become incorporated into the project. This, the court said, amounted to an implied promise to pay for the extra work.

Guided by the principles of equity, the court reasoned that

> the effectiveness of a non-written modification in spite of a contract condition that modifications must be written depends upon whether enforcement of the condition is or is not barred by equitable considerations, not upon the technicality of whether the condition was or was not expressly and separately waived before the non-written modification [*Universal Builders, Inc. v. Moon Motor Lodge, Inc.*, 430 Pa. 550, 244 A.2d 10 (1968)].

> The court's conclusion held that under these circumstances it would be unjust to allow the owner to accept the benefits of the contractor's extra work by refusing payment on the technical grounds that a written authorization did not exist.

CASE 11-7   Contractor's Action Waives Changes-Clause Conditions

The Supreme Court of Nebraska has allowed a subcontractor to recover for extra work, even though it did not comply with the formal requirements of the subcontract's changes clauses.

A prime contractor on two hospital jobs let three subcontracts calling for the installation of millwork. The subcontracts, which were prepared by the prime, required the subcontractor to submit all proposed changes to the contractor before proceeding with the work.

The subcontractor modified the changes clauses to indicate that it was entitled to be paid on a time and material basis for all extra work. It then signed the contracts and returned them to the prime. Before finally executing the contracts, the prime further modified the changes clauses, requiring the subcontractor to submit a price quotation for all extra work.

Later a dispute arose over the subcontractor's failure to obtain written authorization for certain extra work, and the subcontractor sued to recover for its time and material cost.

Reviewing the subcontracts, the court found that the subcontractor was permitted to perform extra work if it complied with formal contract provisions. However, it added that the contractor could waive these requirements through its own words or actions.

Finding that there was clear evidence that the prime was aware that the subcontractor was doing the extra work, the court stated:

> Its conduct indicated approval and authorization for the work to proceed. Under those circumstances, the . . . [prime contractor] cannot now contend that the [subcontractor] is not entitled to compensation because he failed to obtain prior approval of a quotation for the additional work [*Griffin v. Geneva Industries*, 228 N.W.2d 880 (1975)].

As a result, the subcontractor was able to recover from the prime contractor for its time and costs.

CASE 11-8   Work Compensable Even though Unspecified

A contractor was entitled to compensation for work which it did but which was not included in its contract because the owner's tacit approval of the performance of this work was a constructive change order, ruled the U.S. Court of Claims [*Chris Berg, Inc. v. United States,* 455 F.2d 1037 (1972)].

The contractor submitted a payment claim on behalf of its painting subcontractor to the owner, the U.S. Army Corps of Engineers, regarding work completed by the subcontractor but not specified in the contract (NIC). An equitable adjustment is required if either contractor or subcontractor had been ordered expressly or constructively to do the work.

The government argued that painting done by the subcontractor was not covered by contract and was voluntary and therefore not compensable. The Board of Contract Appeals agreed that the contractor had not been directed to do this work.

The question before the claims court was whether or not the work was voluntary. The court found that the Corps' project engineer knew that the subcontractor was painting the NIC areas. Instead of halting this work, he criticized the way it was being done. Evidence indicated that the subcontractor was not totally familiar with the specification requirements and that it relied for guidance on the project engineer, the court said.

Government records showed that "approval was given to paint this area," but this approval had not been given in writing. The court concluded, "We are satisfied that . . . [the contractor] did not act as a volunteer but painted the NIC areas after receiving the tacit and, undoubtedly, oral approval of . . . [the] project engineer."

CASE 11-9   Owner Pays when Specified Directions Proved Inadequate

The Armed Services Board of Contract Appeals has ruled that a contractor was entitled to extra costs when a specified dewatering method proved inadequate [*Appeal of Reid and Hope, Inc.,* ASBCA 17062, 73-1 BCA 9824].

The United States government, the owner, issued revised drawings relocating a new building's underground utility lines. The contractor anticipated subsurface water problems and included in its estimate the cost of well points and sheet piling. The price of the change was negotiated, but the owner specified water pumps and shoring instead.

Water problems were encountered, and the contractor claimed extra costs. The board said the contractor's method would have solved the problem and called the owner's method unsuitable. "The contractor was loath to accept the government's system, but did so in the reasonable belief the government would assist if difficulties were met."

CASE 11-10   Change Removing Subcontractor
is Compensable

A government order that the general contractor dismiss a subcontractor whose work is proved not to be improper is a contract change, and the contractor is entitled to recover its costs resulting from the change, ruled the U.S. Court of Claims.

The paints specified in the prime contract and a second type tried by an approved painting subcontractor proved unsuitable. All parties to the prime contract and painting subcontract tried to resolve the paint problem.

The time spent seeking solutions to the paint problems meant that the subcontractor's work was slower than the anticipated performance rate. The government blamed the slow performance on the subcontractor and ordered the contractor to remove the subcontractor from the job.

261The contractor claimed that the directive was a compensable change to the contract. It said that it was entitled to recover additional costs incurred in getting a second painting subcontractor and damages for which it may be held liable to the first subcontractor for breaching the subcontract.

The Board of Contract Appeals denied the contractor's claim for compensation and found that there was no basis to the government's claim that the subcontractor was irresponsible or at fault for the slow performance rate. The contractor appealed.

On appeal, the court noted that no part of the prime contract had been terminated, and it did not question the power of the government to order the change, but it said it had no right to do so without paying the contractor for its additional costs.

The court held that

> there is no greater interference with the manner and method of performance [permissible under the contract], short of termination of the work itself, than the ordered replacement of the craftsmen originally chosen to do the work.

In concluding that the government must compensate the contractor for the costs incurred in using a different painting subcontractor and for potential damages that the general contractor might have to pay as a result of breaching the subcontract (an independent lawsuit by the subcontractor), the court ruled:

> Specifications may require the prime contractor to utilize approved subcontractors, but they may not impede or restrict his selection from among approved subcontractors without compensable relief when the Government elects so to interfere [*Liles Construction Co., Inc. v. United States*, 455 F.2d 527 (1972)].

CASE 11-11   Contractor Paid for Work
In Exposing Design Deficiencies

The General Services Board of Contract Appeals has ruled that the government was liable to its prime contractor for a subcontractor's drafting and research costs in pointing out discrepancies in contract drawings supplied by the government.

The general contractor filed an appeal on behalf of its mechanical subcontractor claiming compensation for drafting and research time spent exposing discrepancies in the mechanical work of the contract drawings. As a result, the government issued two change orders and paid the contractor for making the changes. But the government denied its claim for researching and resolving the conflicts.

The amount of time and cost were not in question. The government denied the claim on the basis that it was the prime's contractual obligation to submit all discrepancies for resolution. It argued that under this obligation the contractor was required to spend the drafting and research time necessary to submit these resolutions. Therefore, it said, these costs should have been included in the initial contract price.

The board held that,

> The subcontractor's additional efforts . . . were occasioned by faulty contract drawings. Generally, a contractor is entitled to an equitable adjustment for all additional and reasonable costs for changes required because of faulty contract documents. The adjustment is not arbitrarily limited to costs incurred subsequent to formal issuance of a change order [*Appeal of Baltimore Contractors, Inc.*, GSBCA 3425, 72-2 BCA 9622 (1972)].

And, the board said, had the subcontractor not done the preliminary work which was necessary to show the conflicts, the government would have had to do it or pay the contractor to do it. It does not follow that the contractor cannot be adequately compensated for the costs of informing the contracting office of the discrepancies pursuant to the changes clause, the board said.

CASE 11-12   Contract Precludes Extra to Architect-Engineer for Redesign Work

An Architect-Engineer's contract may be so drawn as to preclude extra payment for redesign work, a federal contract appeals board has ruled.

In this case, the architect-engineer had contracted to design a Coast Guard air station and to perform other services for a lump-sum fixed fee. Architectural designs were to be performed in three stages, preliminary, intermediate, and final.

When the Architect-Engineer submitted its preliminary design, it also submitted its cost estimate. The total cost estimate greatly exceeded the available budget. Every item on the estimate was substantially more than the amount that the Coast Guard had estimated. As a result, various alterations were made in the design criteria, and the construction budget was increased.

The Architect-Engineer then submitted its intermediate design incorporating the alterations in design. The new engineering cost estimate was just under the revised construction ceiling. The Coast Guard made various comments which were to be included in the final submittal. On the final submittal the total cost estimate was again above the allotted amount. In addition, certain design and drawing discrepancies were noted by the Coast Guard. The final submittal was rejected. On correction and resubmission they were approved.

After construction bids were opened, and apparently after the contract was awarded at a figure substantially higher than estimated, the Architect-Engineer filed a claim for the additional design work. It claimed that it was entitled to an increase in its fee proportionate to the amount that the construction bid exceeded the estimated cost. It argued that the original budget figure in its contract was unrealistic and that "there is a definite correlation between the construction value of a project and design costs . . . ."

The contracting officer denied the claim and the Architect-Engineer appealed to the Department of Transportation Contract Appeals Board.

On appeal the Architect-Engineer alleged that the Coast Guard's original budget estimate was so low as to constitute a defective specification. The board noted that the Architect-Engineer had originally been furnished with an itemized breakdown of the estimated costs in the early stages of precontract negotiations. Although the total cost and breakdown estimates submitted by the Architect-Engineer with its preliminary design exceeded the corresponding government estimates, this did not mean that the government's estimated budget was wrong, the board said.

> We can find nothing in the record which clearly establishes that the Coast Guard's estimate was so deficient or made so carelessly, or with such gross error, that it must be deemed to be part of a defective specification of the government's requirements [the board said]. In the absence of specific evidence of error or miscalculation, we cannot say that the differences between the Coast Guard's estimate and the architect's estimate or estimates prove substantial defects in the Coast Guard's estimate [*Appeal of Praeger-Kavanagh-Waterbury*, DOT CAB 67-13, 69-1 BCA 7482 (1969)].

The next point of consideration was the Architect-Engineer's allegation that its fee for designing the project should be computed as a percentage of the construction bid price. The board considered the fact that in an architectural service contract the Architect-Engineer has a wide latitude in saying what the design will be, what materials and construction methods will be employed, and many other factors, all of which have a direct and ultimate impact on the construction cost. In ruling that the fixed contract fee represents full compensation in the absence of compensable charges under the terms of the contract, the board held that

> to fix the architect's fee as a percentage of the amount bid to construct the design would build into the architect's contract an incentive to overdesign the project and, hence, inflate the fee.

With regard to compensable changes under the contract, the board referred to the contract clause which provided that

> the contractor will redesign as necessary at no additional cost to the government until a satisfactory low bid for construction has been obtained that is within the amount available and reserved for construction.

Within these guidelines, the board held that all redesign work performed by the Architect-Engineer during its three design phases in order to bring the estimated construction cost within the amount available was not recoverable as a compensable change. The Architect-Engineer would be permitted, it said, to recover only for doing that additional design work where the government demands changes to a submittal after it has been approved or where basic project requirements are so altered as to affect prior design work. Additional design work, the board noted, must always be differentiated from the required redesign work specified in the contract.

The appeal was remanded back to the contracting officer for negotiation on certain specific items for which the board considered the Architect-Engineer entitled to payment under the contract.

CASE 11-13   Approval of Incorrect Plans Not A Change

A contractor was denied its claim for compensation for correcting work that was incorrectly specified in its own shop drawings. The owner's approval of the incorrect drawings did not change the contract requirements, ruled the General Services Board of Contract Appeals.

The contractor was required to prepare and submit for approval to the General Services Administration, the owner, shop drawings showing the fabrication of reinforcing steel. The contract provided that "approval of drawings and schedules will be general and shall not be construed as . . . permitting any departure from the contract requirements."

One of the submitted drawings, which the owner approved, later was found to be incomplete by failing to show the proper use of column ties. But before the mistake was discovered, the rebars were fabricated, put in place, and encased in concrete.

At this point the mistake was discovered, and the owner accepted the contractor's proposal for correcting the problem. The contractor claimed it was entitled to the cost of the corrective work because, it said, "approval . . . of a deficient shop drawing resulted in a change in the contract requirement."

The board rejected this argument. It stressed that deficiencies in the drawings were created by the contractor and its subcontractor. The board said,

> general approval of a shop drawing therefore may be said to be conditional, conditioned, that is, that it also meets all other contract requirements and such approval cannot be used to shift the responsibility of complying with all of the contractual requirements from the contractor to the government [*Appeal of Dawson Constr. Co.,* GSBCA 3685, 72-2 BCA 9758 (Oct. 31, 1972)].

CASE 11-14   Approved Shop Drawings Not A Change Order

A contractor was denied additional costs for removing fixtures specified in its approved shop drawings and replacing them with fixtures specified in the contract. Approval of shop drawings, held the Armed Services Board of Contract Appeals, did not permit deviation from the contract provisions [*Appeal of Whitney Brothers Plumbing & Heating, Inc.,* ASBCA 16876, 72-1 BCA 9448 (1972)].

Before work began, the contractor submitted literature describing the fixtures it intended to use. The government's contracting officer approved the submittal, and the contractor then ordered and installed the units. During installation the government found that one of the characteristics of the fixtures was not as required by the contract.

Even though the contractor's submittals did not describe this one characteristic and did deviate from the specifications, the contractor argued that the fixtures were proper since the contracting officer approved shop drawings specifying these fixtures. This approval, argued the contractor, was its order to deviate from the contract. The government claimed that the contractor was required to specify every instance when it intended to furnish items not in complete compliance with contract requirements. And it cited a contract provision that "approval shall not be construed as authorizing any deviations from the contract plans or specifications."

The board concluded that the contractor was clearly required to furnish fixtures in complete compliance with the contract requirements "unless it first informed the contracting officer it was not, gave its reasons for not doing so, and received the contracting officer's approval for deviating from this requirement."

CASE 11-15 Shop-Drawing Mistake Is Costly

The Armed Services Board of Contract Appeals has ruled that a contractor was not entitled to additional costs for removing and replacing nonconforming equipment that had been installed in accordance with government-approved shop drawings.

A contract for the design and construction of multifamily housing in Georgia specified that a certain thermostat was to be used for that project. However, when the contractor submitted its shop drawings to the government, they called for a different type of thermostat.

After the government approved the shop drawings, the unspecified thermostats were installed. Later, the error was detected, and the contractor was ordered to correct it. The work was performed under protest, with the contractor eventually filing a claim for additional costs.

The contractor based the claim on a contract provision that said the government had "an obligation to scrutinize shop drawings and notify the contractor of any deficiencies and of suggested corrective action." It claimed that the government's approval of the drawings and its silence on the error should make it liable for the replacement costs.

The government, denying the claim, pointed to another contract provision that stated:

> The approval of [shop] drawings by the contracting officer shall not be construed as a complete check, but will indicate only that the general method of construction and detailing is satisfactory. Approval of such drawings will not relieve the contractor of the responsibility for any error which may exist as the contractor shall be responsible for the dimensions and design of adequate connections, details and satisfactory construction of all work.

Siding with the government, the appeals board first noted that there was no evidence that the government had carefully compared the shop drawings against the contract requirements to discover the error. In addition, it found that the government's inspectors would not have known that the nonconforming thermostats were being installed.

Therefore, the board concluded:

> We have consistently held that a "shop drawings" provision such as found in this contract . . . does not relieve [the contractor] of the responsibility for errors or omissions therein nor can [the contractor] normally rely on or derive any benefit from erroneous government approval of shop drawings furnished pursuant to such a clause [*Appeal of Community Science Technology Corp., Inc.,* ASBCA 20244, 77-1 BCA 12,352 (1977)].

CASE 11-16   Work Conflict Due to Lack of Coordination, Extras Denied

A contractor's claim for a compensable change was denied by the General Services Board of Contract Appeals since the additional work was due to the contractor's failure to properly coordinate the work of its subcontractors [*Appeal of Grunley-Walsh Construction Co., Inc.,* GSBCA 3343, 73-1 BCA 9978 (1973)].

The contract called for rehabilitating a government building. A subcontractor claimed it could not install, as specified, a catwalk around the air-conditioning tower because the work conflicted with ducts already installed.

The general contractor, filing a claim on behalf of its steel erector, said the government had approved its shop drawings, which now could not be complied with, and claimed extra costs. In denying the claim, the board said the extra work would not have been required had the contractor properly coordinated the work of its subcontractors.

CASE 11-17   Substitutions Proposed by a Contractor Found Not Reasonable

The Armed Services Board of Contract Appeals has ruled that a contracting officer's refusal to approve the use of substitute doors was reasonable and denied the contractor's claim for additional compensation.

The contract involved construction of an Army laboratory and called for installation of vault doors. The plans specified a set door size. However, the specifications provided that doors of standard size different from those specified "may be furnished subject to approval."

The contractor found that doors of the size specified were not readily available standard sizes. It submitted shop drawings of standard doors substantially narrower than those specified. The government refused to approve the proposed substitute. The contractor was forced to purchase and install doors of the specified dimensions.

The contractor claimed that it was entitled to additional compensation. It argued that the doors it proposed were a standard size and that, since substitution was allowed by the specifications, the government's refusal to accept the substitute was arbitrary and unreasonable.

The board disagreed. In denying the contractor's claim, it said,

> The contract did give the appellant an option to furnish standard size doors. Such door was subject to approval by the contracting officer. This approval could not be withheld arbitrarily. On the other side, the contracting officer could properly reject an unreasonable offer. We find that the proposal to substitute 40-inch doors for doors required by the contract plans to be 64-in. wide was unreasonable on its face. The contracting officer properly refused to approve the proposed substitute [*Appeal of Norair Engineering Corp.*, ASBCA 11615, 70-1 BCA 8082 (1970)].

CASE 11-18   Unit Price Prevails over Lump-Sum Figure

Because of confusion in the wording of a contract, the North Carolina Supreme Court has ruled that a contractor working under a lump-sum agreement could recover for certain work performed based on a unit price [*Wood-Hopkins Contracting Co., v. North Carolina State Port Authority,* 202 S.E.2d 473 (1974)].

A lump-sum contract for a port facility provided that the contractor be paid a unit cubic-yard price for the placement of fill in certain areas.

After construction began, it became apparent that further filling would be needed. When the owner refused to pay for the fill at the unit price, the contractor sued.

In court, the owner argued that since the contract was generally for a lump sum the unit price was not applicable for the extra work.

Noting that the contract had been written by the owner, the court stated, "It is a rule of contracts that in the case of disputed items, the interpretation will be inclined against the person who drafted it."

Another rule of law that the court said supported the contractor's claim was that "when general forms and specific statements are included in the same contract, and there is a conflict, the general terms should give way to the specifics."

The court ruled that in this case the specific provision for a unit price prevailed over the general terms of lump-sum contract. Therefore, the contractor was entitled to be paid for the additional fill according to the unit price.

CASE 11-19   Good Workmanship Does Not Require Extra Work

The Armed Services Board of Contract Appeals has held that the obligation of good workmanship does not require a contractor to perform nonspecified work [*Appeal of Valley Constr. Co.*, ASBCA 13277, 68-2 BCA 7293 (1968)].

The case involved a contractor who claimed that a government directive requiring it to take out noncoded wire and replace it with color-coded internal control wiring was beyond its contract requirements and was an extra. It argued that the specifications, prepared by an independent architect-engineer, did not require color coding.

The government admitted that there was no specific contract provision specifying the use of color-coded wires. However, it claimed that the contractor was responsible for installing color-coded wiring because the obligation of "good workmanship" required it.

The board noted that the noncoded wiring was installed by the contractor without government protest. The board granted the claim for an extra.

TWELVE

Changed Conditions

One of the most misunderstood construction claims relates to the area generally categorized as *changed conditions*. The term is a technical one, more or less restricted to the field of construction contracts. More often than not, no contract clause is entitled changed conditions, even when such a title would be appropriate.

The starting point for considering this area of claim is the fact that there is no implied right to file a changed-conditions claim [*United States v. Spearin*, 248 U.S. 132 (1918)]. The contractor often believes, and erroneously argues, that an automatic implied right is included in every contract entitling it to additional compensation when it encounters conditions which differ from those it unilaterally anticipated. A changed-conditions claim is created only by express contract language. It exists *only* when so provided in the actual contract. The contract is the basis for changed-conditions claims, and all claims depend upon the exact wording of the contract. A proper claim under one contract may not be proper under another.

A properly written changed-conditions clause is for the benefit of the owner, contractor, and subcontractor. It has been deemed to be a fair and equitable clause; it is not exculpatory [*James Julian, Inc. v. President & Commissioners of Town of Elkton*, 341 F.2d 205 (1965)]. The changed-conditions clause eliminates wild guesswork in bidding and large contingencies in the price.

Since the rights for changed-conditions claims arise through the contract, the specific clause must be carefully scrutinized. Two typical but differing changed-condition clauses follow. Although this AIA article is not entitled changed conditions, it is the basis for a changed-conditions claim and provides that

Should concealed conditions encountered in the performance of the Work below the surface of the ground be at variance with the conditions indicated by the Contract Documents or should unknown physical conditions below the surface of the ground of an unusual nature, differing materially from those ordinarily encountered and generally recognized as inherent in work of the character provided for in this Contract, be encountered, the Contract Sum shall be equitably adjusted by Change Order upon claim by either party made within a reasonable time after the first observance of the conditions [American Institute of Architects General Conditions Form A201, art. 12.1.6(1970)].

This clause has now been modified by the more recent AIA 201 (1976) edition. Know your contract. Most existing contracts are patterned after the older AIA general conditions, and it takes years before new revisions become the standard.

On federal contracts, the Armed Services Procurement Regulations provide for a changed-conditions claim under, and pursuant to, the contract clause entitled "differing site conditions." The wording of this clause, although similar in many respects to the 1976 AIA clause, provides for the filing of claims in different situations. This federal clause is probably the model clause most often followed in contract forms. It provides that

(a) The Contractor shall promptly, and before such conditions are disturbed, notify the Contracting Officer in writing of: (1) subsurface or latent physical conditions at the site differing materially from those indicated in this contract, or (2) unknown physical conditions at the site, of an unusual nature, differing materially from those ordinarily encountered and generally recognized as inhering in work of the character provided for in this contract. The Contracting Officer shall promptly investigate the conditions, and if he finds that such conditions do materially so differ and cause an increase or decrease in the Contractor's cost of, or the time required for, performance of any part of the work under this contract, whether or not changed as a result of such conditions, an equitable adjustment shall be made and the contract modified in writing accordingly. (b) No Claim of the Contractor under this clause shall be allowed unless the Contractor has given the notice required in (a) above; *provided,* however, the time prescribed therefor may be extended by the Government. (c) No claim by the Contractor for an equitable adjustment hereunder shall be allowed if asserted after final payment under this contract [G.S.A. Standard Form 23A].

The importance of careful analysis of your particular changed-conditions clause is exemplified by the differences between the quoted AIA and federal clauses. In certain instances entitlement exists under the federal form but not the AIA form. The AIA form is limited to conditions "below the surface of the ground." This is a limitation which does not exist in either the federal or 1976 AIA form, which talk about subsurface conditions as well as latent or unknown physical conditions at the site. These conditions are not limited to conditions below the surface of the ground. A changed condition might exist above ground, especially in renovation and alteration work.

Although the scope and application of the changed-conditions clauses vary from contract to contract, one essential ingredient seems similar, the need for prompt notice. Most contracts specifically provide, either in the changed-conditions clause itself or in a related clause, that before any claim can be recognized, the contractor must comply with the notice provisions, either actually or constructively. Specifically, the contractor is obligated to notify the owner of the changed condition before disturbing the conditions and/or performing the work. The purpose for the notice requirement is to permit the owner to verify the conditions and to allow the owner the right to either exercise the option to have the contractor proceed with the work and pay for a changed condition or to redesign that portion of the work to avoid or reduce the effect of the changed condition. The failure to give proper notice can defeat an otherwise proper changed-conditions claim.

The changed-condition clauses usually categorize and cover two basic forms of claim. The first form of claim is when the actual conditions "differ materially" or are "at variance" with the conditions indicated in the contract. In this instance, the AIA contract form seems more lenient than the federal form. Essentially, the standard clause creates a *contractual right* to recover for what would otherwise be deemed a breach of contract claim. If no changed-conditions clauses existed and the actual conditions encountered differed materially from those indicated in the contract documents, the contractor would have a possible claim for breach of contract [*Hollerbach v. United States,* 233 U.S. 165 (1914)]. Thus, the clause establishes a contractual right in lieu of a claim arising outside of the contract. It is easier to resolve claims based on contractual rights than those which allege a breach of contract.

There has been substantial litigation as to when a fact is affirmatively represented by the contract, so that one can determine whether conditions actually vary or differ materially from that base [*Burgess Mining & Constr. Corp. v. City of Bessemer, Alabama,* 312 So.2d 24 (1975)] (Case 10-2) and [*Wunderlich v. State of California,* 423 P.2d 545 (1967)]. Both parties must review the contract as a single unit in order to determine what is legally represented. The contractor will lose its claim if it should have anticipated the conditions based upon the original contract (Cases 12-1 and 12-2).

General disclaimer and exculpatory clauses denying liability and responsibility for actual conditions which differ from those indicated in the contract have, in many instances, been denied their full force.

> The state should not be thus permitted by general provisions in its specifications, instructions or contract from escaping liability for its direct and patent misrepresentations. The bidder could properly rely upon the clear and unequivocal information contained in the plans, otherwise they would serve no useful purpose. They should reasonably depict the work to be done and where they are definite and plain the contractor is entitled to rely upon them. The positive representations of the plans which refer only to the particular work involved take precedence over specifications applicable to all contracts or the general terms of a uniform contract form [*Young Fehlhaber Pile Co. v. State of New York,* 30 N.Y.S.2d 192, aff'd 37 N.Y.S.2d 928 (1942); see also *County Asphalt, Inc. v. State of New York,* 337 N.Y.S.2d 415 (1972) (Case 10-7) and *Fattore Company, Inc. v. Metropolitan Sewerage Commission, County of Milwaukee,* 454 F.2d 537 (1971)].

On the other hand, there are instances where the disclaimer clauses have been deemed valid, and this validity is enlarged when the contractual statements are not positive representations but statements of possibility or probability. Before a claim of breach of contract for misrepresentation or changed conditions can be asserted, the contractor must prove that positive and affirmative statements were made in the contract, that it relied on these statements, that the statements were inaccurate, that its reliance was justified, and that it incurred damages as a result thereof. When the contractor is able to prove that actual conditions were at "variance" or "differed materially," a changed-conditions claim exists (Cases 12-3 to 12-5). The contractor need not prove any sinister purpose [*Christie v. United States*, 237 U.S. 234 (1915)].

The second form of changed-conditions claims does not have an alternate remedy such as breach of contract. It is one that strictly exists by virtue of the contract. The basis for this claim is not founded upon what was indicated in the contract; instead the claim is founded on the difference between what the contractor should reasonably have anticipated for a particular site, project, and contract and what was actually encountered. As stated by the contract changed-condition clause, a contractor must be able to prove the existence of an unknown physical condition (which by its very fact assumes that the contract does not state that such physical condition will exist) of an *unusual* nature, which differs *materially* from those *ordinarily* encountered and generally recognized as inherent in the work of the character provided in the particular contract. No breach of contract or misrepresentation need be proved.

Before establishing any claim or entitlement, the contractor must be able to prove that it could not have reasonably anticipated the actual conditions. In order to establish this fact, and thereby establish the unknown and unusual requirements, the contractor's obligation to investigate the site, conduct tests, etc., must be considered. Inherent in this obligation is the fact that if a reasonable site inspection would have revealed the physical condition, the actual conditions could not constitute an unknown or unusual condition and thereby could not constitute a reasonably unanticipated condition.

In Illinois, a completion contractor who specifically contracted to complete a defaulted contractor's work was denied additional compensation when it found that part of the original work had to be redone and corrected. The completion contract specifically placed the burden of inspecting all existing work on the contractor, and therefore the completing contractor assumed the risk of acceptability of all prior work, which was discoverable by reasonable inspection [*Kuch and Watson v. Woodman*, 331 N.E.2d 350 (Ill. App. Ct. 1975)].

If a reasonable investigation would have divulged the existence of a physical condition which is not specifically referenced in the contract, such a condition would neither be unforeseen, nor an unknown physical condition, nor of an unusual nature, and therefore no changed condition would exist (Cases 12-6 and 12-7).

The site-inspection clauses often are attempts totally to deny liability for the information furnished either in the contract or other annexed or referenced documents. Such site-inspection clauses and disclaimers are not looked upon favorably by the courts. A contractor was entitled to receive an equitable adjustment under a contract-changed-conditions clause even though a separate clause in the contract tried to disavow responsibility for inaccurate estimated quantities and tried to place on the contractor the obligation to perform its own subsurface investigations.

> There can be little doubt that the contract proposals and plans, as submitted to the bidders . . . constituted material representations as to the location and quantity of undercut excavation. Lowder [contractor] relied on the relative accuracy of the undercut locations and quantities and was reasonably justified in doing so. It had no reason to believe that project 8.11618 would produce an excessive amount of undercut excavation.

These material representations were *not* negated by exculpatory clauses which try to eliminate liability.

> Clauses of this type, stating in effect that the contracting agency does not guarantee the statements of fact in the plans and specifications and requiring the contractor to make his own independent investigation of the site and satisfy himself of the conditions, are not given full literal effect . . . The information in the plans constituted positive representations upon which Lowder was justified in relying. We are of the opinion, therefore, that (1) a contracting agency which furnishes inaccurate information as a basis for bids may be liable on a breach of warranty theory, and (2) instructions to bidders to make their own independent investigations of the conditions to be encountered cannot be given full literal reach . . . It is simply unfair to bar recovery to contractors who are misled by inaccurate plans and submit bids lower than they might otherwise have submitted [*Ray D. Lowder, Inc. v. North Carolina State Highway Commission*, 217 S.E.2d 682 (1975)].

In determining the applicability of such clauses, courts often look at how long the contractor had from receipt of the invitation to bids to the bid date. Often this time is so limited that independent site investigations to the extent demanded by the bid documents are precluded. Where such time has been unreasonably limited, courts have denied the strict enforcement of the exculpatory provisions of site-investigation clauses (Case 12-8). The responsibility for inspecting the jobsite is mitigated by the following:

> Respondent's [contractor] inspection of the job site did not indicate any difficulties as to the location and extent of unsuitable material. Any inspection that could possibly have been made within the three-week period between the advertisement for bids and the opening thereof, would not have revealed the subsurface conditions to the point where it could be said that the prospective bidder should be forced to rely on this limited exploration over the misleading information supplied by the State which was a result of over three years of investigation, particularly in view of the omissions of information in the contract estimate of which the State had knowledge [*County Asphalt, Inc. v. State of New York*, 40 App. Div. 2d 26 (3d Dept. 1972)] (Case 10-7).

The establishment of a changed-condition claim under the second approach is not predicated on the representations in the contract. It is assumed the contract has not misrepresented the true facts. Whether the encountered conditions fall within the stated basis for a changed condition must necessarily depend upon the contractor's obligations to inspect and investigate the site and such knowledge that *should have been* gained as a result.

In the Lowder case, the contractor, walking over the jobsite, did not observe any major conditions which would indicate that the bid documents were inaccurate. This investigation was deemed to be a reasonable site inspection and did not eliminate a changed condition. However, "had Lowder's difficulties not arisen from a latent geological problem, but from a failure to inform itself of reasonably observable physical factors, we would be disposed to reach another conclusion." The contractor was entitled to an equitable adjustment of its unit price when it encountered substantially increased excavation beyond the approximate units indicated in the contract, as a changed condition even though the owner denied any guarantee for the accuracy of the estimated units.

If, as a result of the contract review and site investigations, the conditions are still classified as unknown latent physical conditions and fulfill the requirements of the contract clause and are not precluded by exculpatory language, then the contractor is entitled to submit its claim for a changed condition as specified in the contract (Cases 12-9 and 12-10).

Once entitlement is established, the contractor is faced with proving the damages or equitable adjustment which it is entitled to receive. In construction claims, the courts normally require and always prefer that the contractor prove *each* dollar claimed as a result of each specific changed condition. Although the courts normally deny granting an award on a total-cost approach, under certain circumstances, a contractor has been found entitled to all its additional costs, above the base contract, resulting from the changed condition. The equitable adjustment to which the contractor is entitled is those provable increased costs which are the direct and necessary result of changed conditions (Case 12-11).

Conclusion   It is of the utmost importance that before bidding the contractor review the contract documents to ascertain the existence of any changed-conditions clause. In addition, the contractor should be fully apprised of its further obligations to perform site investigations. The contractor cannot unilaterally discount disclaimer and exculpatory clauses inserted by the owner; however, neither can the owner believe it has achieved total safety by the disclaimer clause. If the contractor believes a changed condition exists, immediate notice must be furnished to the owner's designated representative and all documents necessary to prove actual costs must be carefully and totally prepared. The changed-conditions clause should prove to be a valuable asset to both the contractor and the owner, especially when a continuing relationship exists.

**CASE 12-1   Contractor Loses
Borrow-Pit, Extra Claim**

If the borrow-pit material found at a site is similar to that indicated in the specifications, the contractor cannot recover extra costs incurred in reworking the material to meet the specifications' requirements, according to a federal contract appeals board [*Appeal of Robert L. Helms Construction Co.,* DOT CAB 67-1, 69-2 BCA 7883 (1969)].

The case involved a contract with the Bureau of Public Roads. It called for construction of a base course and surfacing of a Nevada highway. The contract documents indicated the existence of two borrow pits.

The contractor claimed that the government had misrepresented the materials to be found in the borrow pits, forcing it to incur additional costs to produce materials acceptable under the specifications. The additional costs formed the claim, which was considered under the contract's changed-conditions and changes clauses by the Department of Transportation Contract Appeals Board.

The borrow pits were designated as type B material sources under the contract. For type B sources, the contractor was obligated to

> satisfy himself as to the quantity of acceptable material that may be produced in accordance with paragraph 2

of the contract. The paragraph provided

> Should the contractor elect to obtain material from a type B source and it is subsequently found that the source contains insufficient acceptable material to meet the contract needs and it becomes necessary for the contractor to select a new source, or if the contractor chooses, for some other reason, to change the source of material, no adjustment in payment or contract time will be made.

The contractor's problem arose in making a material taken from one of the borrow pits conform to the plasticity-index requirements of the contract. Using certain alleged detailed information furnished by the government, the contractor followed a single procedure for intermixing pit material to arrive at an anticipated acceptable blend. The result of the intermixing did not, however, meet specification requirements, apparently because the type of materials the contractor anticipated was not found in the pits.

The use of a single intermixing procedure, the board noted, was of the contractor's own choice and was not specified in the contract. In fact, the board found that the proposed contract documents clearly informed the contractor "that at least two operations had to be performed on the pit-run material before it could be expected to meet the specification requirements" and that the contractor's method was not feasible. In addition, the contract language put the contractor on notice that the borrow pit was a marginal source of material and that the material would require extensive processing to be useable under the contract. Since the material found at the site was not different from that indicated by the contract, and since the amount of work should have been anticipated by the contractor, the board held that no claim existed under the changed-conditions or changes clauses of the contract.

**CASE 12-2   Architect-Engineer Denied
Additional Design Fee for
Unexpected Conditions**

An Architect-Engineer was denied an increase in its fee when it encountered poor subsurface soil conditions that required exceptional design work. The Postal

Service Board of Contract Appeals held that the possibility of poor soil conditions could have been anticipated and that the design work based on these conditions was part of the original contract [*Appeal of John J. Flad & Associates,* PSBCA 466, 71-2 BCA 9090 (1971)].

The contract with the Post Office Department called for Architect-Engineer services, including complete building design drawings and specifications. In addition, the Architect-Engineer was to arrange for and supervise subsurface investigations, tests and borings and then to prepare an engineering report of the results. The analysis revealed adverse soil conditions, which the Architect-Engineer says were not contemplated and which required additional design work to the foundation, for which it seeks payment.

The contract contained no changed-conditions clause. The board said that the parties never discussed subsurface conditions before execution of the contract and that the contract made no specific representation of what conditions were to be anticipated.

The board ruled that the contract contained no clause providing for adjustment of compensation if unusual conditions were encountered. It held that the conditions ought not to have been totally unexpected and that even had the conditions been totally unexpected, they did not present problems of design or construction of such magnitude as to render the contract voidable as having been made under a mutual mistake of fact.

There is no evidence that the department withheld any special information it had concerning the site, and in the absence of a contract provision placing the risk on the government that poor subsoil conditions would be present, the Architect-Engineer must assume the risk, the court ruled.

CASE 12-3   Sewer Depicted in Drawings Ruled a Changed Condition

A storm sewer shown in the contract drawings but not anticipated by the contractor was held to be a differing site condition by the federal Engineering Board of Contract Appeals [*Appeal of Excavation Constr. Co.,* ENGBCA 3646, 77-1 BCA 12,224 (1976)].

While performing work on the Washington Metropolitan Area Transit Authority system, the contractor discovered that the placement of several bearing piles would be affected by a storm sewer line that the drawings indicated as abandoned in place. When notified of the problem, the owner told the contractor that it was its responsibility to remove the storm sewer or redesign the pile structure.

The contractor argued that, according to the contract, a line could be abandoned, without requiring removal. As further proof, it showed that the drawings specified twenty-five utilities to be abandoned but only four were to be removed. The sewer in question was listed as a utility to be abandoned but not marked for removal on the drawings.

The board held that "since no provision for the removal of the storm sewer appeared on the contract drawings, the [contractor] reasonably concluded that it would not have to be removed and on that account included no amount of money in its bid estimate for that purpose."

It concluded that the actual location of the sewer, which required either removal of the sewer or redesign and relocation of the cast-in-place bearing piles, was a differing site condition in accord with the contract.

The contractor's interpretation, it said, was reasonable. It was therefore entitled to recover for the additional cost of performance.

CASE 12-4   Inaccurate Boring Data Are a Basis for Liability

The Postal Service Board of Contract Appeals (PSBCA) has ruled that a contractor is entitled to recover the additional costs incurred due to subsurface conditions inaccurately depicted by the boring data of the contract documents, even though rock outcroppings existed at the site.

The contract called for the construction of a postal maintenance facility in Texas. McCann Co., the general contractor for the project, contended that the boring data included in the project specifications led it to believe that it would encounter soft to medium-hard limestone within the excavation area and that hard limestone existed only outside of the work area.

In actuality, the contractor encountered hard limestone throughout the site and was required to alter its excavation procedures drastically at a greatly increased cost. McCann argued that it was entitled to additional costs because the actual conditions it encountered were materially different from those indicated in the contract.

The Postal Service denied liability on the basis that two rock outcroppings existed on the site. This condition, the government argued, negated any changed condition claim.

The board found that McCann's subcontractors relied upon the boring data in determining their estimates for excavation work. It further noted that although the prime contractor did not make any independent estimate of the excavation work, the closeness of the subcontractor bids received, as well as the government's independent estimate, confirmed that all persons interpreted the boring data in the same fashion.

Ruling against the government, the board noted that even the Postal Service's architect testified that the actual existence of the rock outcroppings could not indicate whether the rock was hard or soft. It merely indicated the existence of limestone.

After reviewing the evidence, the board upheld the contractor's claim, saying:

> Neither the [contractor], its two excavating subcontractors, nor the government, nor, for that matter, any other bidders had actual knowledge of the real subsurface conditions. Neither has it been shown that actual pre-bid site inspection would have revealed the problem later encountered.
>
> [The board concluded that the contractor is chargeable] only with that knowledge which it would gain from a reasonable visual inspection of the site and/or examina-

tion of the core borings [*Appeal of McCann Co.,* PSBCA 152, 76-2 BCA 12,219 (Nov. 18, 1976)].

CASE 12-5   Contractor Collects Extra Costs When Site Did Not Meet Specifications

A U.S. Court of Appeals ruled that an owner implies a warranty to a contractor when a contractor is forced to base its price and schedule on certain specified site conditions. If the site does not meet these specifications at the time construction is scheduled to begin, the court held that the contractor is entitled to recover its total additional cost under the contract's changed-conditions clause [*Moorhead Constr. Co., Inc., v. City of Grand Forks,* 508 F.2d 1008 (8th Cir. 1975)].

The owner divided the construction of a sewage-treatment plant into two phases, each to be performed by independent prime contractors. The first phase, earthwork and site preparation, was to be completed before the start of the second phase, which involved general construction work.

The phase II contract was awarded substantially before completion of the site work. It included a changed-conditions clause, stating:

> Should the Contractor encounter or the Owner discover during the progress of the work subsurface or latent physical conditions at the site differing materially from those indicated in this contract, or unknown physical conditions at the site of an unusual nature, differing materially from those ordinarily encountered and generally recognized as inherent in work of the character provided for in the contract, the Engineer shall be promptly notified in writing of such conditions . . . . The Engineer will thereupon promptly investigate the conditions and if he finds they do so materially differ and cause an increase or decrease in the cost of, or time required for performance of the contract, an equitable adjustment will be made.

The phase II contractor was not given access to the site until two months after work was originally scheduled to begin. This delay forced the contractor to work during winter months. In addition, the contractor encountered unanticipated unstable soil conditions. Both these problems forced the contractor to use more expensive building methods than those originally planned.

Although the engineer agreed with the contractor that these problems constituted changed conditions, the owner refused to adjust the contract to cover the builder's increased costs. As a result the contractor sued to recover additional costs, charging the owner with a breach of implied warranty.

The owner argued that phase I specifications were not part of the phase II contract and that the follow-on contractor should have inspected the site before submitting a bid. Rejecting this argument, the lower court said:

> At the time Moorhead [the contractor] bid on phase II contract, the phase I earth work had just commenced. Because an inspection of the site would not have disclosed the difficult site conditions which it would later face due to excess moisture and lack of compaction, . . . [the contractor] in estimating its bid necessarily relied upon the city [the owner] to provide a construction site prepared in accord with the specifications of phase I.

The court ruled in favor of the contractor, holding that phase I specifications were implied warranties in the phase II contract.

On appeal, the higher court affirmed the district court's ruling and took up the question of damages.

In presenting its damage claim, the contractor fully documented its total cost of actual performance, subtracted the contract price and sought the balance. The lower court allowed this method of computing the damages. As part of its appeal the owner argued that this total-cost approach was not the proper method of assessing liability. Acknowledging that this total-cost theory is not a preferred method of calculating damages, the appeals court said it is justified in this case. "As a practical matter, the [lower] court found no other method was feasible and that the supporting evidence was substantial," the higher court said. "The contractor was obviously confronted with a situation not of its own making, but one induced by the . . . [owner's] delay and failure to prepare the site properly." The court said the total-cost method could be used to assess the damages.

CASE 12-6   An Inadequate Site Inspection
Defeated Contractor's Claim

The Armed Services Board of Contract Appeals has ruled that a government contractor who was required to excavate more rock than it had anticipated could not recover the extra costs because a reasonable inspection of the site would have led to a proper estimate of the rock excavation required.

The primary work requirement of the contract, to be performed at Camp Drum, New York, was installation of 50 miles of cable. The manner and method of excavation for the installing of buried cable was set forth in the specifications. However, the contract neither stated the quantity or type of rock to be found nor the percentage of rock excavation anticipated for the 50-mile run. The responsibility for checking the nature and location of the work was to be the contractor's.

Before the contract award, the contractor visited the site and spent about six hours inspecting 20 to 25 miles of the cable route, taking probes every so often. No inspection was conducted of the rougher terrain, where its car could not go. As a result of this inspection, the contractor estimated that approximately 10 percent of the route would require rock excavation and submitted its bid based on this fact. After it received the contract and started work, it discovered that substantially more than 10 percent rock excavation was required. The contractor then filed a claim for the increased costs of the work.

In opposition to the claim, the government stated that a bidder's conference was held at the site which the contractor failed to attend. For those at the conference the government furnished four-wheel-drive vehicles and conducted an inspection tour of the cable route. The inspection tour covered a different area of the cable route, which was not accessible by ordinary car, and rock was clearly observable and prevalent throughout the area. If the contractor had availed itself of this tour, it could have estimated the required rock excavation properly, the government said.

The board agreed with the government. In denying the contractor recovery, it held:

> Since the contract documents are silent as to the surface and subsurface conditions and since the board finds that no representations regarding these same conditions were otherwise made, it cannot be said that appellant [contractor] met any condition differing materially from that shown in the contract or in the accompanying plans, specifications and drawings or which was otherwise represented.
>
> Reasonably thorough inspection of the sight would have apprised appellant of the need for rock excavation beyond its 10 percent estimate. The appellant did not participate in the government-conducted tour of the site . . . . Covering but half the route and driving in a probe every 1.5 to 2 miles to the inadequate depth of 30 in. did not constitute an adequate inspection and the board so finds [*Appeal of Utilities Contracting Co.*, ASBCA 13261, 69-2 BCA 7932 (1969)].

CASE 12-7   Dry Lake Bed Turned Into Lake
Not a Changed Condition

A contractor's claim that it encountered a changed condition requiring it to fill in a haul road before it could be used was denied by the Agricultural Board of Contract Appeals.

In testimony, the contractor claimed that when it visited the site, it observed that a portion of the haul road crossed a dry lake bed but that there was no visual indication that this area held water. After the contract was awarded and work began, it rained and about ¼ mile of the road became a lake.

Although the contract provided that no payment would be made for borrow material used to build a haul road, the contractor claimed that the clause was not applicable since the present condition constituted a changed condition. It sought compensation for placing about 35,000 tons of fill.

In denying the contractor's claim, the board concluded

> that the weather conditions were not unusual and that the ground conditions during the course of construction were essentially the same as those which were observable at the prebid time when the site was available for inspection . . . . While the contract allows additional time for bad weather, it does not provide additional compensation for unfavorable weather such as is here alleged to have been encountered [*Appeal of F. H. Antrim Constr. Co., Inc.*, AGBCA 307, 72-2 BCA 9475 (1972)].

CASE 12-8   Bid Time Inadequate,
Earth Estimates Used

A contractor that has been allowed insufficient time to investigate a site fully while preparing its bid has sufficient reason to rely on the owner's earthwork estimates even though the owner rules out responsibility for the estimates [*Appeal of Raymond International of Delaware, Inc.*, ASBCA 13121, 70-1 BCA 8341 (June 12, 1970)].

The Armed Services Board of Contract Appeals ruled that the contractor's resulting overruns constituted a changed condition and that the owner's (United

States government) failure to award a time extension was a valid basis for an acceleration-of-work claim.

The contract called for construction of two separate 75-mile-long roads in northern Thailand. The roads were more than 500 miles apart.

Separate contracts for a topographic survey and highway design had been awarded to an architectural-engineering firm before signing the contract. The topographic survey was complete, but the design survey was not. This meant that the project's specifications published with the bid advertisement were "either not final or had been prepared by the government in general terms," the board said.

When the contractor completed performance, it submitted a claim for additional costs incurred as a result of having relied on the owner's inaccurate estimates of the quantity of earthwork. The material moved amounted to more than twice the amount estimated, but the government denied responsibility, saying that it was the contractor's obligation to determine actual quantities during the project's bidding period. The government pointed out that it did not guarantee accuracy of the estimates and the amounts shown were furnished only as a guide.

The board considered the extensive size and scope of the construction contract, the length of time that it took the government and its architectural-engineering firm to design the project and prepare specifications and the relatively short period (less than two months) allotted the contractor to prepare and submit its bid.

From these facts, even though the contractor was shown to have known about the project before the advertised invitation for bids, the board concluded that a changed condition existed and that the contractor was entitled to an equitable adjustment in its contract price. It said the contractor could not prepare a bid until it had definite and specific information of the work to be done and that the development of logistics of a large project in two separate and remote areas could not be undertaken until the project had been formulated.

> It allowed no time for a detailed survey [explained the board]. The only possible relevance of the government quantity estimates was to provide a basis for bidding, and appellant had no alternative than to rely upon them. No bids could have been otherwise made. Under these circumstances, it is well established that a material overrun of these quantities is a changed condition within the terms of the contract.

Acceleration of Work   Another claim submitted by the contractor was to recover extra costs incurred as a result of the government's alleged acceleration of work on the second road covered by the contract.

The contractor's approved progress schedule indicated that it would move its equipment to the site of the second road upon completion of the first. Prolonged use of the equipment on the first road because of the massive amount of overruns delayed this move, and the second road was not completed by the date set in the original contract.

The board noted that the contractor was not at fault for delays that carried work on the second road beyond the original contract completion date. Due to the earth-overrun problem on the first road, the contractor was entitled to time extensions, it said. However, during performance and before any time extensions were granted, the contractor was told by the government "that no extension would be given, and that it [contractor] must take any measure necessary to finish the job by the original completion date. . . ."

This action by the government, held the board, constituted an acceleration of performance and the contractor was entitled to recover the expenses it incurred in trying to comply with the acceleration order.

**CASE 12-9   Contractor Not Bound by Soils
Report It Did Not Read**

The federal Engineering Board of Contract Appeals has upheld a contractor's claim for damages for a changed condition based upon its reasonable interpretation of boring data, even though the contractor did not refer to the soils report included in the contract [*Appeal of Jackson-Swindell-Dressler, a joint venture,* ENGBCA 3614, 76-2 BCA 12,222 (Sept. 22, 1976)].

The contract called for the construction of a section of the rail transit system in Washington, D.C., by the joint venture of Jackson-Swindell-Dressler (JSD). In preparing its bid, the contractor reviewed the plans, specifications, and boring logs and conducted a site inspection, but it did not refer to the soils report that was mentioned in the physical data clause of the contract.

As a result of its bid review, the contractor anticipated encountering boulders only while excavating soldier-pile holes in certain areas of the project and not in others. The excavation subcontractor did not originally submit a bid on the project and did not review the soils report.

When excavation began, the subcontractor encountered an unexpected layer of boulders, causing production delays in two areas. It instituted a claim under the differing-site-conditions clause of the contract, which JSD passed along to the owner.

The board denied the contractor's claim of encountering unanticipated conditions in one of the two areas because the testimony was vague and the actual daily reports did not indicate the extent of the problem alleged by the contractor and subcontractor. The unfavorable ruling appears to be the result of JSD's failure to maintain proper records.

In the second area, the contractor alleged that the boring logs represented conditions that differed from those actually encountered. The joint venture argued that it anticipated gravelly material with some boulders in no way comparable to the quantity of boulders actually encountered.

An expert witness for the contractor testified that a reasonable review of the contract bid documents "would indicate a low probability of encountering boulders."

The government, however, presented another expert witness with a conflicting interpretation of the bid documents. According to his testimony, the documents would have placed the contractor on actual notice of the high possibility of boulders in the area. This being the case, the government argued that the borings were not misleading and therefore no changed conditions were encountered.

The government's expert also indicated, however, that the contractor's interpretation was not unreasonable, and that there was a wide latitude for interpretation of the documents.

Using these facts, the board held that the contractor's interpretation was reasonable and that a high percentage of boulders was not anticipated from its reasonable interpretation of the documents.

The owner presented a second argument claiming that the contractor was bound by the data included in the soils report referred to in the physical-data clause of the contract. The soils report specifically indicated that a continuous layer of boulders might exist.

JSD testified that it did not consult the report.

In concluding that the contractor was not bound by the soils report, the board held "that we do not construe that clause as requiring [JSD] to place reliance on the referenced data instead of the actual representations made by the specifications and drawings."

Because neither the contractor nor the subcontractor had reviewed the soils report, they were not bound by its contents, according to the board.

CASE 12-10   Wet Site Warrants Extra Pay

The U.S. Court of Claims has ruled that a contractor was entitled to an equitable adjustment in the contract price for having to perform its work in quagmire caused by an inadequate site drainage system designed by the government. The ruling affirmed and adopted the Board of Contract Appeals' finding that a changed condition existed [*Phillips Constr. Co., Inc. v. United States.*, 394 F.2d 834 (1968)].

The contractor was to construct 800 family housing units in a complete community setting. It made an adequate prebid site inspection, and there was nothing indicated in the site inspection, drawings or specifications to put it on notice that a major site-drainage problem would exist. It was reasonably anticipated that the drainage system, designed by the government, would be adequate to disperse surface waters.

The general scheme of the drainage system called for the final disposal of collected waters by connecting an off-site swale with an outfall ditch that was to empty into the Atlantic Ocean. Neither the specified drainage piping nor the outfall ditch was adequate for proper drainage. The outfall ditch often clogged, resulting in prolonged ponding and flooding back on the construction site. Surface water was collected, not dispersed. These inadequacies were found to be a major contributing cause to the quagmire condition that resulted in extra costs to the contractor.

The board concluded and the court affirmed the fact that this quagmire condition constituted an unknown physical condition at the site, differing materially from that reasonably anticipated, and constituted a changed condition. The contractor, they said, was accordingly entitled to an equitable adjustment in its contract price.

CASE 12-11   Changed-Conditions Payment Includes All Direct Costs

A general contractor working on a government project has been allowed to recover extra costs incurred on work performed under the changed-conditions clause of its contract.

The contract called for construction of a federal post office and courthouse in Bangor, Maine. It contained the standard changed-conditions clause, but no suspension-of-work or similar provision that would allow compensation for delays caused by the government.

During the initial phases of construction, the pile-driving subcontractor encountered numerous boulders that interfered with and disrupted its work. The site condition was determined to be a changed condition by the contracting officer, and the general contractor was directed to move the boulders.

The contractor argued that it was entitled to all costs attributable to the changed condition. These included the cost of having to work in a disjointed manner, of having to perform certain work in the winter months, and of having to pay higher labor wage rates and material prices because work was now being performed at a later date.

The General Services Board of Contract Appeals allowed the contractor to recover these costs, subject to substantiation, even though the contract did not contain a suspension clause.

The board held:

> The "changed conditions" clause permits an equitable adjustment to cover increased costs which are the direct and necessary result of changed conditions where the changed conditions lead directly to disruption, extra work, or new procedures [*Appeal of Electronic & Missile Facilities, Inc.*, GSBCA 2203, 69-2 BCA 7781 (1969)].

THIRTEEN

Owner-Furnished Property

There seems to be an endless list of circumstances in which an owner purchases materials, equipment, or other property from one source and furnishes it to the contractor for inclusion as part of its work. The reasons for such a procedure include the hope of acquiring the materials more cheaply, without the contractor's markup, the avoidance of certain taxes, maintaining certain proprietary rights, better buying power, the necessity of ordering the property sufficiently in advance of entering the construction contract due to lead times, and various other good or fallacious reasons. It is noted that the same reasons often are the cause for the contractor's purchasing materials and furnishing the property to another subcontractor for installation into the work. In addition, the more prime contractors on the project the more often the owner or others furnish the property.

If the owner furnishes property, a series of different legal responsibilities and problems come into existence, and both the owner and contractor may encounter problems they had not taken into consideration. The idea of the owner's furnishing property can be worthwhile and sometimes even mandatory. Both contractor and owner are warned of the attending additional responsibilities.

The property to be furnished is that property specifically set forth and itemized in the contract documents. The contractor should never assume that any major item of property is being furnished to it for its inclusion in the work. If you as a contractor believe that property is to be furnished, specify it; otherwise you are not entitled to it. There may be some exceptions, but none is widely recognized. Included within the listed items, and sometimes implied as an exception, are the "necessary related data" needed for using the property, e.g., special handling instructions, instructions on how to put it together, and instructions on maintenance. The right to unspecified related data is specified in the federal government furnished-property clause.

The delivery schedule for the property is a major concern which seldom is given the necessary and proper consideration. The contract should spell out, in detail, the time schedule and factors relating to delivery. Specifically, whose obligation will it be to pick up the materials, to transport them to the site, to unload them, and to store them until needed? Most important are the dates of delivery. If substantial properties are being furnished, a detailed construction schedule should be incorporated as part of the contract. Property which comes late can cause tremendous obstacles and damages to a contractor. The federal clause specifically provides that if the materials are not provided on time and as agreed, the contractor shall be entitled to an equitable adjustment in its contract price and time. This is fair to both. If no clause granting a contractual right to an equitable adjustment is included, the owner may be liable for breach-of-contract damages for failure to abide by the schedule. This assumes that time is a material factor (and it should be made material by the contractor), that it is the owner's obligation to furnish supplies on time (which again should be so stated by the contractor in the contract), and that there has been a default of that obligation. Remember that early materials can cause as many problems as late materials.

It seems that every time that there is an equitable clause, someone comes along and rewords it. In order to avoid (or at least attempt to avoid) liability for improper delivery dates, many owner-furnished-property clauses have integrated exculpatory no-damage-for-delay provisions. Owners are now stating that they should deliver by a set date but that if they do not, they are not liable for delays. When this no-damage-for-delay clause is specifically incorporated into the owner-furnished-property clause, it would appear that the clause would overcome the objection that it is not specific. The contractor is forewarned that such an exculpatory clause may be valid. The owner must also remember that if such a clause is used, the contractor will put in a contingency factor to cover this possibility. If the contingency does not arise, the owner has paid more. In other words, in the long run it appears that the owner has gained very little by such a clause.

Under the normal situation when the contractor purchases the property as part of its contract, it is liable for late deliveries and responsible for defects in the materials. If the owner purchases the material, this responsibility is taken off the contractor's shoulders and put onto the owner's. If the materials are defective, are not suitable for the intended use, or are unsuitable for the particular use, this is the owner's problem. Again, the federal clause specifically provides for an equitable adjustment in the contract price and time if the property is not suitable for its intended use. The damages incurred by a contractor can be substantial if the property is not in accordance with the contractual requirements and must be replaced or causes damage to other property. In trying to avoid this liability, the owner has, in some contracts, started to add the clause that the contractor shall inspect and accept the property furnished before installation. This puts an added degree of responsibility on the contractor. It appears, however, that this clause might relate only to patent defects and not to latent defects; this is a speculation, however.

It is true that the owner may be reducing its price to a certain extent, but the owner should realize that it is also accepting substantial additional responsibilities and liabilities. However, the contractor cannot consider itself void of responsibilities, and compensation should be included in its price, but this point is often overlooked.

After the property has been delivered to the site, the question often arises: Who has the *risk of loss*? *Title* and *risk of loss* are two separate and distinct legal considerations. In the true owner-furnished-property situation the contractor never has title, which remains with the owner; but when the goods are furnished to the project and the contractor, the contractor then has care, custody, and control of the property and probably has acquired the risk of loss. The contractor may have to accept the responsibility for moving it on the project, for damage or theft of the goods, for protection, etc. Once these points are considered, the contractor will realize that it will have to perform certain work and take certain responsibilities and therefore must receive some consideration, even though it is not furnishing the property.

The owner-furnished-property provision can be equitable and fair to both parties, granting each reasonable rights, and should be written in such a fashion.

FOURTEEN

Delays and Suspensions

The most important determination in claims of delays or suspensions is whether or not a specific contract clause exists permitting or denying the recovery of delay damages. At one pole there is the no-damage-for-delay clause, specifically precluding, on its face, any right to recover damages. The no-damage-for-delay clause attempts to avoid liability, sometimes successfully, even when there would otherwise have been a breach-of-contract claim. Contractors should note that although many contracts do not have a no-damage-for-delay clause in the "standard" general conditions, the clause is often inserted in supplemental conditions. These documents must be reviewed carefully. At the opposite pole is the suspension-of-work clause, as found in the Federal Conditions Standard Form 23A. If there is a suspension-of-work clause, the contractor will submit its claim as part of, and through, the actual contract. If there is no suspension-of-work or similar clause, the only means for recovering delay damages is by proof of default and breach of contract. The suspension-of-work clause has been labeled as the administrative or contractual equivalent to a breach-of-contract action for delays. If one is confronted with a factual situation where a suspension-of-work clause exists but no formal stop-work or suspension order was issued, a constructive suspension-of-work contract claim should be pursued [*Chaney and James Constr. Co., Inc. v. United States,* 421 F.2d 728 (1970)] (Cases 14-1 and 14-2). However, as with all contractual rights, each and every right depends upon the specific contract language. Changing a word within the clause or altering another contract clause (which will be interpreted together with the suspension-of-work clause as it is part of the same contract) may well call for different decisions from case to case. Seldom is a suspension-of-work clause, granting a contractual right to delay damages, inserted in private contracts gratuitously. The negotiation of its inclusion should be considered and pursued.

Because the scope of damages which can result from a delay is extremely difficult if not impossible to estimate or even appreciate at the time of the delay, delay claims are often overlooked until it is too late. Often the cause for loss on a contract cannot be pinpointed, even in a broad sense, because the delay is not a single catastrophic event but a cumulative, continuing loss-of-efficiency problem. Frequently the cause is not determined because of poor communications between field and administrative personnel. It is essential that the delay or suspension be recognized immediately, since notice of the suspension within a prescribed time is usually a necessary condition precedent for a contract suspension-of-work claim. If one is pursuing a delay claim, notice of the breach and protesting the breach are essential; otherwise the breach may be deemed to have been waived. Irregular filing of notice is permitted only where serious prejudice is not caused by the lack of notice (Case 14-3).

In that the delay claim is typically a breach-of-contract argument, the claimant must be able to ascertain and prove that the other party had a contractual obligation running to the claimant and that a default of *that obligation* has occurred. The obligation, default, and effect should be material in scope, else the court may well rule that an immaterial nonsubstantive breach, if any, has occurred, and deny the right of action. However, at the very outset, when the breach occurs, one is normally not able to determine the scope of the breach and therefore in order to protect itself the claimant must go on record.

Proving that an obligation exists normally requires proof that time limitations and periods, in some respect, were specifically incorporated as a material part of the contract. The time periods must be contractual obligations and not just reference points [*Burgess Constr. Co. v. M. Morrin & Sons Co., Inc.*, 526 F.2d 108 (10th Cir. 1976)]. Before the contractor can say that the owner defaulted because the owner delayed performance, the contractor must be able to prove the obligation of the owner and what was delayed. The same principle is true if it is the subcontractor who claims delay by the prime contractor [*Longview Constr. & Dev., Inc. v. Loggins Constr. Co.*, 523 S.W.2d 771 (Tex. 1975)]. This creates a major obstacle for many contractors. Although universally most construction contractors take strong exception to the court's ruling, courts have established the general rule of law that *time is not of the essence of a contract unless so specified.* Although time can be inferred to be of the essence, under certain limited circumstances, the trend appears to be to treat time *not of the essence* or as a mandatory requirement, the breach of which might have been a material breach [*Kingery Constr. Co. v. Scherbarth Welding, Inc.*, 185 N.W.2d 857 (1971)] (Case 14-4). In one case a subcontractor was denied its claim for delay damages against a general contractor since it failed to prove that the general contractor breached the contract by failing to perform its work within a reasonable period of time. Since the contract did not contain a specific completion date, the court ruled that the contractor was only obligated to perform within a reasonable time

[*H. Piken & Co., Inc. v. Planet Constr. Corp.,* 326 N.E.2d 725 (Mass. App. 1975)]. In fact, the inclusion of commencement and completion dates was deemed not to be an absolute time period or to even imply that time was of the essence, since in construction contracts, the court felt neither party believed or acted as if these were mandatory. Still another decision went one step further and indicated that the existence of a liquidated-damage provision and a prescribed time-limitation period implied that time was not of the essence [*Carter v. Sherburne Corp.,* 315 A.2d 870 (1974)]. Although this case limited an owner's rights to the specified liquidated damages, the ruling was still that time was implied not to be of the essence by the existence of a liquidated-damage provision. Such a ruling might hold true even if it were the contractor trying to assert a delay claim. In another decision a court precluded termination of a contract which had gone beyond the completion date, since the contract had a changes clause; and a changes clause, whether or not a change exists, implies that time was not intended to be of the essence [*Kole v. Parker Yale Development Co.,* 536 P.2d 848, *cert. denied* (Colo. 1975)]. These court decisions might be distinguished in a given factual situation, but to avoid that concern and obstacle, it is strongly recommended that if the contractor is concerned with time and the extended costs incurred by delays, it specifically state that "Time is a material provision of this contract. Time is of the essence." Beware, it is a double-edged sword and cuts both ways.

It appears that the establishment of time's being of the essence and a material provision of the contract can be further clarified by inserting specific progress schedules as part of the contract, by incorporating provisions for termination if the time limitations specified in the contract are not adhered to, or by specifying the right to collect damages for delay. The establishment of time limitation as a material part of the contract still does not, in and by itself, establish the obligation or the default on which to base the delay claim. The obligation is often spelled out in different paragraphs in the contract. This obligation might be the owner's obligation to furnish the site, a reasonable work area, proper surveys, or access to the site (Cases 14-5 and 14-6); to issue interpretations and clarifications of the contract, review of contract submittals such as shop drawings, catalog cuts, or other documents within a specified time (Cases 14-7 and 14-8); to furnish materials, equipment, or other services by a set date; to obtain permits, variances, rights-of-way, or similar items (Case 14-9); to coordinate the work of the various independent prime contractors or subcontractors (Case 14-10); to pay by a specified time; to perform certain aspects of work within a specified period of time (Case 14-11); to furnish punch lists at various stages or within a certain time after notice; to deal properly with change orders (Cases 14-1 and 14-12); to furnish nondefective contract documents (Cases 14-13 and 14-14); or any one of hundreds of other reasons.

A contractor was found to be entitled to its actual unit-price costs, in excess of its contract unit prices, resulting from delays occasioned by the presence of a utility contractor on site. The owner knew of the requirement for the utility company's exclusive presence on the site but did not disclose this fact to this contractor in its bid documents [*Commonwealth, Department of Highways v. S. J. Groves & Sons Co.,* 1343 A.2d 72 (Penn. Commonwealth Ct. 1975)].

The most important obligation is the implied obligation of one contracting party not to interfere unreasonably or intentionally with the performance of another contracting party (Case 14-15).

> It is a well-settled rule that where one party demands strict performance as to time by another party, he must perform on his part all the conditions which are requisite in order to enable the other party to perform his part, and a failure on the part of the party demanding performance to do the preliminary work required in order to enable the other party to complete within the time limited, operates as a waiver of the time provision in the contract [*Dannatt v. Fuller,* 120 N.Y. 554 (1890)].

This obligation is not only implied but should be specified and expressed in the contract. The question of how it is expressed, in addition to the other specified obligations, raises another question and is another double-edged sword. In that both parties are assumed to enter the contract in good faith with the expectation of proper performance, it is not unreasonable to insert a clause indicating "it is expressly understood and agreed by and between the parties hereto that neither party will interfere with the performance of the other." The real concern is whether or not the word "unreasonably" should be inserted so that it reads "would not unreasonably interfere." The question of what is interference is again one of degree. Without the word "unreasonable," a court might find that any interference is a breach of an obligation, but will normally permit certain minor immaterial interferences and infer the word "reasonable" in most situations. If greater latitude is sought, the word "unreasonable" should be inserted.

The implied obligation not to interfere with the performance of another not only relates to the possibility of a delay claim but is simply another item for breach. Once performance is interfered with, as ruled by the court, the defaulting party may have lost its only right to assert liquidated or delay damages (Case 14-15) and subjects itself to a lawsuit for breach. Deliberate delays, unjustified delays, or failure to perform properly can lead to proper withholding of payments to subcontractors [*Bart Arconti & Sons, Inc. v. Ames-Ennis, Inc.,* 340 A.2d 225 (Md. 1975)].

The next component which must be proved is the default of the obligation. When no time is specified in the contract, a reasonable time will be allowed. The time needed for a reasonable delay to become unreasonable, so that a default may exist , can be quite long. Situations can arise where if no time is specified, no obligation is inferred; and even if there is an obligation, its default may never come into existence because of the elasticity of the word "unreasonable." Even when a time is specified, it is subject to the court's legal inclusion of the word and principles or "reasonableness and equity."

EXCUSABLE DELAYS

Proving of a default, although a legal problem, requires hard cold facts showing how the obligation was not adhered to. This technical default, the failure to perform by a specified date or a reasonable date, is often excused because the defaulting party may be contractually excused for the delay since it is entitled to an extension of time. Most major contracts include a clause relating to a party's entitlement to an extension of time due to excusable delays. The clause is also known as a force majeure clause.

A party's entitlement to an extension of time is of utmost importance in a delay claim; it often determines whether or not a default legally exists. If the party is entitled to an extension of time, its obligation deadline is extended for the period of time allotted by the contract or the court. Once there has been an extended time period, the default may become nonexistent (Case 14-16).

Most contracts contain a clause permitting the contractor to seek extensions of contract time for specified excusable delays, which include acts of God, strikes (Cases 14-17 and 14-18), hurricanes, floods, embargoes, epidemics, riots, national emergencies, acts of the other party, changes, and unusually severe weather conditions (Cases 14-19 and 14-20), or other cause (Case 14-21). Most of these comprehensive clauses have a catchall phrase like "or any other reason not due to the fault or negligence or within the control of the contractor." Some forms limit this last statement by adding at the end the words "or its subcontractors" (Case 14-22). There does not appear to be any general policy or definitive statement of the contractor's right to an extension of time if no contract clause exists, although it does seem that if the event was truly unforeseeable, the courts would be lenient and equitable. The right to an extension, e.g., one based upon a flood or other weather conditions, is not an automatic extension right, even with the clause. The contractor is under the obligation to include in its estimate of performance time the normal weather conditions for the area in which the work is being performed. The contractor assumes the risk of normal local conditions. If tropical storms and hurricanes are the expected normal conditions during that time of year, they must be anticipated as such. The question, again, is one of degree (Case 14-23). In like fashion, the contractor assumes the risks and obligations related to labor shortages (Case 14-24 and 14-25).

There is great debate over the right to time extensions for weather conditions. Some contract forms deny time extensions for "normal" conditions, or "daily" weather variations. But, isn't a hurricane a daily condition? The federal government places the burden on the contractor to prove that the weather conditions were "unusually severe," which seems equitable. For unusually severe weather to exist, one must consider the type of work being performed. Although the weather conditions may not be physically severe, they may be unusually severe for that time of the year so that they greatly hinder the performance of a particular type of work. The severity can be evidenced by going back five to ten years and proving, with climatological data, what is normal and what could have and should have reasonably been anticipated.

The right to a contractual extension of time is usually not an automatic right. Most clauses require that notice be given by the person claiming the extension within a specified time. This notice requirement is generally recognized as being proper and has been enforced so as to deny many unclaimed extensions, but, as with all rules, there are exceptions. Seemingly, if the event which gives rise to the request for an extension is so severe that it should have been common knowledge that it had to affect the work, then the technicalities of the notice requirement are often disregarded. The purpose of the notice provisions is to avoid surprise and prejudice to a party, but if the event itself is of a great magnitude, the notice requirements may be reduced. Remember, however, that every additional obstacle in the attorney's path which must be overcome creates a greater likelihood of the claim's being denied; therefore, give proper notice.

The extension of time is of great importance, since it not only allows a greater period of time in which to complete the work and can reduce the inefficient and costly obligation to accelerate work, but also many times saves a contractor from a default situation and puts it on schedule, thus eliminating the assessment of liquidated damage for that period of time. However, it seems to be the federal court rule that if the claimant is delayed from two causes, one being attributable to a breach of the other party's obligation (thus being the basis for a compensatory delay claim) and the other being the result of an excusable delay (without the fault of either party), and if performance would have been delayed as a result of that excusable delay, whether the other party had been in default of an obligation or not, then the claim will be denied. Keeping track of excusable delays is of great importance, whether an extension of time has been requested or not.

Although the claimant may not be entitled to recover for the default delay when it would otherwise have been precluded from performing due to an excusable delay, the contractor may be able to turn a subsequent excusable delay into a compensatory delay for time and money. This comes into existence when, but for a prior compensatory default delay, your performance would have been sufficiently advanced to have avoided that subsequent excusable delay. Simply put, the default delay forced you into a further formerly excusable delay. This is very difficult to prove and is an overwhelming reason for keeping good solid daily records and other documentation.

A compensable delay does not require that the entire contract be delayed or that the entire project be affected. A delay claim may exist even if only a part of the project is affected and even though the contract is completed on time or ahead of schedule (Case 14-26). The cause of the delay may be overt acts or even a failure to act. Check your facts and your contract.

Compensatory delays, based upon default, take various forms (Cases 14-27 and 14-28)—so many that they cannot all be listed. As already indicated, the real concern is proving that time is a material element of the contract, that an obligation existed, and that there has been a material default. A large proportion of delay claims arise from the proposition of law that the owner warrants the accuracy of its contract plans and specifications; that if they are defective, there is a breach of warranty; and that "every second" necessary to correct defective contract documents is automatically compensable [*Luria Bros. & Co., Inc. v. United States,* 369 F.2d 701 (1966), and *Laburnum Constr. Corp. v. United States,* 325 F.2d 451 (1963)].

FAILURE TO COORDINATE

Delay claims often arise from the owner's failure to coordinate the work of the various prime contractors or the prime contractor's failure to coordinate the work of its subcontractors. The owner takes responsibility for potential delay claims by letting separate prime contracts. As stated in a New York case:

> When the claimant made its bid, it contemplated the work would be progressed by the general contractor according to its contract. Upon receipt of the contract, it proceeded to plan its work so as to coordinate its various operations with those of the general contractor, and made the necessary commitments for material, labor and equipment, so that the work could be performed in accordance with contract requirements, and completed as agreed. The claimant moved on to the job promptly, and at all times was able, ready and willing to progress the work according to schedule. Actually it was not able to do this. The general contractor fell behind the schedule for many reasons, principally because it failed to progress the work in accordance with approved engineering and construction methods, and there were times when it performed no work at all. Some of these delays were authorized by the State engineer in charge, and other delays were allowed to continue without objection or any affirmative effort to apply the remedies authorized to compel compliance with the contract, with the result that the site, for long periods of time, was not available to the claimant, and it could not progress its work as planned. This we hold amounts to a breach of contract by the State. The interference and delay occasioned to the claimant by this breach of contract was of sufficient consequence to compel the claimant to rearrange its progress plan in a manner not originally contemplated, and to perform various phases of its work in a different sequence and piecemeal manner, thereby adding greatly to its costs.
>
> Under such circumstances, the claimant is entitled to reimbursement for the damages sustained, as it is well established that the State is liable for the damages occasioned by the default of a separate contractor who undertakes contemporaneously to perform and complete work on the same completion date [*Heating Maintenance Corp. v. State,* 47 N.Y.S.2d 227 (1944); see also *Snyder Plumbing and Heating Corp. v. State,* 198 N.Y.S.2d 600 (1960)].

This obligation of the owner to coordinate is not an absolute one but an obligation to use all reasonable efforts in trying to coordinate. In an action by a subcontractor against a general contractor for the failure to coordinate, the subcontractor lost when the court found:

> nor did Rugo's [general contractor] responsibility to Brown [subcontractor] as enumerated in the subcontract include the advanced scheduling of work for the latter's convenience. Furthermore, Brown was unable to prove that scheduling was a custom of the trade. While we might agree that Rugo's failure to provide such scheduling was ungenerous, the irritation to Brown caused by such failure was not a breach of the subcontract . . . . Brown inserted many amendments in the subcontract, and it seems to us that, if it felt its schedules were that important, it should have added a clause requiring the same [*Drew Brown Limited v. Joseph Rugo, Inc.,* 436 F.2d 632 (1971)].

Thus, the obligations cannot be taken for granted, and if the delay claim is asserted, it must be on firm ground.

ACCELERATION

The assertion of acceleration claims is founded on several bases. There is the obvious claim where one party directs another to accelerate. If the contract provides for the method of payment for the acceleration, obviously there is a contractual right to proceed and be paid. If the contract does not grant the other party the right to direct acceleration but the contractor is forced to accelerate, it must protest. The question becomes: Was there a right by one party to direct acceleration since the other party was behind schedule and possibly in breach of contract (Cases 14-29 and 14-30)? If the contractor protests the acceleration order on the basis that it is entitled to a denied extension of time and that with this time it would be on schedule, and if it is able to prove that it was entitled to the extension of time, the courts are apt to find the existence of an acceleration claim. In fact, cases have held that the denial of extension of time and forcing completion by the original completion date can amount to a constructive acceleration order. For this reason both parties should be fully aware of all rights regarding extensions of time.

Delays and accelerations cannot be taken lightly, as their impact can be devastating. Damages are substantial.

CASE 14-1 Delays Caused by Change Orders Recoverable

The U.S. Court of Claims has ruled that a contractor working on a government contract is entitled to the extra costs incurred by the government's defective specifications, even if only part of the job is delayed.

The case involved a Federal Aviation Administration (FAA) contract for an Air Force traffic-control center.

While the contractor was laying pipe for a subsurface roof-leader drainage system called for by the specifications, the government ordered that the pipe be lowered. The contractor complied. The government then decided that the original elevation was the proper one and directed the contractor to raise the elevation, which it did.

The government acknowledged its two directives and issued a change order extending the contract performance period and compensating the contractor "for the additional cost incurred in effecting the changes."

The contractor claimed the changes caused delays that were not covered by the compensation for additional costs.

The contract contained a standard construction-changes clause under which the government had allowed the extra compensation. It also included a suspension-of-work clause under which the contractor claimed the additional compensation.

The claim was denied by the FAA Contract Appeals Board. The board said the government did not unreasonably delay issuing the change orders, the overall job was not delayed, and the contractor's remedy was limited to the changes clause.

The Court of Claims, to which the contractor appealed, ruled that the contractor was entitled to additional compensation under the suspension-of-work clause.

The delay period for which a contractor may recover in defective government specification cases is all the delay, not "just the unreasonable part of the delay," the court said. "All delays due to defective or erroneous Government specifications are per se unreasonable and hence compensable," it explained. As a result, the court said, the contractor could recover for a delay to any part of the project.

Had the contract contained no suspension-of-work clause, the contractor could recover under breach of contract, the court said. Under that remedy, it said, recovery is not limited to an equitable adjustment for changes. Accordingly, it ruled, the contractor could recover under the contract clause as if it were a breach-of-contract claim.

> The Suspension of Work clause [the court said] has two main functions: it negates the notion that a contractor's exclusive remedy for delays caused by acts of the Government is a time extension, and it provides an administrative remedy for losses and increased costs incurred by the contractor because of suspension of work caused by the Government . . . . Since the Suspension of Work clause is an administrative substitute for an action at law for breach, . . . the contractor should be entitled to get the same relief under the clause that he could get in the absence of the clause if he sued for breach of contract [*Chaney and James Constr. Co., Inc. v. United States*, 190 Ct. Cl, 699, 421 F.2d 728 (1970)].

CASE 14-2   Lack of Suspension of Work Order Does Not Defeat Claim

A contractor forced to halt work for a year on a dam it was building was entitled to suspension costs even though the government issued no formal suspension of work order, the U.S. Court of Claims has ruled.

The contract involved construction of a rock-fill dam and related works in Oregon for the federal government. The dam was to be built across a narrow river.

Preliminary inspection by the government indicated that a suitable foundation for the dam would be about 10 feet below the existing riverbed. The contractor encountered an ancient riverbed and immediately notified the government that it had hit a changed condition that was not anticipated.

The government directed the contractor to engage in further exploration and to proceed with corrective action. The contractor worked on this phase of the problem for over a year, during which the government issued sixteen change orders. At the end of this period the contractor was back to the stage of construction it was at when it encountered the changed condition. Having reserved under the change orders its right to submit delay claims at a subsequent date, the contractor then claimed suspension costs. It said it was constructively suspended from moving forward on the original contract during the period when it was engaged in remedial and corrective work.

The government claimed the contractor had received just compensation for the work performed during the period of corrective work and that the suspension-of-work clause in the contract did not apply.

The court ruled that the construction contract had been constructively suspended and that the contractor was entitled to its provable costs. In upholding the contractor's claim, the court said:

In the case before the court, the foundation originally planned was deemed to be "unsuitable" by the Government. The initiative of determining whether to proceed, and how to proceed at that point, lay with the Government, not with the plaintiff. The contractor could have proceeded as originally planned if it had been permitted to do so. Instead, the Government elected in effect to suspend construction of the dam, and then to engage the contractor for a substantial period of time in exploratory work designed to determine the extent of the problem, and how best to proceed from there.

This was a classical example of the type of factual situation for which the "Suspension of Work" clause was apparently created because it authorized the contracting officer to "order the contractor to suspend all or any part of the work for such period of time as may be determined by him to be necessary or desirable for the convenience of the Government.". . . When the contractor, as here, is effectively suspended but the contracting officer has declined to issue the actual order of suspension, "the law considers that done which ought to have been done" and characterizes the circumstances as a constructive (or de facto) suspension [*Merritt-Chapman & Scott Corp. v. United States* 429 F.2d 431 (1970)].

CASE 14-3   Irregular Notice of Claim
Allowed by Court

The United States Court of Appeals, Fifth Circuit, has ruled that a subcontractor complied with the notice provision of its contract for filing delay claims even though it did not follow the procedure specified in the contract.

The plaintiff, an electrical contractor, had negotiated a contract with the owner but was assigned to act as a subcontractor under the general contractor. Its contract provided that it would be able to work in an orderly manner on an established schedule.

When it became apparent that the work on the job would be delayed by other contractors, the subcontractor sent a letter of protest to the general contractor stating,

> We cannot be held liable for late start dates beyond our control without additional compensation and/or extension of time. Our proposal for compensation for this late start will be forthcoming when the work presently under construction is completed and an official start date is assigned.

After delays had disrupted performance dates, the subcontractor sued both the owner and the general contractor for breach of contract. The lower court rejected the suit because the subcontractor had not followed the notification procedure of the contract. This provision required that all notifications of claims be submitted in writing with a statement of the exact amount of the damages to the architect-engineer and to the owner's purchasing department.

In its appeal the plaintiff argued that it had been advised at progress meetings to send all communications through the general contractor. The plaintiff also claimed that it could not specify the exact amount of the claim at the outset of the extended delay.

The court of appeals stated that the purpose of the notice provision "is to alert the other party that the claimant has a grievance against it." The court noted that the plaintiff was a subcontractor and stated that there was clear evidence that the owner had knowledge of the subcontractor's hardships.

The appeals court struck down the provision's requirement that the amount of the claim be submitted. Stating that the length of the delay

> would have practically required the appellant [the plaintiff] to give daily notice [the court concluded]. We think the giving of such daily notice is more of a burden than a contract or the law should impose.
>
> [In its final decision the court warned] Our decision here should in no way be construed as relieving the parties to a contract of strict compliance with notice provisions and the like. To the contrary, it results from our conclusion that, under the particular facts of this case, [the] Appellant complied with the notice provision . . . of this contract to the extent reasonable [*E. C. Ernst, Inc. v. General Motors Corp.* 482 F.2d 1047 (5th Cir. 1973)].

CASE 14-4   Time Is Not of the Essence unless Specifically Stated

A subcontractor that was not given notice to proceed with its work until the day it was supposed to have completed the contract breached the subcontract by refusing to perform, the Supreme Court of Nebraska has ruled. The delay by the prime contractor was not a defense because time was not of the essence, the court said [*Kingery Constr. Co. v. Scherbarth Welding, Inc.,* 185 N.W.2d 857 (1971)].

The general contract called for construction of three steel storage tanks. The subcontractor, under its contract, was to start its part of the work within three days of a notice to proceed and to finish the work within five weeks after the general contractor had completed the preliminary foundation work. The date for completion of the entire job under the general contract was June 15.

The general contractor encountered several problems and the foundation work was delayed. It so informed the subcontractor. On June 15, the scheduled completion date, the general contractor notified the subcontractor that the foundation work had been completed and to proceed with the tank installation.

The subcontractor did not proceed and was sued for breach of contract and damages after the general found another subcontractor.

The court rejected the defense that the general contractor had breached the contract by delaying the start of work. Noting that building contracts usually specify a time for starting work and a time for completing it, the court said, "Generally, neither of these times is considered to be of the essence to the contract unless there is a special stipulation to that effect."

Here there was no such stipulation, and neither party, prior to the notice to proceed, considered the June 15 date important enough to make time of the essence, the court explained.

As a result, the general contractor's delay did not relieve the subcontractor of its contractual duty to perform.

**CASE 14-5   Lack of Promised Work Area
                      Creates Constructive Suspension**

The government's failure to make the proper work site available for a contractor as warranted constituted grounds for a suspension of work claim, the U.S. Court of Claims has ruled. The court held that the contractor's right to file such a claim was not affected or waived by the contractor's receipt of a separate time extension by contract modification to cover such delays [*Merritt-Chapman & Scott Corp. v. United States*, 439 F.2d 185 (1971)].

The contract called for construction of a system of locks and a dam in the Ohio River at a site where there existed a state highway, which the government contracted with the state to relocate. Because the highway was not relocated on schedule, the contractor was not afforded as complete a work area as anticipated. While the contractor was forced to alter its work schedule and to incur substantial delays and additional costs, a contract modification did extend the completion date.

The contractor subsequently submitted a claim for additional costs resulting from the delays and from being forced to work in a narrow, unproductive area. Denied recovery by the Corps of Engineers Board of Contract Appeals, the contractor appealed to the U.S. Court of Claims.

The court discounted the government's defense that the contractor had no claim because of an accord and satisfaction, namely the granting of a time extension regarding the completion schedule. The court noted that the extension was granted under the clause relating to time extensions and not pursuant to the suspension-of-work or other monetary-relief clause.

The time extension did not preclude a claim for suspension costs due to that delay, held the court. Also, it said, the only accord and satisfaction reached through the contract modification related to the length of delays and not to compensation for the delays.

On the question of whether the contractor was entitled to rely on getting a more complete construction site, the court noted that the very first thing the contract covered was that the old highway running through the construction site would be made available as soon as the relocated highway was open to traffic, about December 1, 1955. When it was not available to the contractor within a few days after the given date, the court held that the government had failed to fulfill its warranty and therefore had failed in a legal obligation.

This legal failure, noted the court, came within the coverage of the contract's suspension-of-work clause, and the withholding of a formal suspension order did not defeat a suspension claim since the suspension is considered a "constructive suspension." The court remanded the appeal to the board for a determination of damages and costs due the contractor.

CASE 14-6   Owner Pays for Delays

A contractor was entitled to damages when the government's site survey was found to be defective and caused the contractor's planned work sequence to be disrupted, the U.S. Court of Claims has ruled [*H. John Homan Co., Inc. v. United States*, 418 F.2d 522 (1969)].

The contract called for extension and modernization of a post office in New Jersey at a fixed price. The specifications required the contractor to follow a definite work sequence because the government insisted that the postal facility remain in continuous operation. Contract completion was to be within 270 days. Actual substantial completion was not obtained for an additional 80 days.

When work was started, problems immediately began to appear. The site survey shown on the site plan was defective, and the metes and bounds would not close. The contract discrepancy was brought to the government's attention as well as the fact that work could not proceed properly until the discrepancy was corrected. The preparation of a new survey was started by the government but was not completed until approximately seven weeks later.

Although a set work sequence had been scheduled at the time the contract was executed, the contractor had to change its planned sequence during the time the government was preparing the new survey. The contractor was required to work in a disjointed, inefficient out-of-sequence manner. Since the contract did not contain any suspension-of-work-clause the contractor sued for breach of contract to recover the additional disruption and inefficiency costs incurred. The basis of its claim was that its contract progress was unreasonably delayed by the government.

After reviewing the facts, the court found that the delays were not due to the fault of the contractor and that the contractor had worked efficiently under the circumstances. The major portion of the completion delay "was attributable to the disruption to the work caused by the defective contract specifications . . . . " The court concluded that the government had implicitly warranted that its contract documents were adequate for satisfactory performance, and since the documents were defective and were the cause of the contractor's disruptions and damages, the contractor was entitled to recover its breach-of-contract damages.

**CASE 14-7   Contractor Recovered for Delays
Caused by Slow Decision Making**

The Armed Services Board of Contract Appeals has ruled that a contracting officer unreasonably delayed a project by taking eight days to render a decision on certain disputed work. Although the contractor was required to perform the work in question, it was able to recover for the delay under a work-suspension clause in its contract [*Appeal of Royal Painting Co., Inc.*, ASBCA 20034, 75-1 BCA 11,311 (1975)].

During the performance of a painting contract at a Florida Air Force base, a dispute arose over whether certain garages had to be painted. The contract administrator indicated that he would get an opinion on the work from the contracting officer and that an authoritative decision would be forthcoming. Eight days passed before the contracting officer ordered the contractor to do the work. During that time, work was suspended on the project.

The contractor appealed the decision to perform the work and filed a claim for delay caused by the government's failure to make a timely decision. The contracting officer denied the contractor's claim, saying that the delay was the fault of the contractor because the government had never instructed it to stop work. The contractor then appealed to the Armed Services Board of Contract Appeals.

Reviewing the terms of the contract, the board found that the painter was required to paint the garages, and it ordered the work performed without any additional compensation. However, the board said that it was not unreasonable for the contractor to request a decision on whether the work was required or to delay its work in that specific area pending a decision by the government.

On the other hand, the board said that

> it was unreasonable for the government to take eight days to furnish its decision. One day appears to have been enough time under the circumstances. Accordingly, an adjustment shall be made for any increase in the cost of the performance of this contract (excluding profit) necessarily caused by such unreasonable suspension.

The board remanded the matter to the parties to negotiate the increased costs of the delay.

CASE 14-8   Owner Must Respond Promptly

The Armed Services Board of Contract Appeals has ruled that a contractor is entitled to an equitable adjustment in its contract price if the government fails to respond promptly to its requests for engineering information [*Appeal of Hardie Tynes Mfg. Co.*, ASBCA 20582, 76-2 BCA 11,972 (1976)].

That ruling was made in a case involving a manufacturer that had contracted to supply several valve assemblies to the Navy. Over the term of the contract the manufacturer was forced to wait more than 400 days for replies to nine requests for information.

Arguing that the government should have responded to each of its requests within five calendar days, the contractor claimed it should be compensated for the delays.

The board said that the government had the right to approve or disapprove engineering information requests. "However," the board added, "[the government] was obliged to notify the contractor of its decision on each request in a reasonably timely manner."

If the government failed to respond promptly and as a result of the delay the contractor was injured, the board said the contractor would be entitled to an equitable adjustment in its contract price.

In this case, the board said the government should have notified the contractor of its decisions within 20 days. It said the contractor was entitled to an adjustment for 239 days that the work was delayed.

CASE 14-9   Contractor Paid For
Right-of-Way Delays

A state's incorrect assurance to a highway contractor that right-of-way had been obtained for a project nullified a contract provision that provided "no damages" for right-of-way delays, according to the Appellate Division of the Superior

Court of New Jersey [*Franklin Contracting Co. v. State of New Jersey*, 365 A. 2d 952 (1976)].

A New Jersey highway contract called for the relocation of certain sewer lines. At a preconstruction conference the contractor asked the state's Department of Transportation about the availability of access and was orally assured that easements had been obtained.

Later, however, a landowner refused to grant right-of-access, and the state was forced to institute formal condemnation proceedings. When the contractor filed a claim for delay damages, the state refused to pay.

Initially, the state claimed that it was the contractor's responsibility to investigate the site and to make sure that it "had available means of access." After examining the specific wording of the contract, however, the court said the clause the state referred to related to "physical rather than legal access." The contractor's duty under this clause, the court said, was limited to ascertaining the "status" of the right-of-way acquisitions.

The state then denied liability on the basis of a contract clause that stated: "The contractor shall make no claims for additional compensation on account of delays or necessary alterations in the procedure of his work that may be caused by delays in the vacating or removal of buildings by others and/or the acquisition of right-of-way."

In order for such a clause to be enforceable, the court said, it must be clear and unambiguous and must "effectuate the contemplation" of the parties involved.

The court said that if at the outset the state had informed the contractor that all the right-of-ways had not been obtained, the "clause would be operative in foreclosing the contractor from making any claim for delay."

But in this case, the court concluded, "it can hardly be claimed that this clause was intended to render the state immune from liability or that the parties contemplated delay because the state did not have a valid right-of-way."

CASE 14-10   Owner Liable for Delay
Caused by Site Contractor

A contractor that has received an owner's notice to proceed but is effectively prohibited from commencing work because a prior contractor is still on the site can submit a claim for damages against the owner, according to the federal Engineering Board of Contract Appeals [*Appeal of Head Constr. Co.,* ENGBCA 3537, 77-1 BCA 12,226 (1976)].

An electrical contractor had a contract with the Washington Metropolitan Area Transit Authority requiring it to start work no later than 10 days after receipt of the notice to proceed and to complete work within 240 days. There were also intermediate completion dates. The contract provided for liquidated damages for late completion on each phase and on the final contract.

When the contractor received the notice and attempted to start work, it discovered that the site contractor had still not completed demolition and removal work, thus preventing the electrical contractor from starting work. It then notified the owner of its intention to submit a claim for damages.

The owner later rejected the claim, saying that it was not the contracting officer but the site contractor that delayed the work and that the electrical contractor had prior notice that another contractor was working on the site.

The contractor claimed that the suspension-of-work clause permitted it to receive compensation if it were unreasonably delayed due to the acts of the owner.

The board held that the notice to proceed "is equivalent to an order to begin the work . . . [and] there was an implied contract that the site was available for work." When the site was not available, it said, the owner became liable for breach of contract even if there were no suspension-of-work clause.

It further noted that the owner's liability existed "whether or not it was negligent in meeting its obligation to provide the work site."

CASE 14-11 Contractor Liable to Subcontractor For Delay Damages

Ruling that a prime contractor breached a subcontract by failing to keep a delivery schedule, the Massachusetts Court of Appeals has ordered the contractor to compensate the subcontractor for the time that its crew and equipment sat idle [*Dorel Steel Corp. v. Modular Constr., Inc.,* 334 N.E.2d 76 (1975)].

The subcontract clearly stated that the subcontractor's price was "based on continuous operation" of its crew. It further provided that the contractor would furnish all materials and deliver them to the jobsite in such a manner as "to avoid any delays in unloading of materials."

When the contractor did not meet its delivery schedule, the subcontractor's men and equipment sat idle for nine hours. The subcontractor sued to recover for its delays, claiming that the contractor had breached its contract.

From the evidence and the testimony of the subcontractor the court concluded that the "[prime contractor] had broken the subcontract in this regard and was liable to the . . . [subcontractor] for damages caused thereby."

CASE 14-12 Contractor May Collect for Owner's Delay

The Armed Services Board of Contract Appeals has ruled that a government contractor was entitled to reimbursement for the increased costs it incurred when it was forced to suspend work because of the government's delay in issuing required change orders [*Appeal of A. F. Drexler, d/b/a Drexler Constr. Co.,* ASBCA 12249 and 12316, 69-1 BCA 7572 (1969)].

The contractor, for a fixed price, had agreed to perform marine construction work involving the repair of barge piers and ferry landings at two locations in Texas. At a preconstruction conference the government informed the contractor that either the barge or ferry facilities must be operable at all times. In compliance with the request, the contractor prepared a progress schedule outlining its anticipated work phases which would continuously allow the use of one facility. The progress schedule was approved. The contractor then ordered its material so that it would be delivered to the sites to coincide with its scheduled work.

After starting work, the contractor encountered several defective conditions at the site. These conditions were immediately called to the attention of the government inspector. In addition, letters were sent to the contracting officer requesting contract changes and also indicating that the entire work schedule was being disrupted. Further, the contractor stated that if the changes were not promptly issued, it would be forced to work in winter months which would cause even longer delays.

Although a government engineer visited the site and noted that deficiencies existed, no commitment was made to issue changes because there was a question whether sufficient funds were available. Subsequently, the contractor was informed that the proposed changes were being held up until funds were made available.

About one month later, the contractor was unilaterally directed to perform the corrective work. The contractor agreed to the price for the corrective work but specifically stated that the change did not include its claim for suspension costs caused by the government's delay in issuing the changes.

The contractor appealed from an adverse decision by the contracting officer to the Armed Services Board of Contract Appeals. The board first disposed of the government's argument that the contractor should have discovered the defective conditions on its site investigation. The conditions were not of such nature as would normally be discovered by a bidder, and the contractor could not be charged with any knowledge of their existence, it said.

The board also found that the contractor had originally scheduled its work and progress so that it would first be able to do that portion of work where the materials and supplies were readily available and that work requiring special material would be done later. The contractor had planned its work and progress so as to coordinate it with the delivery capabilities of its suppliers.

When these facts were reviewed in conjunction with the requirement that one system of water transportation be kept operable at all times, the board concluded that after the contractor started on either the barge or ferry work and ran into a defective condition, it was unable to stop work on one area and start work on another.

The board held that the contractor was entitled to an equitable adjustment because its work was suspended "when action was deferred on required proposed changes because of lack of funds."

CASE 14-13 Owner's Defective Drawings Create Compensable Delays

A contractor was entitled to recover all its delay costs because any delay resulting from defective government plans and specifications was unreasonable, held the Corps of Engineers Board of Contract Appeals [*Appeal of Desonia Constr. Co., Inc.*, ENGBCA 3250, 73-1 BCA 9797 (1972)].

During excavation the contractor encountered a gas line at a much higher elevation than the contract plans indicated. The contractor incurred delay costs because it had to halt excavation while the owner, the United States government, lowered the gas line.

The contract contained a standard changes clause and a suspension-of-work clause which said, "If performance of all or any part of the work is, for an unreasonable period of time, suspended, delayed or interrupted by an act of the contracting officer . . . an adjustment shall be made for any increase in the cost of performance of this contract . . ."

In finding the government liable, the board held that "any delay to a contractor as a result of defective specifications is a suspension of work for an unreasonable period of time" and under the contract all incidental costs are recoverable.

CASE 14-14   Erroneous Plans
Cause Extra Costs

Increased costs incurred by a contractor in Panama were recoverable when its work sequence was changed and delayed because of errors in government plans, held the Armed Services Board of Contract Appeals [*Appeal of Kemmons-Wilson, Inc., and South & Patton, Inc., A Joint Venture,* ASBCA 16167, 72-2 BCA 9689 (1972)].

During excavation, the contractor discovered that the site plans drawn by the government were incorrect. Work was slowed while the government investigated and found that the errors were substantial. The board found that, "The errors affected all construction including . . . the earth pads, roads, drainage structures and . . . the land between the buildings."

The drawing errors required the government to redesign the project and to issue many changes. The effect of the errors and the time needed for redesign caused the contractor to proceed in an irrational work sequence and to backtrack in some instances.

The sequence change forced the excavation to be performed during the area's rainy season and delayed completion of this phase three months past the scheduled date. The change also caused conflicts in the trades which followed the excavation work.

Data were collected on causes and effects and pointed to a delay of six months. The contractor claimed that these conditions caused it to incur substantial increased costs which it sought to recover.

The board, in holding that the costs were recoverable, said that because of the delay in the earth work, the prime contractor was delayed in starting building construction. And when it began, access to building areas was impeded by the absence of planned interior roadways, and much of the construction had to be performed in a tropical rainy season, it added. When the excavating subcontractor returned to the job to complete its work, there was interference between its men and equipment and those of other contractors, the board said.

CASE 14-15   Owner's Delay Bars It
from Suing for Delays

An owner is not entitled to withhold liquidated damages for delayed performance of a construction contract if the delay is caused by its own acts. This is the case even though the contractor failed to request an extension of time within the limit specified in the contract, the California Court of Appeal for the Second District has ruled [*General Insurance Co. of America v. Commerce Hyatt House,* App. 85 Cal. Rptr. 317 (1970)].

The case stemmed from a contract for building a hotel and related facilities. After the general contractor defaulted during performance of the contract, its surety, under a performance bond, completed the contract. After the job was finished, the surety sued the owner for the balance due.

The owner, as one of its defenses, counterclaimed that it was entitled to substantial liquidated damages for late completion. The project was finished seventy-one days after the completion date.

The contract was a standard American Institute of Architects form. It provided that in case of certain itemized events or "any causes beyond the contractor's control," the architect could extend the contract completion date. However, the contract provided that no extension could be made for a delay occurring "more than seven days before claim therefor is made in writing to the architect." And it stated that "in the case of a continuing delay, only one claim is necessary."

Completion of the project had been delayed by various events, including heavy rains, floods, contract discrepancies, jurisdictional disputes, changes in design and contract work, and time to perform extras. Some of these were listed in the contract as excusable delays or beyond the control of the contractor. However, no time extensions were requested within the seven-day limit imposed by the contract.

The court found that many of the delays were caused by the owner's acts and that the delay in substantial completion was the result of those acts.

In the light of these facts, the court denied the owner's right to withhold liquidated damages. "An owner whose acts have contributed substantially to the delayed performance of a construction contract may not recover liquidated damages," it said.

Failure to give notice of the delays within the seven-day period was immaterial, the court said. "Noncompliance with a provision requiring an application for an extension of time is not a proper basis for holding a contractor liable in liquidated damages for late completion caused by the owner's conduct," it explained.

The surety's claim was accordingly upheld and the owner's counterclaim denied.

**CASE 14-16   Contractor Required to Bear
                Heating Costs during Strike**

The Armed Services Board of Contract Appeals has ruled that a contractor cannot claim the cost of heating an incomplete building despite the fact that completion was delayed by circumstances beyond its or the owner's control [*Appeal of Hoel-Steffen Constr. Co.,* ASBCA 15233, 70-2 BCA 8470 (1970)].

The contract called for the erection of a dormitory at an Air Force base. As the project approached final completion, the job was halted in November by a local carpenters' strike that lasted until the following April. During the strike, the contractor requested that the government accept the portion of the dormitory that was almost complete so that the contractor would not have to undertake the cost of heating the dormitory to prevent freezing and rupturing of installed water pipes. The government refused, and the contractor heated the building.

In denying the contractor's claim for the cost of heating the dormitory, the board noted the fact that the building was not 100 percent complete when the contractor requested the government to take it over. Furthermore, although the contract permitted the government to take over and use any completed or partially completed segment of the building, the board held that the contractor could not compel the government to accept partial completion of the project.

CASE 14-17   Strike Starting after Completion Date Is Excusable Delay

The General Services Board of Contract Appeals holds that a contractor may be excusably delayed in fulfilling its contract even though a strike that delayed work did not occur until after the contract should have been completed. The board granted the contractor's request for a time extension to complete work lost as a result of a sheet-metal-workers' strike, because the delay was beyond the contractor's control [*Appeal of George E. Jensen Contractors, Inc.,* GSBCA 3280, 71-1 BCA 8841 (1971)].

The contract called for completion of work at a federal building in Mississippi within sixty days and provided for late-completion assessment of liquidated damages. Work was not substantially completed until fifty-five days after the scheduled date.

In denying the government's claim that no delay after the scheduled completion date was excusable, the board held, "The resulting principle would preclude any delay from being declared to be excusable which begins or extends beyond the scheduled completion date because it could not have prevented the contractor from completing the contract on time. This conclusion, we know, is not accurate." The board went on to state, "Only time that is lost as a direct result of the strike is excusable."

CASE 14-18   Contractor Cannot Recover for Excess Labor Costs Caused by Strike

The U.S. Court of Claims has ruled that a contractor working under a fixed-price contract is not entitled to recover for excess labor costs that are the result of severe labor problems [*McNamara Constr. of Manitoba, Ltd. v. United States,* 509 F.2d 1166 (1975)].

A contract for the construction of a canal lock in Michigan specifically stated that it was the contractor's responsibility to ascertain general and local labor conditions in the area. It further provided that if the job was delayed by a strike, a time extension would be given.

When severe labor problems stopped the job, the project's owner, the Corps of Engineers, extended the project's completion date but rejected the contractor's request that the contract be reopened and that $6 million be added to cover excess labor costs.

In its suit to recover these costs, the contractor claimed that a mutual mistake in fact had existed at the time the contract was signed because neither party could foresee the unreasonable attitude and conduct of the local unions. As a result of this mistake, the contractor claimed the additional compensation.

Noting that "the risk of strikes and other labor problems is inherent in the vast majority of construction contracts," the court said, "neither the contractor nor the Government could be presumed ignorant of this risk."

Rejecting the contractor's response that it assumed the risk for normal strikes but did not anticipate the severe difficulties that it actually encountered, the court said, "the distinction is unworkable as a practical matter, because there is no such recognizable concept as a 'normal' strike, and no clear line between 'normal' and 'severe' difficulties."

In its conclusion, the court said the contract both explicitly and implicitly placed the risk of labor strife directly upon the contractor.

CASE 14-19   Weather Does Not Excuse Delay

The General Services Board of Contract Appeals has denied a time extension requested by a contractor whose progress was delayed by bad weather [*Appeal of T. C. Bateson Constr. Co.*, GSBCA 2656, 68-2 BCA 7263 (1968)].

The contractor claimed the bad weather entitled it to an extension because the contract specifically excused delays caused by "unusually severe weather."

In denying the claim the board indicated that merely showing that rain, snow, high winds, or unsettled weather conditions prevented or hindered performance is not enough to excuse a delay. For example, it said, a showing that rain or snow on a specific day exceeded the average for that day is insufficient proof of an excusable delay. Daily variations in weather patterns should be expected, it said. The board defined the kind of "unusually severe weather" that constitutes an excusable delay:

> In brief, unusually severe weather means adverse weather, which at the time of year in which it occurred is unusual for the place in which it occurred. No matter how severe or destructive, if the weather is not unusual for the particular time and place, or if a contractor should have reasonably anticipated it, the contractor is not entitled to relief.

Under this ruling, a contractor must determine whether the weather it encountered falls within this definition of unusually severe weather before it claims an excusable delay. The contractor's consideration should necessarily include an analysis of the seasonal weather variations for past years for the project area so that it can show that the current weather conditions are in fact unusually severe.

CASE 14-20   Winter Not Severe
Enough for Extra Delay

A contractor was properly assessed liquidated damages because it was unable to prove that the closing of its project during winter months was not reasonable or anticipated. The Armed Services Board of Contract Appeals ruled that the contractor failed to show that the weather was so unusually severe that it would constitute an excusable delay [*Appeal of Arndt Brothers,* ASBCA 17186, 72-2 BCA 9672 (1972)].

The contract specified that construction of a sewage-treatment and disposal plant in Alaska would be completed within 270 days of the notice to proceed. It also required certain excavation and prohibited the use of frozen backfill. Liquidated damages were set at $120 per day.

The government granted the contractor two short time extensions, but the contractor claimed additional time because of a seven-month job shutdown, due, it said, to unusually cold weather. The government argued that both it and the contractor should have anticipated the closing since excavation could not be done during the winter, and, it said, the shutdown was not due to unusually severe weather.

The board said that the contractor had provided no proof of why it did not resume work until May 21, since, the board said, work could have continued on May 1. The question, it said, was whether the contractor should have reasonably expected the weather conditions.

The contractor argued that it was impossible to complete the contract within the time specified because the weather conditions interfered with the excavation and because the use of frozen fill was prohibited.

In denying a time extension, the board said that the weather was not unusually severe and that under the contract, the builder assumed the risk that normal weather could prevent the completion of the contract within the time allowed.

CASE 14-21 Vandalism Excuses a Delay

The Court of Claims has held that a contractor could not be assessed liquidated damages for delays to a project when the delays were caused by unforeseeable vandalism [*Wertheimer Constr. Corp. v. United States,* 406 F.2d 1071 (1969)].

The case involved a general contractor on a housing project in Washington, D.C. Under the terms of the contract, the owner, National Capitol Housing Authority, assessed the contractor liquidated damages for late completion. The contractor claimed that its late completion was excusably delayed and that it was therefore entitled to an extension of time and the return of liquidated damages.

One of the reasons for claiming excusable delay was that the project was hit by vandalism. The contracting officer initially stated that it was the contractor's responsibility under the contract to protect the project from vandalism. Therefore, no time extension was allowed. This denial was based on the general conditions article of the contract entitled "Care of Work," which provided:

> The Contractor shall be responsible for all damages to persons or property that occur as a result of his fault or negligence in connection with the prosecution of the work and shall be responsible for the proper care and protection of all materials delivered and work performed until completion and final acceptance . . . .
>
> In the event of delay in completion of the contract work due to loss or damage caused by failure of the contractor to adopt reasonable and continuous protective methods, the contractor shall not be relieved from payment of liquidated damages.

The court noted that the general conditions did not completely deny the right to an extension of time due to vandalism. Rather, it stated the type and degree of care that the contractor must use to protect the work. The court further noted that the contractor could be exonerated from liquidated damages if the delays were "due to unforeseeable causes beyond its control and without its fault or negligence." Based on these propositions, the court's conclusion was that if the contractor adopted reasonable and continuous protective methods required by the general conditions, and if the vandalism that occurred delayed completion and was unforeseeable and not due to the contractor's fault or negligence, it would be relieved from payment of liquidated damages.

The evidence clearly indicated that the contractor anticipated that some vandalism might occur during construction. Expecting this possibility, it apparently included in its bid the costs for a reasonable protective system. Throughout the entire project it had two or three watchmen on duty at all times. In addition, the police had been alerted. Nevertheless, vandalism occurred and delayed job completion.

The court held that the contractor had employed a reasonable and continuous protective system, that the vandalism that occurred was unforeseeable and was beyond its control and without its fault or negligence. It granted the contractor relief from liquidated damages for the delay.

CASE 14-22   Delays by a Second-Tier
             Subcontractor Excuse Prime Contractor

A prime contractor's failure to complete a project substantially within the scheduled contract time because of a second-tier subcontractor's delay was considered excusable by the Armed Services Board of Contract Appeals. The board concluded that according to the facts presented, a second-tier subcontractor's dilatory actions could not be attributed to the prime contractor and that the prime contractor, not being in default of its contract, could not be assessed liquidated damages [*Appeal of Reynolds Constr. Co.*, ASBCA 12015, 68-1 BCA 6756 (1967)].

The prime contract called for construction of two airport hangars at a government air base in Turkey. The contract allotted 360 days for completion after receipt of the notice to proceed. One of the hangars was not substantially completed until over two months after the scheduled completion date. The prime contractor was assessed liquidated damages on a daily basis for this delay.

The question before the board was whether the contractor was excusably delayed under the contract's default clause. The late completion was a result of late delivery of certain items of electrical equipment. The electrical part of the contract had been subcontracted to a first-tier subcontractor. The first-tier subcontractor further subcontracted out the part of its contract that required the use of nonstandard, specially fabricated panel-box components. The second-tier contractor's late delivery of the panel-box components delayed the total job completion, for which liquidated damages were assessed.

The board found that the prime contractor and the first-tier subcontractor had both diligently attempted to expedite the second-tier subcontractor's delivery of the panel-box components and that neither could have foreseen or controlled the problems and delays caused by the second-tier subcontractor. On the basis of these findings, the board cited and followed the ruling in the landmark decision of *Schweigert, Inc., v. United States,* 388 F.2d 971 (U.S. Ct. Cl. 1967). It held that since the prime contractor's failure to perform on time was due to a second-tier subcontractor's actions whose acts and omissions were beyond the control and without the fault or negligence of either the prime contractor or the first-tier subcontractor, the prime contractor's late completion was excusable, and assessment of damages was improper.

CASE 14-23   Contractor Relieved from Liability for Damages Caused by Storm

A contractor was not responsible for rebuilding part of its work destroyed by an unusually heavy rainfall prior to acceptance of the work by the government, the Interior Board of Contract Appeals has held [*Appeal of Ray W. Lynch,* IBCA 764-2-69, 69-2 BCA 8026 (1969)].

Part of a contract with the Bureau of Indian Affairs called for installation of corrugated culvert pipe. Several weeks after the culverts were put in place and backfilled, a severe rainstorm washed out the fill, collapsing the pipe. The government had not accepted the work and required the contractor to replace the pipe. It did this under protest and filed a claim for additional compensation.

The contract contained a clause relating to the allocation of risk prior to final acceptance.

> Until the final acceptance of the work by the contracting officer [it said] the contractor shall be responsible for the work . . . and shall take every precaution against injury or damage to any part thereof by the action of the elements, or from any other cause, whether arising from the execution or from the nonexecution of the work. The contractor, at his own expense, shall rebuild . . . and make good all damages to any portion of the work, except those damages due to unforeseeable causes beyond the control of and without the fault, or negligence, of the contractor, including, but not restricted to, acts of God (or) extraordinary actions of the elements. . . .

The contractor argued that the rainstorm was unusually heavy and amounted to an "extraordinary action of the elements." This was essentially the issue before the board.

The board noted that there is no absolute measure to determine extraordinary characteristics of a storm and that the various factors of each individual case must be reviewed. "Thus, to gage whether the event in issue approached the standard of 'extraordinary action of the elements,' one must take into account not only the intensity and volume of the rain and flood themselves, but also the design characteristics of the destroyed structure," it said.

The board concluded that the culvert was designed to withstand "a 10-year average frequency maximum one-hour rainfall" and that the particular storm came closer to a 25-year frequency in intensity. It accordingly ruled that the damage was caused by "extraordinary action of the elements" beyond the contractor's control and without his fault or negligence, putting the risk of loss on the government.

**CASE 14-24   Contractor Loses Claim
For Its Overtime Costs**

A federal board of contract appeals has ruled that a contractor was not entitled to increased overtime and labor inefficiency costs stemming from labor shortages allegedly caused by the government.

The case involved construction of a building at the Manned Spacecraft Center in Texas for the National Aeronautics and Space Administration (NASA). On behalf of its mechanical subcontractor the general contractor submitted a claim for overtime-labor and labor-inefficiency costs. The contractor claimed that the government had ordered that work be done seven days a week, twelve hours a day, by other contractors under other contracts in the same geographical area. As a result, it said, there was a labor shortage in the area and this forced it onto overtime and caused a loss of productive efficiency due to the longer working hours.

On appeal to the Corps of Engineers Board of Contract Appeals, the contractor argued that the government was responsible for unfair competition and that it was entitled to the additional costs it incurred. The board set forth the general principle of law that governs this type of appeal and stated, "In order to recover on account of such acts a contractor must prove that the government concealed information known to it on the date of contract and also that the contractor could not be expected to possess the pertinent information at that time."

In denying the contractor's claim, the board held,

> There is no allegation, much less proof, that NASA or the Corps of Engineers knew at the time of execution of appellant's [contractor's] contract that any of the contractors at the Manned Spacecraft Center would be ordered to work overtime or that planned completion dates on contracts would be so tight as to require overtime or disrupt the labor market. Nor did appellant make any attempt to establish that it was reasonable for it or its subcontractor to assume that the contract work could be completed on time without resort to overtime or that the labor market would be better than it turned out to be except for government actions [*Appeal of Baxter Constr. Company, Inc.*, ENGBCA 2870, 69-2 BCA 7893 (1969)].

**CASE 14-25   Labor Shortage Not Excusable;
Liquidated Damages Assessed**

The General Services Board of Contract Appeals reduced the liquidated damages assessed a contractor for delays caused by the failure of two utility companies to finish their work on schedule but refused to excuse the delay caused by a shortage of masons [*Appeal of Clyde Burton & Son Constr. Co., Inc.*, GSBCA 3227, 71-2 BCA 9152 (1971)].

A contractor completed a laboratory complex in Oklahoma 118 days late. When it was assessed liquidated damages for the overrun, the contractor appealed, stating that the delays were excusable because they arose "from unforeseeable causes beyond the control and without the fault or negligence of both the contractor and any such subcontractors or suppliers" as provided in the contract.

Delays were caused by gas and water companies charged with running utility lines to the site for connection by the contractor. Because this work was not part of the prime contract but did affect completion of the contractor's work, the contractor argued that it should be excused for its delays. The board agreed with the contractor, stating that it could not be charged liquidated damages for this time.

The contractor claimed a second extension of time because construction was delayed by the shortage of masons in the labor market. The board recognized the contractor's exhaustive but unsuccessful efforts to recruit both union and non-union masons and called the lack of masons a local and national problem. However, it concluded that a delay due to a labor shortage is not excusable grounds on which to grant an extension of time.

The board stated that "it is a well established rule that the contractor is responsible for providing the labor forces needed to perform the contract into which he has entered with the government . . . unless, of course, the government by some act has caused the labor shortage."

CASE 14-26   Damages for Delay Awarded
Despite Early Completion

The New York Supreme Court, Appellate Division, has ruled that a contractor is entitled to damages for delay caused by inaccurate contract documents, even though the contractor completed work ahead of schedule [*Grow Constr. Co., Inc. v. State of New York,* 56 A.D.2d 95 (1977)].

The contractor, working on a state highway project with state-designed plans, encountered various unanticipated difficulties. Although it finished work ahead of schedule, the difficulties prevented it from completing the job even earlier, it said.

Arguing that the plans were inadequate, misleading, and not in accordance with good engineering practice, the contractor sued the state for interference.

Most significant, it said, was the difference between the rock elevations in the plans and those actually encountered. The plans indicated a low permeability for subsurface soils when, in fact, the opposite condition existed, requiring extensive dewatering operations.

The state attempted to show that the contract denied liability, but the court said that it could not escape liability if "inspection would have been unavailing to reveal the incorrectness of the representations . . . or [if] the representations were made in bad faith."

The state was liable, the court found, not only because a site inspection would have been unavailing but also because the state withheld information that might have alerted the contractor to the problems.

The state then argued that damages were not necessary because the project was actually completed early. However, the court rejected this defense as well, saying that a contractor had the right to perform its work "free from needless interference."

CASE 14-27   Contractor Liable for Inexcusable Delay Caused by Supplier

A contractor was properly assessed double liquidated damages due to an inexcusable delay caused by a supplier, ruled the General Services Board of Contract Appeals [*Appeal of Howard L. Dressler Co.,* GSBCA 3616-9; 73-1 BCA 9818 (1972)].

The contractor was delayed in installing air-conditioning systems at four postal facilities because, it said, the equipment supplier was so "swamped with orders" that it could not meet delivery dates. The contractor said that this was an excusable delay and that it had not contacted other suppliers because they too were "in the same predicament."

Because of the delay, the government assessed the contractor on each of its four contracts liquidated damages for every day the project was unfinished beyond the scheduled completion date and also for each day's failure to achieve beneficial operations of the air-conditioning system. The government argued that the damage provisions were valid and enforceable and that the double damages were separate and distinct. One portion, it said, was a measure of loss of employee efficiency in the absence of air conditioning and the other covered extra administration costs required because the contract was not completed on time.

The board said that the contractor based its claim on a contract clause allowing delays when they arise from unforeseeable causes "beyond the control and without the fault of or negligence of both the contractor and subcontractors or suppliers." This, it said, requires both contractor and supplier to be free from fault.

But the court said that the delay was the fault of the supplier and was not excusable because the supplier accepted more orders than it could fill, a situation within its control. In finding the contractor liable, the board concluded, "The derelictions of the supplier are not abrogated by the absence of fault or negligence of the contractor."

CASE 14-28   Impact Costs Not Recoverable

The General Services Board of Contract Appeals has rejected a contractor's claim for extra costs incurred when the sequence of its work was changed [*Appeal of Terminal Constr. Corp.,* GSBCA 2694, 68-2 BCA 7322 (1968)].

The contractor had a fixed-price contract with General Services Administration for construction of a federal office building in Newark, New Jersey. During performance of its work numerous contract changes and work directives were issued by the government.

The contractor claimed that as a direct result of the various changes and directives, it was forced to perform unchanged work out of sequence and incur additional costs. The contractor sought recovery of the additional impact costs on the unchanged work. The costs for performing the specific changed work had already been agreed upon and became contract modifications.

The board noted that the contract contained the normal construction-changes clause but did not include any type of suspension clause that would allow the contractor recovery for either government-caused delays or for increased costs incurred in performing the unchanged work. The board stated that the amount and time the contractor is entitled to as an equitable adjustment under the changes clause is limited to those costs involved in performing the changed work and the additional time necessary to perform it.

The board concluded that it must dismiss the appeal since the contractor was claiming "costs incurred due to the impact of performing changed work on other work not changed," and since these costs are not compensable under the changes clause, and since the contract did not include any suspension-type clause allowing recovery for impact costs.

The board, in dismissing the appeal, held that it had no jurisdiction to review this claim because it has jurisdiction only over those claims which are directly compensable under a specific contract clause.

CASE 14-29 Acceleration Claim Denied

The General Services Board of Contract Appeals has ruled that a contractor incurring additional costs in acceleration of performance as a result of the owner's urging cannot recover those costs unless there has been an affirmative act by the owner [*Appeal of Guaranty Constr. Co., Inc.,* GSBCA 3109, 70-2 BCA 8483 (1970)].

The contractor in the case had agreed with the owner, the United States government, to complete a new office building in 240 days but was delayed by a series of strikes and work stoppages. The building, originally scheduled for completion in October, was not finished until the end of the following March.

When all the striking tradesmen had returned to work, the government called a contractor meeting in November at the job site. The owner stressed the urgent need for quick completion of construction and said that it was imperative for the building to be ready for occupancy by the end of December.

The contractor stepped up the pace of the work and was able to give the owner beneficial occupancy by mid-January rather than the end of March. The contractor then submitted a claim for additional costs incurred in completing the project in January.

Although acknowledging that the acceleration was a result of the owner's urging, the board stated that the question of recovery rested on

> whether the government [owner] took such action to accelerate the performance under the contract as to amount to a constructive change under the changes clause.

The board relied on the principle of law governing acceleration cases:

> Where a contractor is entitled, by circumstances beyond his control, to an extension of his contract time, and the owner denies him such an extension, thereby compelling the contractor to accelerate his performance to meet the original contract deadline, contract appeal boards have held that there is a "constructive acceleration"

which will entitle a contractor to compensation under the changes clause for the additional costs incurred as a result of such acceleration.

In this case, however, the board held that there was no specific affirmative act by the government to serve as a basis for an acceleration claim. In denying the contractor's claim, the board pointed out that the contractor had been entitled to an extension of up to 160 days but that at the government's urging had voluntarily accelerated its performance and completed the work within an eighty-one-day extension. The board ruled that the government had not denied the contractor the full time extension to which it was entitled, but if it had, such an act would have constituted an affirmative act.

CASE 14-30   Owner Not Liable for
Proper Acceleration Orders

The Appellate Division of New York's Supreme Court has ruled that the state did not breach its contract with a road builder when it directed the contractor to hire additional workers in order to complete a project on schedule.

The highway contract had a completion date of October 1963. In the early part of 1962, the contractor fell behind schedule, and that summer the state ordered it to finish the job on time. After the contract's completion date was extended, the contractor finished the project and the state accepted it about one year late.

The contractor then sued for breach of contract, claiming that the state had interfered with its performance and improperly accelerated the pace of the project. A lower court awarded the contractor $3 million in damages caused by alleged breach of contract, delays and acceleration.

On appeal, the state argued that it had not accelerated the contractor's performance but merely demanded that the contractor meet the original completion date specified in the contract. It also claimed that many of the delays were caused by the contractor's own inexperience.

The appellate court found that

> the [contractor] experienced numerous delays, but that these were caused by the [contractor's] ineptness and lack of diligence, particularly in the early stages of the project . . . .
>
> [Other delays were] caused by actions of third parties over whom the State had no control and for whose conduct the State is not . . . liable.
>
> [Reversing the lower court's ruling, the appellate court concluded] The State did not accelerate performance of the project in the summer of 1962 or thereafter . . . . [It] cannot be held liable for breach of contract because it urged completion of the contract by the agreed completion date [*Merritt-Chapman & Scott Corp., and the Mount Vernon Contracting Corp. v. State of New York*, 386 N.Y.S.2d 894 (1976)].

FIFTEEN

Completion Schedules and Terminations

Whether time is or is not a material provision of the contract plays an important part not only in ascertaining and presenting delay claims and the assessment of possible liquidated damages, but also in relation to completion schedules and terminations. The right to, and extent of, an extension of time, for whatever reason, is evidence of whether the contractor is on time, behind schedule, or in default. When time is a material item of the contract and the contractor is in default of its obligations, the contract often provides for termination. Termination of the contract, either pursuant to contract or as a result of a breach of contract, is normally in addition to the owner's other legal rights resulting from the default. There are numerous different types of terminations, by one party or the other, which will be discussed in two categories, termination for convenience and termination for default.

One of the most important clauses for the insertion into a prime contract by an owner is the termination-for-convenience clause. Without a termination-for-convenience clause the owner is legally subjected to breach-of-contract damages for changing its mind. Specifically, if an owner enters into a contract for the construction of a building, and if after the execution of the contract the owner determines that it would not be financially advisable to build the proposed plant, or if the owner discovers that its major tenant is no longer interested in the space or has gone bankrupt, or if for any other reason the owner decides not to proceed with the construction, the owner has no implied right to stop the contractor's performance without being subjected to liability. In fact, if the owner decides to terminate the contract without the contractor's being in default, it is generally recognized that the owner will be liable for all damages incurred by the contractor *plus* all lost anticipated profit the contractor anticipated earning as a result of full performance of the contract. Thus, if the contract is a $10 million contract with an anticipated 10 percent "profit", and if the day after execution of the contract the owner determines to terminate it without a termination-for-convenience clause, the owner is liable for the contractor's actual damages, which will probably be its out-of-pocket costs or a percentage of the work performed to date, plus the 10 percent anticipated profit on the unperformed work, or $1 million. No party has an *implied* right to terminate the contract for its convenience (Case 15-1). Termination without the default of a material provision of the contract by the other party is in fact a breach of contract.

The termination-for-convenience clause grants to one of the parties (or both, but normally the owner as against the contractor) the right to terminate the contract for its "convenience" whether or not a default exists and without constituting a breach of contract. This clause takes it out of the realm of breach of contract. It becomes a contractual right between the parties. When properly written, termination-for-convenience articles are not against public policy and are enforceable. In fact, in federal contracts the termination-for-convenience article had been implied to be part of the contract when its inclusion was mandated by the enabling legislation, even though it was not, in fact, included in the contract documents.

The benefits of the termination-for-convenience clause depend upon its wording. One of the more equitable termination-for-convenience clauses appears in the federal contracts. It provides, in essence, for a right to terminate the contract for the convenience of the government, as in its sole discretion it determines, and that it will pay for all costs to date and liabilities, based upon the contract price, but no lost anticipated profit on work to be performed (Case 15-2). The contractor is only entitled to receive earned profit on work *performed.* In addition, the contractor is entitled to receive its costs which might well include preparatory work, mobilization, partial performance, materials and specialty items ordered but not incorporated into the work, and numerous other considerations.

On the other hand, contractors are specifically warned to beware of the excessively restrictive termination-for-convenience articles which may or may not be enforceable. An example would be one not only granting the owner the right to terminate for its convenience, precluding unearned profit, but limiting payment to the contractor to that percentage of the work which is "accepted and in place" at the time of termination. This percentage would be based upon the actual contract breakdowns. The road to bankruptcy is paved by such a clause: what happens when the contractor has ordered, built, and even stored in its own warehouse or on site specialty items which have no salvage value but which have not been incorporated into the work? These items of work can be a vast percentage of the overall contract price but by the very terms of the termination clause are not subject to remuneration. The contractor should take careful steps in trying to include within the termination-for-convenience article the right to collect from the owner *all* its costs (even when based upon a percentage allocation of the total contract price) incurred to the date of termination, including its potential liability to subcontractors, although this liability may exclude the subcontractors' unearned profit. Thus, after the specialty item has been ordered and the termination comes into existence, the contractor will be able to pay the subcontractor or supplier its damages, excluding unearned profits, with the right to collect them from the owner. Upon payment the property, if it is tangible, becomes the property of the owner. This form of clause offers a certain degree of equitable consideration to the contractor and still reserves for the owner a substantial right it would not have had without a termination-for-convenience clause.

The contractor should take great care to include in its subcontracts and purchase orders termination-for-convenience clauses when its prime contract incorporates one. If it does not, the contractor may find that it is paying the subcontractor substantial monies with no right to recover from the owner. Another consideration for the contractor is the inclusion of a termination-for-convenience article in the subcontract whether there is one in the prime contract or not. This offers the contractor a greater range of conduct when dealing with its subcontractors and suppliers. Write an equitable clause; read the clauses given to you.

In the second general category of terminations, the termination for default, there are several subdivisions. The first is the contractual right to termination. Most contracts have specific clauses specifying the circumstances under which one party may terminate the contract of the other. When such a clause exists, it is essential that each party follow the mandates and procedures of the clause to the letter in order to effect a proper contractual termination. This is especially true when the cause for the termination may not otherwise be deemed a material default. However, just because the clause indicates a basis for termination, this does not necessarily mean it is a proper termination and not against public policy. Taking it to an absurd end, a clause stating that if a contractor hired anyone of other than a specified race or religion it would be a basis for termination would be subject to immediate attack of unconstitutionality in the courts. Again it can be seen that just because the contract says something is so does not necessarily mean that it is so.

Contract-termination clauses often specify reasons for termination, e.g., the contractor's filing voluntary or involuntary bankruptcy proceedings, assignment for benefit of creditors, failure to pay subcontractors and materialmen, breach of contract, failure to progress the work properly, or failure to complete on time.

A subcontractor was improperly terminated since, although the subcontractor did not resume work when directed by the owner and contractor's representatives, it was not substantially behind schedule and in default when the contractor terminated the subcontract. The contractor was held to have terminated the subcontract improperly and to be in breach of contract [*Rimmer & Garrett, Inc. v. Donnell & Fussell,* 306 So.2d 74 (La. App. 1975)].

The owner is faced with a substantial liability possibility if it enforces some of these clauses (Case 15-3). For example, the mere claim by a subcontractor that it has not been paid should not be a basis, by the owner, for termination of the prime contract without substantial additional evidence. If, in fact, the subcontractor has been "properly" paid, whether or not it has been paid the full amount it claims, the owner could be subjected to substantial liability if it terminates the contractor on that alleged basis. Often the threat of termination is more effective and less painful than actual termination pursuant to a contract clause.

The next termination relates to the contractor's failure to complete by a specified date. Obviously, this again necessitates the determination of whether time is a material part of the contract and whether a specific date was contractually specified. If no date was specified, the courts will permit a reasonable period of time for performance before a default can be inferred. It has been said that the right of termination for default by a specified date is evidence that time is of the essence, whether it is so stated or not. If there has been a failure to complete by the specified date, the right of termination for default arises. In the case of supply contracts, the purchaser seems to have the right to refuse to accept any supplies not furnished by that date. This could be true even though the supplies have been partially or completely manufactured but not delivered. The construction of a building offers other considerations. The right to termination for failure to complete by that specified date might be an overreaction and excessive use of force if the contractor had substantially completed and performed its work and only a minor item had to be completed. In such a case the contractor seemingly has the right to claim substantial performance and recover for the work performed, less some minor reduction (Case 15-4). On the specified date, if the contractor still had substantial work to perform, it appears that the termination would be upheld and the contractor could be held liable for the damages incurred by the owner. Thus, even the contractual right to terminate for failure to complete by a set date is a matter of degree and subject to the discretion of the judge.

Again it is emphasized that if the contractor is entitled to an extension of time, the originally specified date must be modified accordingly.

A contractor terminated a subcontractor after the scheduled completion date specified in the contract. The subcontractor argued that the completion date was no longer binding and that the termination was therefore improper. The contractor had issued various changes during the performance to the subcontractor. The court concluded that when the contractor's own actions prevent performance, it is precluded from claiming nonperformance of the contract by the subcontractor. "The delay in performance of a contract may be waived by conduct indicating that the contract is still in effect," and the delay occurred when the subcontractor was permitted to perform after the original completion date without reservation of rights. In addition, "After delays in performance have been waived a contract cannot be rescinded for failure to strictly perform without giving notice and a reasonable opportunity to perform. . . ." The completion date having been waived, the termination became improper and its own default [*Gamm Constr. Co. v. Townsend,* 336 N.E.2d 592 (Ill. App. 1975)].

It is amazing to find that at many termination meetings the termination officer is totally unaware of various prior requests by the contractor for extensions of time. At several meetings various documents have been put in front of terminating officers, who with great dismay have indicated "I didn't know that." These threatened terminations are not only abusive but improper, if the termination is effectuated when an extension of time was yet to be granted; as a result the alleged right party is in breach of the contract. In addition, while the contractor continues to operate under the threat of termination and is being forced to work toward a completion date which should have been extended, it is amassing an acceleration claim.

For these reasons, when dealing with any of the terminations for default, it is important for the potential terminating party to find out the facts. This can best be done by writing the alleged defaulting party, indicating your intent to issue a termination for default, requesting a written document from it within a specified period of time, and directing it to set forth any and all reasons why it believes termination should not be effectuated. A list of all open requests for extensions of time should also be asked for. Although the other party may not be under a legal or contractual obligation to furnish this type of statement, clearly it is a fair procedure. The respective parties will then know where they stand at the time of their acts. It must be noted that in some federal contracts there is a mandatory procedure for filing cure, or default, notices and show-cause letters and that under their contract (and possibly others) it is mandatory to respond, else the party be deemed to have waived its rights to object. In such cases the words of the contract must be followed by both parties.

The termination for failing to make proper progress is often an invitation for litigation. Even if the right exists, by contract, to terminate for this cause, the problem is still horrendously complex. What is proper progress? What is a failure to perform? Who determines these answers? Is there any contractual requirement that the contractor have a set percentage complete by specified dates during performance? The same problems over entitlement to extensions of time are present, but in this situation, more often than not, the alleged threat of termination is not based upon any contractual obligation of the contractor to be at a set point in construction at some intermediate point. Just because 50 percent of the contract time has elapsed does not necessarily mean that 50 percent of the work should have been completed. The simple question is: What does the contract require? As in all other situations of breach, the threatening party had better be able to prove that the alleged defaulting party had a contractual obligation and that it was in default of that obligation. Easier said than done.

The question of failing to make proper progress brings into consideration the problems of a completion schedule, progress schedule, CPM, PERT, bar graph, or any other schedule. The first question which must be asked regarding these schedules is whether or not they are contract documents. Many of these progress schedules are not contract documents but merely guidelines, and the failure to comply with them may offer no rights to allege a breach of contract. Even though some noncontractual progress schedule shows that at the 50 percent point 50 percent of the work should have been completed, this does not mean that the contractor still might not be able or is not entitled to do 50 percent of the work in the last 25 percent of the time. This fact must be ascertained before any termination. Again, the alleged defaulting party should show cause why it believes it should not be held in default for failing to make proper progress. Many progress schedules, even when prepared after the contract is executed, still only require that the progress schedule show how the contractor *intends* to perform the work. Intents change. Many contracts require continuous updating of progress schedules, but somehow or other they are never updated. This failure to have them updated may be a waiver of the requirement that the contractor follow a specified progress schedule and may imply that the work need only be completed by the required date. If the issuing authority wants total compliance with a progress schedule, the bid documents and contract should be so written that (1) if possible the proposed contract performance schedule or intermediate completion dates are specified in the contract as being mandatory; (2) the progress schedule will be made a contract document; and (3) the progress schedule will be continuously updated. A major concern with many progress schedules is that even when they exist, they do not show what percentage of work should have been completed by a given date. On a bar chart the excavation line might run for half the performance time and have no percentage breakdown on the line. In fact, the contractor may not be behind schedule even when there is a progress schedule since the progress schedule may not really have any intermediate-stage dates. Another question which seems to be coming to the forefront on CPM schedules is who has the entitlement to float time. The courts are just being faced with this problem.

Progress schedules, with a certain degree of latitude, seem to be desirable for both contracting parties. Remember that progress schedules, in whatever form, are double-edged swords. Not only can they be used to show how the contractor might be failing to make proper progress but in the reverse situation they can be used to show how the contractor has been delayed. That document will become a vital document in proof and substantiation of the delay claim.

Thus, although terminations for default are remedies which should be considered, their use and enforcement should be tempered by great discretion. Once a contractor is terminated, the terminating party is either all right or all wrong, and there is very little room for negotiation. All alternate avenues of recourse and considerations should be completely investigated before terminating a contract.

Another basis for failure to comply with the performance requirements, and thus excuse a delay default, is commonly referred to as *impossibility of performance*. Impossibility of performance is a legal excuse which forgives performance, but it is one of the hardest legal arguments to prove and sustain. There is no single definition of impossibility of performance. Court decisions seem to run from subjective impossibility to objective impossibility. On the one hand some jurisdictions have gone so far as to indicate that partial performance negates the legal argument of impossibility of performance (Case 15-5); i.e., if it is possible under any contractual condition, it is not impossible. In jurisdictions which seem to adhere to the state-of-the-art concept, i.e., the absolute-impossibility theory, one would imagine that impossibility would not depend upon financial considerations. This does not seem to be the court's approach, however, in several decisions. The door has been left ajar for a financial argument of impossibility since the decisions have discussed the financial burden placed upon the contractor as a factor to be considered.

In one case the contractor's building of 45 columns was proof that construction of 200 columns was not impossible. The court indicated that it was guided by the objective-impossibility argument [*Ballou v. Basic Constr. Co.,* 407 F.2d 1137 (1969)] (Case 15-5). There seem to be diametrical statements in the court's decision since it talks about loss of profit while applying the objective standard. Still another court denied any impossibility argument and stated:

> Mere inconvenience or substantial increase in the cost of compliance with a contract, though they might make compliance a hardship, cannot excuse a party from the performance of an absolute and unqualified undertaking to do a thing that is possible and lawful. Courts cannot alter contracts merely because they work a hardship. A contract is not invalid, nor is the obligor therein in any manner discharged from its binding effect, because it turns out to be difficult or burdensome to perform [*Hudson v. D. & V Mason Contractors Inc.,* 252 A.2d 166 (1969)] (Case 15-6).

However, use of the word "substantial" seems to suggest that possibly there is a degree beyond which financial compliance would become unconscionable and impossibility would set in. It must be noted, however, that this is merely an argumentative statement, as the cases stand for what is written. Therefore, the claimant is specifically warned that from case law it appears that eating up all profit and substantial increases in costs do not render a lawful and possible contract impossible and do not excuse performance.

On the other side of the coin are federal contract cases, where the doctrines of equity seem to have greater effect. These decisions talk in terms of "legal impossibility," "commercial impossibility," and "commercial impracticality." Although leniency is involved, it is doled out very sparingly and should be an argument only of last resort. More often than not impossibility arguments stand or fall on the testimony of the expert witness [*Appeal of Instruments for Industry, Inc.,* 69-2 BCA 8025 (1969)]. The arguments of impossibility, other than absolute impossibility, gain a small degree of support by the Uniform Commercial Code, § 2-615. This statute has been labeled by some to allow for impossibility of performance to be argued when there has been a frustration of purpose. This section of the Uniform Commercial Code excuses nonperformance

> if performance as agreed has been made impracticable by the occurrence of a contingency the non-occurrence of which was a basic assumption on which the contract was made or by compliance in good faith with any applicable foreign or domestic governmental regulation or order whether or not it later proves to be invalid [Uniform Commercial Code, § 2-615].

As previously noted, this code normally is not applicable, in the strict sense, to construction contracts, although it may be applied in dealings with suppliers and merchants. However, it will be looked to as a guide even for construction cases.

The beauty of the Uniform Commercial Code is the use of the word "impracticable."

Thus it can be seen that the right to termination, even when provided by contract, is one which should be used sparingly. There is never a simple answer or resolution. If this is understood, the parties are more apt to sit down and negotiate.

CASE 15-1   Court Turns Deaf Ear to New York City's Fiscal Woes

Even though New York City was teetering on the brink of bankruptcy, it could not cancel a contract without liability, ruled the New York Supreme Court, Appellate Division [*Pettinelli Electric Co., Inc. v. Board of Education of the City of New York,* 56 A.D.2d 520 (1977)].

The excuse of impossibility of performance, it said, means more than economic hardship.

The contract called for construction of two New York City schools, which were planned and designed in conjunction with a state housing project. Due to fiscal problems, however, the state's Urban Development Corporation (UDC), decided to scrap the housing portion.

The New York City Board of Education, the owner on the school project, then canceled its contracts for the school construction, and the contractor sued for breach of contract.

New York City's financial problems, argued the school board, necessitated canceling the contracts. The emergency, it said, was a reasonable and proper basis for breaching the contracts without liability.

However, the court was not swayed by the school board's plight, and it ruled that "financial difficulty or economic hardship, even to the extent of insolvency or bankruptcy, is not such an impossibility as to excuse [an owner] from liability."

The school board then mounted a second defense, arguing that the contract was "frustrated" because of UDC's failure to build the housing project. The school projects, it said, were conditioned upon the housing projects being built.

The court rejected this defense as well, saying that the housing projects were not "the foundation of the contract" between the school board and the contractor.

It noted that the city, even with its fiscal emergency, did not cancel all its capital construction projects. This project was canceled because of a "business decision," it said, not because the contract was frustrated.

After all, the court concluded, if the owner had decided to construct the schools, the contractors "would not have been excused because of an implied condition that the housing project should continue."

CASE 15-2   Government Contract Cancellation not a Breach

A termination-for-convenience clause in a government contract precludes a contractor from recovering unearned anticipatory profits if the contract is canceled, the U.S. Court of Claims has ruled [*G. C. Casebolt Co. v. United States,* 421 F.2d 710 (1970)].

The case in which the ruling occurred goes back to 1968, when the federal government solicited bids for sewer and roadwork. After the bids were opened, the contracting officer verbally informed the contractor that it would be awarded the contract. A written notice of award was then placed in the mails but retrieved before delivery. The government informed the contractor that no contract was to be let. The contractor sued for the profits it would have made had it received the contract.

A combination of circumstances led the government to conclude "it would be in the Government's best interest to reject all bids . . . " and postpone the contracting until another fiscal year, the court said. The contractor turned out to be the second low bidder, there was a question whether the low bid had been properly disqualified, and the fiscal year was drawing to a close.

The court assumed, without ruling on the issue, that the contractor had a valid contract either because of the oral notification or the mailing of the notice. But, "even if a valid contract were consummated, the contractor would still not be entitled, under our decisions, to the anticipatory profits now asked," the court said.

The government's action had to be considered under the standard termination-for-convenience clause written into the contract between the parties, the court explained. The rejection of all bids and the directive not to perform any work did not represent a breach of contract under that clause, the court ruled. And, it said, "anticipated but unearned profits . . . are not allowable under a convenience-termination" clause.

CASE 15-3   Contract Improperly Terminated

The government was liable for costs paid by a defaulted contractor and its surety company to a completing contractor when the termination for default was deemed improper, held the U.S. Court of Claims [*J. D. Hedin Constr. Co., Inc. v. United States,* 456 F.2d 1315 (1972)].

During performance of the contract the government terminated the contractor for default, allegedly for failing to perform its work diligently. The contract was completed with a second contractor on a cost-plus basis.

The court decided that the termination was improper because the government failed to grant a time extension the contractor was entitled to receive because of an excusable delay. This additional time would have meant that the contractor was not in default when the contract was terminated. The improper termination was held to be a breach of contract. The question was what damages the defaulted contractor was entitled to recover.

The contractor claimed that the completion costs it paid far exceeded its anticipated completion costs "calculated on the basis of its original bid estimate applied to the amount of work remaining to be accomplished." It claimed the difference as damages. The government disputed the amount of work to be completed and argued that the completion costs of the terminated contractor should not be based on the original bid estimate.

The court agreed with the contractor about the status of work when the contract was terminated. It also rejected the government's attempt to use the pre-termination rate of progress as a basis for estimating the time it would have taken the contractor to complete its work had no default been issued.

The court determined a completion cost based on the cost escalations that the contractor would have incurred while on the job longer than estimated due to excusable delays for which the government was not liable. It concluded that the contractor was entitled to recover "completion costs in excess of those plaintiff reasonably would have incurred had there been no termination."

When the contract was terminated, the government confiscated tools and equipment on the site. The contractor argued that it was entitled to "the market rental value of the items during the periods it was deprived of their use, plus interest as part of just compensation."

Although interest was denied, the court held that since the termination was improper, the plaintiff was wrongfully deprived of the use of the items. Damages may be measured by the rental value of the equipment from the time plaintiff was deprived of their use to the dates that they were returned to plaintiff or consumed as part of the project operations, the court ruled.

CASE 15-4   Recovery Allowed for
Work Performed

A subcontractor whose contract was terminated was entitled to full payment from the contractor for all work completed even though the architect had not approved the subcontractor's progress-payment requisitions, a New York court has ruled [*Arc Electrical Constr. Co., Inc. v. George A. Fuller Co. Inc.*, 24 N.Y.2d 99 (1969)].

The electrical subcontract in this case was on the contractor's standard form, which it had drafted. The subcontract contained two separate payment clauses. The first clause provided for 90 percent monthly progress payments for work done the preceding month. The remaining 10 percent was retainage payable on completion of the project. For its monthly payments the subcontractor had to submit its monthly requisitions and obtain approval from the contractor and the architect.

The second payment clause gave the contractor the right to terminate the subcontract at any time before final completion. In this case the subcontractor was to receive the entire amount due at that time. The clause neither called for any retainage nor specified the need for the architect's approval of requisitions.

During its performance, the subcontractor had most of its monthly requisitions approved by the architect and received payment in accordance with the first payment clause. However, the subcontractor's last four requisitions were not approved and were not paid. Subsequently, the contractor terminated the subcontract. The subcontractor sued to recover the full value of its work for which requisitions had not been approved, plus the 10 percent retainage previously withheld.

The contractor refused payment and claimed that even though the architect's approval was not specified in the second payment clause, it must be read into the clause. "Otherwise," it said, "Arc [subcontractor] would be able to obtain payment under the termination provision for work which had already been found to be defective and had been properly rejected."

The New York Court of Appeals rejected the contractor's argument. The architect's original refusal to approve the subcontractor's requisitions "did not mean that its efforts would go permanently uncompensated," the court said. The lack of approval, the court noted, might postpone the subcontractor's compensation until it could reasonably satisfy the architect, but it did not foreclose all possibilities of recovery. While the subcontractor was on the job, it was still able to perform the work necessary to satisfy the architect, the court explained, but once the contractor terminated the subcontract, the subcontractor lost all possible power to correct the deficiencies that had prevented the architect's approval of the work.

The court stated that it would not change the contract terms and read into the second payment clause the need for the architect's approval. "Indeed, even if a requirement for the architect's approval was expressly incorporated in article XXXIII [the second payment clause], it would not be enforceable."

On this basis the subcontractor was entitled to the payment that it demanded, the court ruled. If there were any deficiencies in the subcontractor's work when its contract was terminated, this would reduce the amount due the subcontractor but it would not entirely preclude some recovery, the court said.

**CASE 15-5   Part Performance Defeats
            Contractor's Claim**

A U.S. Court of Appeals ruled that a subcontractor who was able to furnish only 45 acceptable columns out of a required 200 did not substantially complete performance of its contract. The fact that it furnished 45 columns defeated its claim that the contract was impossible of performance, the court said [*Ballou v. Basic Constr. Co.,* 407 F.2d 1137 (4th Cir. 1969)].

The case involved work on a community hospital under construction in Virginia. The subcontractor had the contract to produce 200 concrete facade columns to be set around the hospital.

After the first 50 columns were installed, the architect rejected 41 of them because they did not meet the specifications' minimum requirements. He eventually rejected all but 45 of 139 columns the subcontractor had fabricated. The general contractor directed the subcontractor to replace them. The subcontractor, however, was financially unable to continue its contract performance. The general declared the subcontractor in default and let a new contract. After the original subcontractor's performance-bond surety refused any payment to the general contractor, the lawsuit was initiated.

The subcontractor argued it was not liable for breach of contract because it had substantially performed the contract and because strict compliance with the specifications was impossible.

The court rejected both arguments. Furnishing 45 acceptable columns did not amount to substantial performance, it said. Under Virginia law, it said, "breach of contract is excused only by objective impossibility of performance." The fabrication of 45 acceptable columns "proves that it was feasible to make columns conforming to the contract terms," it noted. "The manufacture of 200 acceptable columns might have been extremely difficult or so expensive as to consume any profit the contractor may have contemplated, but neither factor excuses . . . failure to meet its contractual obligation."

The court granted the general recovery against the subcontractor and its surety.

CASE 15-6   Contractor Stuck with Increases after Award

Increased costs incurred by a builder-seller after contract award do not constitute impossibility of performance so as to excuse nonperformance, a Delaware court has ruled.

In this case, a contractor had agreed to construct a house at a set price to be completed by a set date. Subsequently, the contractor informed the buyer that completion would be delayed and then claimed that the house could not and would not be built for the agreed price. The buyer sued, alleging that the contractor had breached its contract.

The contractor opposed the breach-of-contract argument on the grounds that the contract was impossible to perform. The impossibility of performance, it said, excused its nonperformance. The contractor based its impossibility claim on the fact that since the original contract date construction financing interest rates had increased; "points" paid by a builder-seller, relating to an FHA mortgage, had substantially risen; construction costs had gone up, and the labor market was "almost unavailable."

The Superior Court of Delaware recognized that in certain instances impossibility of performance would excuse performance. However, when the work remains the same and when the alleged impossibility is merely due to "increased cost considerations," the contract should specifically reference these factors as excusing performance in clear and unambiguous language, it said. No provision, the court held, was included in the contract relieving performance.

The court further noted that the contractor's mere allegation of scarcity of labor was not sufficient by itself to prove that it was substantially affected and unable to complete performance because of a labor shortage.

The general principle of law, as quoted from a prior decision, the court said, is

> Mere inconvenience or substantial increase in the cost of compliance with a contract, though they might make compliance a hardship, cannot excuse a party from the performance of an absolute and unqualified undertaking to do a thing that is possible and lawful. Courts cannot alter contracts merely because they work a hardship. A contract is not invalid, nor is the obligor therein in any manner discharged from its binding effect, because it turns out to be difficult or burdensome to perform [*Hudson v. D & V Mason Contractors, Inc.*, 252 A.2d 166 (1969)].

SIXTEEN

Liquidated Damages

The inclusion of a liquidated-damage clause in a contract has been said to be the contractors' enemy. They shudder at the thought of it and normally try to seek its exclusion. Often this action by the contractor is detrimental to its own interest. The inclusion of a liquidated-damage provision in a contract often works against the owner's interests.

Before seeking to exclude a liquidated-damage provision, the contractor should keep in mind that the liquidated-damage provision is generally deemed to be in lieu of actual damages for delay. If there is no liquidated-damage provision, the contractor is liable for the actual damages it causes by its delay. These damages are often greatly in excess of the stipulated liquidated amount. Conversely, the owner often believes that it has no right to withhold monies from the contractor without a liquidated-damage provision. However, since the contractor would otherwise be liable for actual damages, if the contract specifically so states, the owner could withhold actual damages.

Admittedly, the main benefit from a liquidated-damage provision is the possible avoidance of subsequent litigation. The parties can know what each day's delay and breach will cost. This prior knowledge and avoidance of litigation is the major reason for the court's approval and recognition of liquidated-damage provisions. However, if the liquidated-damage provision is against public policy or is unconscionable, it will not be enforced by the courts. Penalty provisions are unconscionable and will not be enforced.

In determining the public policy question whether or not a given clause is a liquidated-damage provision or penalty provision, the courts will interpret the specific clause in question in accord with intent of the parties. There seems to be a split among the courts on the presumption of whether the clause is to be deemed a liquidated-damage or penalty provision. This presumption is often the determining factor when neither the intent of the clause nor of the parties can readily be ascertained. In determining the intent of the parties, the clause is the first item to be reviewed. The mere fact that a provision is entitled "liquidated damages" and says that it is "not a penalty provision" does not necessarily mean it is so. Interpretation is a court function. In reviewing this question a court has held:

> Parties to a contract may not fix a penalty for its breach. The settled rule in this State is that such a contract is unlawful.
> *Liquidated Damages* is the sum a party to a contract agrees to pay if he breaks some promise, and which, having been arrived at by a good faith effort to estimate in advance the actual damage that will probably ensue from the breach, is legally recoverable as agreed damages if the breach occurs. A *penalty* is the sum a party agrees to pay in the event of a breach, but which is fixed, not as a pre-estimate of probable actual damages, but as a punishment, the threat of which is designed to prevent the breach [*Westmount Country Club v. Kameny*, 197 A.2d 379 (N.J. 1964)].
> In order for an agreement fixing the amount of damages made in advance of a breach to be enforceable as a contract it must be shown that (a) the amount so fixed is a reasonable forecast of just compensation for the harm caused by the breach, and (b) the harm that is caused by the breach is one that is incapable or very difficult of accurate estimate [*Barr & Sons, Inc. v. Cherry Hill Center Inc.*, 217 A.2d 631 (N.J. Super. Ct. 1966)].

To substantiate the validity of a liquidated-damage provision the party who seeks its substantiation or the party who seeks the assessment of liquidated damages must be able to prove (1) that at the time the contract was executed it made a *good-faith* estimate of what actual potential damages might be as a result of the breach which is covered by the liquidated-damage provision; (2) it ascertained that that potential damage was hard, incapable, and very difficult of accurate estimate; and (3) that it took that unascertainable amount and inserted it in the liquidated-damage provision. If the parties cannot prove these essentials, the provision will be deemed a penalty provision.

In the case of *Staten Island Rapid Transit Railway Co. v. S. T. G. Constr. Co.* the owner had been awarded its actual costs, computed by the lower court as $36,416.04, which included compensation for extra time and expenses of employees, engineers, personnel, and overhead charges. However, the owner appealed, arguing that it was entitled to the liquidated-damage assessment of $161,250. The owner argued that the liquidated-damage clause was valid and not a penalty provision. It claimed the right to enforce the liquidated-damage provision based upon additional damages consisting of interference to navigation and other intangible delays. However, the mere assertion of the intangible delays is not all conclusive. In upholding the lower court's decision that the provision of $250 per day was a penalty provision, the court concluded:

that the Railroad had not shown that it could have reasonably expected the delay in the completion to prevent it from using the bridge, and that it had not adequately shown the nature of the additional damages it claimed. As a result the court found the liquidated damages provision to be unrelated in amount to any possibly foresee-able real damages and hence to be a penalty provision, not allowable under New York law. We agree. The standard applicable under New York law in upholding or rejecting a liquidated damages provision in a contract is whether the provision con-stitutes a reasonable attempt to estimate damages which, though real, may be uncer-tain in amount [421 F.2d 53 at 58-59 (1970), *cert. denied* 398 U.S. 951 (1970)].

There seem to be conflicting decisions whether or not a party is entitled to assess liquidated damages for that portion of time for which the other party was responsible when, in fact, the party seeking the assessment was responsible for other portions of delay [*Nomellini Constr. Co. v. Dept. of Water Resources*, 96 Cal. 682 (1971)]. Some courts have simply indicated that if a clear concise line between the delaying parties cannot be drawn from the evidence, liquidated damages cannot be assessed. Under all circumstances it is recognized that if one party is delayed by the party who is seeking its enforcement for that portion of the delay caused by the latter party, no liquidated damages will be assessed.

> It was in mind, presumably, that to agree to liquidated damages, covering each day's delay, would act as a spur upon the contractor and would save to the owner the delays and expense of an action at law to recover the actual damage he might be able to prove. But it is obvious, as I think, that the very reason for his sustaining the validity of an agreement for liquidated damages, in such contracts as the present ones, as a reasonable and fair provision, also, suggests how essential it is that the owner shall be able to show strict compliance on his part and that the contractor's obligation has not been released, nor effected, by his interference, or dilatory action. In requiring this agreement to pay liquidated damages, it is to be presumed that the appellant intended, when called upon to act, to co-operate with all possible diligence with the contractor and that the latter's situation was such at the time and its ar-rangements were so ordered as to enable it to complete the work within the time fixed.
>   While such an agreement has not the harshness of a penalty, it is, nevertheless, in its nature, such that its enforcement, where the party claiming the right to enforce has, in part, been the cause of delay, would be unjust [*Mosler Safe Co. v. Maiden Lane S. D. Co.*, 199 N.Y. 479 (1910)].

Once the provision has been ruled to be a penalty, there seems to be an indication that at that juncture the defaulting party, normally the contractor, would still be subjected to actual damages. Thus, looking at it from the owner's point of view, if the clause sets an amount so high as to be unrealistic, it will become a penalty and the contractor will be subjected only to actual damages. If, however, the court finds that the amount set was intended to be a penalty provi-sion, without any relationship to the original contract, some court might rule that due to the intentional act of the owner in establishing a penalty amount, it might deny all damages, even actual. This last step has not been taken; however, the ever-changing trends of the law may yield this result. It is still generally recognized that once the penalty provision is established and invalidated, actual damages become the compensatory measure.

Since the validity of the liquidated-damage provision is determined by the acts which occurred at the signing of the contract, the actual sums specified in the contract need not bear any major relationship to what actual damages eventually are. However, the trend seems to be that if the actual damages are negligible, and even if the liquidated-damage provision is proper, in a growing number of jurisdictions the courts are ruling that it would be unconscionable to charge the contractor the unrelated damages (Case 16-1). Thus, if the inserted amount is too high, the contractor will argue that it is a penalty provision; if the amount inserted in the contract is substantially lower than actual damages, the contractor will pay the liquidated amount and argue in favor of the clause; but if the actual damages are so small, even with a valid liquidated-damage provision, the contractor will argue for equitable relief. It would seem advantageous in many instances for the contract specifically to require the payment of all actual damages and to specify the general categories of damages.

Depending upon the contract words, there also seems to be substantial question whether the prime contractor may assess a subcontractor liquidated damages in a sum greater than what it has paid or for a period of time longer than it is required to pay (Case 16-2). However, the prime contractor should keep in mind the fact that it might not only have to pay liquidated damages to the owner, as a result of its subcontractor's delays, but the subcontractor's delays might cost the prime contractor substantial additional costs of its own. These costs should be specified as being in addition to liquidated damages. They are, in fact, separate and distinct and should be so indicated.

The period of time for which liquidated damages can be assessed is subject to much debate. The commencement date for the running of liquidated damages is the date normally specified in the contract. However, if no completion date is specified, the door is open for wide disagreement. It would appear that the date would commence at the conclusion of a reasonable period of time or after the delay has become unreasonable. These might not necessarily be the same times. If a date is specified, it must be further extended for all excusable delays and extensions of time the contractor is entitled to. As previously mentioned, no party has a right to interfere with the work of the other; and the owner cannot demand liquidated damages for the period of time it adversely affected performance. After ascertaining the extended or modified completion date, the next question is: On what date does the liquidated damage assessment stop? Most contracts provide that liquidated damages will discontinue on the date of completion. The courts have generally recognized that this date of completion is the date of substantial completion. Substantial completion is probably not before the date that beneficial use and occupancy can be tendered to the owner. However, often the owner refuses occupancy for some reason, whether justified or not. Therefore, courts might deem the owner reasonably able to take beneficial occupancy and declare that date the date of substantial completion and termination of the liquidated-damage assessment.

Although liquidated damages are to stop on the date of substantial completion, it is the contractor's obligation to prove the date of substantial completion. "To support a claim of substantial completion, appellant [contractor] must establish that the project was capable of adequately serving its intended purpose" on that date [*Appeal of David M. Cox, Inc.,* IBCA 1079-10-75, 76-1 BCA 11,821 (1976)]. When, however, the contract specifically provides that the assessment continues until 100 percent absolute complete and final acceptance, an immediate attack will be taken against the clauses as being a penalty. When the owner tries to assess liquidated damages even when one minute item on the punch list has not yet been completed, attack is probable. Seldom is there any reasonable basis for the assessment for liquidated damages on a per diem basis for this type of item. As a general rule it might be said that the courts will assess liquidated damages from the extended contract date to the constructive date of substantial completion.

The federal contractor must be aware of the various statutes involving liquidated damages; 10 U.S.C. § 2312 and 41 U.S.C. § 256a relate to military agencies and civil agencies, respectively. The provisions of these statutes specifically provide that even though the contractor is not entitled to an extension of time, and even if the liquidated-damage provision is valid, the contractor has a means of seeking a remission of liquidated damages. The remission of liquidated damages would be a waiver of the assessment and return of the monies. The procedures are not easily complied with, but they cannot be overlooked.

The enforcement of a liquidated-damage provision, as written, for the full amount of time claimed by the owner is seldom fully sustained in court. However, the contractor must come forward with some proof of excusable delays (Case 16-3). Numerous factors come into play, and the larger the assessment the more often it appears in court. Although the liquidated-damage provision is intended to keep people out of court, it often does not have that result. The greatest aid of the liquidated-damage provision is the psychological effect on contractors to move faster (even though they might be liable for greater amounts as actual damages) and as a negotiating instrument to resolve the claims of the respective parties. The purpose of the liquidated-damage provision should be reviewed before it is inserted into the contract, and contractors should be constantly aware of their potential liability thereunder and their right to extensions of time to avoid its assessment.

CASE 16-1   Liquidated Damages Barred

A contractor that failed to complete a drilling contract on time should not be assessed for liquidated damages by the owner although the contract contained a liquidated-damages clause, the Supreme Court of Oregon ruled [*Harty v. Bye,* 483 P.2d 458 (1971)].

The owner withheld liquidated damages at the rate of $50 a day for every day of late completion. When the contractor sued, claiming that it was improperly assessed because the owner suffered no damages due to the delay, the owner was unable to prove it had sustained losses by the late completion.

The court held that the liquidated-damages provision should not be enforced because the plaintiff's breach caused the defendant no harm.

CASE 16-2   Subcontractor's Liquidated-Damage Liability Limited

A state court has ruled that a subcontractor is not liable to a general contractor for liquidated damages for a period of time greater than that for which the general is liable to the owner.

The subcontractor involved in the case specialized in membrane curing, joint sawing, and sealing for highway construction projects. It had subcontracted to perform this work on an Idaho state highway project. The general contract specified a completion date and contained a liquidated-damage provision for each day's delay. The general contractor incorporated a similar clause in the subcontract. After various time extensions the project was completed three days beyond the completion date, and the general contractor was assessed liquidated damages.

The subcontractor sued the general contractor for payment, and the general contractor claimed that the subcontractor was liable to it for liquidated damages for fifty-one days. The general contractor argued that the time extensions granted to it by the state were for its own benefit and not for the benefit of its subcontractor.

The Idaho Supreme Court denied the general contractor the right to assess liquidated damages against the subcontractor beyond a period for which it was liable to the state. The time extensions granted by the state, the court said, were for the entire project and not just for the general contractor's benefit. In addition, since the subcontractor's work depended upon the general contractor's completion of its work and since most of the time extensions granted by the state were for causes which happened before the subcontractor's ability to start its work, the subcontractor was entitled to an extension of time for its completion.

In response to the general contractor's claim for assessment of liquidated damages, the court stated:

> Furthermore, this claim is also based upon the assumption that a liquidated damage clause placed in a contract in order to compensate a party for delay in construction will be enforceable even where the beneficiary [general contractor] of such a provision contributes to the delay or where causes beyond the control of either party contribute to the delay. The proper rule of law is to the contrary, however. There is evidence in the record showing that Parson [the general contractor] itself contributed to the delay in completion of the project to a time beyond the original completion date. Much of the delay was caused by bad weather, and this was the reason for the time extension given by the State for the whole project. In these circumstances . . . it would be entirely inequitable to allow Parson to recover against Hunt [the subcontractor] liquidated damages for delay, especially to an extent greater than that to which Parson itself was held liable by the State [*State of Idaho ex rel. Pierce R. Smith et al. v. Jack B. Parson Constr.* 456 P.2d 762 (1969)].

CASE 16-3   Liquidated Damages Upheld,
                Excusable Delay not Proved

A liquidated-damage assessment was upheld by the U.S. General Services Board of Contract Appeals despite the contractor's allegation of excusable delay. The board also stated that the government's nonoccupancy of the building for more than a year following its completion had no bearing on the propriety of liquidated damages [*Charles N. Landon, Inc.,* GSBCA 3230, 71-1 BCA 8808 (Mar. 31, 1971)].

Notice to proceed with construction of a building to be completed by April 8, 1969, was received by the contractor on June 13, 1968. The project was not completed until mid-May, and the contractor was assessed thirty-six days of liquidated damages. The contractor claimed excusable delay, arguing that the government had failed to have an architect-engineer on the project until mid-July, 1968. The government freely admitted this but contended that the contractor was not delayed by the architect-engineer's absence.

The board indicated that the absence of the architect-engineer could be grounds for excusable delay but that the contractor must prove how it was delayed and to what extent, which it failed to do in this case.

The board also denied the contractor's argument that liquidated damages were improperly assessed because the government did not immediately occupy the building. "The fact that the building was not placed into beneficial use or occupancy for more than a year after construction was completed does not militate against the assessment of liquidated damages, for beneficial occupancy was not a prerequisite. . . ."

SEVENTEEN

Contract Warranty and Guaranty

The contractor's contract warranty and guaranty is a creature both of the express terms of the contract and of that which is implied by law. The extent of the warranty or guaranty depends not only upon the written word but also, more important, upon the freedom of choice for design and construction left with the contractor. A contract which is purely a plan and specification contract will have a much more limited warranty imposed upon the contractor than one which is a performance contract. The terms *warranty* and *guaranty* should first be defined. Although there may be certain trade customs and trade practices applying to the definition of these two terms, there does not appear to be any universally recognized differentiation in the construction industry. In fact, several dictionaries have the word "guaranty" as their definition of "warranty" and vice versa. The world of the tort warranty, which is quite different was covered in Chapter 2.

The first source for determination for the warranty is the contract. Contract clauses normally define the scope of the contractor's warranty to the owner. In similar fashion the subcontract, either by incorporation by reference to the prime contract or by separate provision, specifies the scope of that warranty. Expressed warranties normally expand those which are implied by most contracts. In fact, they often go even beyond the extent that the courts will enforce. Where there is no specific clause, the courts will normally read into the contract the contractor's warranty that its work will be done in a good workmanlike manner, that the materials and equipment will be free from defects, and that the work will be done in accord with the contract documents.

Where a party contracts to build a building for a specified purpose, the law reads into the contract a stipulation that the building shall be erected in a reasonably good and workmanlike manner and when completed shall be reasonably fit for the intended purpose [*Minemount Realty Co. Inc. v. Ballentine,* 162 A. 594 (N.J. 1932)].

These implied warranties usually appear as express warranties in the contract. However, many written warranty provisions in plan and specification contracts, where the contractor is granted no choice in the selection of the changes to be incorporated in the work, will also mandate some form of performance criteria warranty. These performance criteria are not absolutes. There must be a balancing of the two warranties, to wit: the warranty of the owner, who drafted the plans and specifications, that if they are followed, a satisfactory product or building will result, as against the warranty of the contractor that it will follow the contract documents in a reasonable fashion, will perform the work in a reasonably workmanlike manner, and will not furnish defective materials. If the contractor fulfills its warranty and the desired results are not attained, it is generally recognized not to be the responsibility of the contractor (Case 17-1).

The original design is not guaranteed by the contractor. That responsibility lies with the designer. If the equipment specified, even when operating properly, cannot achieve the desired results, the responsibility for the defect is the designer's and not the contractor's. However, contractors continuously try to make repairs and corrections under their warranty and guaranty clauses for weeks and years after completion in the hope of avoiding ruffled feathers, to get their retainage, and for many other reasons. When the contractor believes that the work being corrected is not due to its fault, even though it intends to correct that work, it should give notice to the party demanding the action and state its denial of responsibility or liability. The contractor can still make the corrections, but it should put its position on record.

A primary source for warranties is found in the Uniform Commercial Code. This code, the law of merchants, specifies various types of warranties which might flow from the original manufacturer, supplier, jobber, distributor, subcontractor, prime contractor, and owner to the next in line or a third party. Even if the Uniform Commercial Code is not specifically applicable between the prime contractor and owner, the courts will often look to it for guidance. The Uniform Commercial Code provides for the following types of warranties:

1. Section 2-312 relates to the warranty of title and against infringement. It specifies the seller's obligation to convey free unencumbered title to the buyer.

2. Section 2-313 is entitled Express Warranties by Affirmation, Promise, Description, Sample. In essence, the seller must live up to those statements which reasonably became the basis of the bargain. The item delivered must meet the standards of the prior affirmation, promise, description, and sample. The buyer must beware of mere "sales talk," as reasonable reliance might be questioned.

3. Section 2-314 relates to the implied warranty of merchantability. This implied warranty of merchantibility is subject to the trade custom and practice of

that particular trade. One of the warranties is that the particular item will be "fit for the ordinary purpose for which such goods are used."

4. Section 2-315 creates the implied warranty of the seller that the goods will be fit for a particular purpose when it can be proved that the buyer was relying upon the skills of the seller and the seller had knowledge of that fact.

The Uniform Commercial Code is constantly being interpreted by the various courts, and each state's decisions must be reviewed. The code further specifies bases for the exclusion or modification of the warranties, and if a seller wants to modify its warranties, it had better follow the code to the letter.

Many of the questions relating to warranties, whether under the Uniform Commercial Code or relating to construction contracts, deal with who designed the item. As indicated above, the contractor's obligation is not normally to warrant the design of the owner. However, it is often the contractor, under a change, who raises the question of altering the design or comes up with a better method of doing the job. When these changes are now raised by the contractor, the original design responsibilities and warranties of the owner are lessened and those of the contractor raised. This is especially true when the contractor makes affirmative representations and promises results. At that time the contractor might be entering a performance-type contract. On the other hand, the contractor might merely be making suggestions for the owner's review and decision, subject to the review and decision by the owner's architect and engineer, who are the professionals. Thus, it can be seen when the contractor raises the question of changes, a lot will depend upon its presentation, whether the contractor has now accepted the responsibility for performance or whether that responsibility still rests with the owner. The contractor is advised to obtain from the owner a written consent and approval, including that of the architect, authorizing, and possibly directing, the contractor to proceed.

If the owner believes that a right to demand compliance with the warranty provision exists, the question arises upon whom the burden lies to prove that the alleged defect is within the coverage of the warranty clause. It has been recognized that where the government asserts a right under a guaranty clause to demand repair or replacement of defective materials, it has the burden of showing the existence of that defect. At this point the burden shifts from one party to another, back and forth.

> Once Appellant has shown that it has complied with the express provision of the contract, the burden of going forward with the evidence shifts to the Government. . . . It must show wherein Appellant's work was deficient. Subsequently, if Appellant is able to rebut this showing, Appellant must bear the burden of proving that the corrective measures were ordered and were in excess of the requirements of the contract [*Appeal of Arthur Venneri Co.*, 65-2 BCA 4976 (1965)].

The mere allegation that something does not work as intended does not prove the contractor is liable. Testing procedures may not be proper, or the administration of those procedures, even if they are proper, may be improper.

Where a contract contains certain specified tests of performance and provides that the passing of such tests shall be deemed conclusive proof of performance, the contract is conclusively presumed to have been performed upon the completion or fulfillment of the conditions constituting such tests. . . . Failure to pass the test may defeat a recovery . . . but a party cannot rely on a condition precedent, such as the fulfillment or passing of a test, where the nonperformance of the condition was caused by or consented to by the party itself . . . Where the work, in fact, has been substantially performed in accordance with the provisions of a contract, the failure to take or pass stipulated tests, due to the fault or neglect of the party for whose benefit they were to be accomplished, should not bar recovery. . . .[*McIntosh Ready Mix Concrete Corp. v. R. D. Battaglini Corp. and County of Broome,* 317 N.Y.S.2d 692 36 A.D.2d 561 (N.Y. 1971)] (Case 10-8).

Thus, the party seeking the protection of the warranty clause must be able to prove that it has complied with the contract and that the contract was capable of compliance.

The warranty and guaranty clauses must be read hand in hand with the inspection and acceptance clauses. Many contracts specifically provide procedures whereby the owner or its duly authorized representative shall inspect and accept the work. Some of these clauses may well affect the warranty and guaranty. The federal government contract provides that acceptance shall be final and conclusive except as to latent defects, fraud, such gross mistakes as may amount to fraud, or as regards the government's rights under any warranty or guaranty (Cases 17-2 and 17-3). Other contract clauses state that inspection and acceptance by the owner shall, in effect, mean nothing as the contractor is still bound to do everything. Although these clauses do exist, their enforcement is not as literal as written. It appears from federal decisions, as well as some state decisions, that if the owner is exercising inspection activities, and if it was aware of defects in the contractor's work, and if the contractor is acting in good faith, and if the owner did not advise the contractor of the defect, then after the work is inspected the owner cannot now demand that corrective action must be taken by the contractor where such corrective action might result in inequitable burdens placed on the contractor (Case 17-4). However, the fact that the owner reserved the right to inspect does not place upon it the total obligation to inspect or to conduct all inclusive tests.

The right to inspect does not imply a duty to inspect. . . . It did not place any duty on the Government to conduct such tests at the risk of assuming responsibility for any deficiencies which it might have discovered. [However, had the government conducted the tests, then] the failure of the Government to discover an obvious error in construction would have relieved plaintiff of its responsibility to insure the tower and derricks were properly constructed [*Kaminer Constr. Corp. v. United States,* 488 F.2d 980 (1973) (Case 17-2)].

The inspection activities, with lack of notice to the contractor of such deficiencies, may be deemed a waiver of the owner's rights "to recover damages for all defects which were known to it or which were discoverable by a reasonable inspection [*Town of Tonawanda v. Stapell, Mumm & Beals Corp.,* 270 N.Y.S.

377, *aff'd* 265 N.Y. 630 (1934)]. Thus, it becomes a question of the inspection activities and what a reasonable inspection would have discovered. Patent defects, i.e., those which are readily discoverable by a reasonable inspection, are arguably waived by the failure to notify the contractor with reasonable promptness of the defect; however, latent defects, i.e., those which are not reasonably discoverable during the inspection being performed, will not be waived.

Before a contractor can be relieved of responsibilities under its warranty to perform in accord with the contract by arguing that the shop drawings it submitted called for different performance and were approved by the owner, the contractor must be able to show by absolute evidence that the owner was aware of the proposed change or should have been aware of it. The mere approval of shop drawings normally does not permit changing a contract requirement. Thus, the original contract requirements still remain, and the contractor may be responsible for correcting the work even though the approved shop drawings show otherwise. If the contractor wishes to change any requirements in the contract by shop drawings, it is first advised not to do so; more important, if it does, it had better have on the submittal sufficient clear notice that a change is incorporated therein. That notice should be in a separate document as well as on the shop drawing itself.

The extent of the corrective action required under a warranty clause is normally to correct that to which the warranty legally relates. Because a particular spot on the roof leaks does not mean that an entire new roof system is to be installed. The obligation is one of corrective action. To take advantage of the warranty and corrective action the owner must give notice within the time specified in the contract. The duration of the warranty is that which is specified. The contractor is warned to read the contract carefully to determine this time limitation. Many times it will be one year from (1) date of completion, (2) date of substantial completion, (3) date of performance of the work, (4) date the material was installed, (5) date the material was delivered to the job site, (6) date the material was manufactured, and others. What often happens is that a supplier will give a guaranty, even when of equal time duration, from date of manufacture, whereas the prime contractor might be giving a warranty from the date of final completion and acceptance of the entire project. What may happen is that the supplier will no longer be responsible under its warranty and guaranty, which expired before the job was even completed. Contractors should take great pains to have their subcontractors' and suppliers' warranties coincide with the contractor's warranty to the owner. The owner should also demand this, if possible, since many times it is the major supplier's warranty and manufacturer's warranty that the owner is interested in receiving, not the prime contractor's.

Whether the responsibility is expressed or implied, the contractor is responsible for performing its work in a good workmanlike manner, free from defects, and in accord with the contract. It must be prepared to prove this at all times. It must have sufficient and proper documentation to show that it has met both its implied and its expressed warranties. It should also keep accurate records of cost and time expended in performing corrective work under the warranty clause.

These records and proof often have been the substance to a litigation when a contractor is trying to prove that its work was not defective, that it had performed properly, and that it is entitled to additional costs for doing this work and is not liable for damages under its warranty.

CASE 17-1 Contract Not Total Guarantee

The highest court in Wisconsin has ruled that a contractor does not absolutely guarantee its work against defects or losses prior to the owner's final acceptance [*E. D. Wesley Co. v. City of New Berlin*, 215 N.W.2d 657 (1974)].

A contract for the construction of a pumping station provided that "Guarantee: Each contractor shall be responsible for his own work and shall make good, repair or replace, at his own expense, as may be necessary, any defective work, or material which may show itself within one (1) year after issuance of final certificate of the engineers."

Before the owner's acceptance of the work, a problem developed with a booster pump, and the owner withheld the contractor's final payment. To recover this payment, the contractor brought suit. The owner counterclaimed seeking the cost of the repairs.

Since it had not accepted the work, the owner argued that the contractor was absolutely liable for all repair costs. "Under a contract to furnish a working unit and until it is accepted by the owner, the contractor assumes all risks," the owner claimed.

The contractor replied that it had performed its work in a proper fashion and was not liable for any damages that may have arisen from causes totally outside its control and not due to negligence.

The court noted that to determine the contractor's liability the specific guarantee clause must be reviewed. "Under the guarantee clause, the damage to the booster pump was not proved to be caused by a defect in the booster pump," the court found. "The only evidence showed the cause to be an electrical phenomenon, which was neither the fault of the . . . [Contractor] or the manufacturer of the pump."

Therefore, the court ruled that the damage was not within the scope of the contractor's liability either before or after the acceptance of the work. "The present contract does not make the contractor an insurer," the court said. "The risk of loss to property generally follows ownership unless the contract provides otherwise."

CASE 17-2 Contractor's Use of Undersized Bolts Ruled a Latent Defect

The U.S. Court of Claims has ruled that a contractor's use of undersized bolts in the erection of a derrick constitutes a latent defect and that the government's final acceptance of the work does not bar recovery against the contractor [*Kaminer Constr. Corp. v. United States*, 488 F.2d 980 (1973)].

Nine months after the government had accepted a structural-steel tower with two attached derricks at the Marshall Space Flight Center, one of the derricks collapsed under testing. The contractor and the government agreed that the derrick collapsed because 1¼ inch high-strength stud bolts had been used in 1⅜ inch holes in the sill plate.

The contractor performed that repair work under protest. Then, citing the contract, which provided that "acceptance shall be final and conclusive except as regards latent defects, fraud, or such gross mistakes as may amount to fraud, or as regards the Government's rights under any warranty or guarantee," the contractor sued the government for what it considered an equitable adjustment.

The question before the court was whether the use of the undersized bolts constituted a latent defect, which the court defined as "one which cannot be discovered by observation or inspection made with ordinary care."

The contractor argued that the undersized bolts were not hidden from sight and should have been discovered by the government through the exercise of reasonable care and customary inspection procedures. Therefore, the contractor said the bolts were a patent defect and did not survive final acceptance.

Responding to the contractor's contention that the defect was patent because the government had the right to inspect and should have discovered the defect, the court said:

> Just because the material was to be subject to inspection and tests, did not impose upon the Government the duty to conduct all-inclusive tests. The right to inspect does not imply a duty to inspect. It did not place any duty on the Government to conduct such tests at the risk of assuming responsibility for any deficiencies which it might have discovered.

The court concluded that it was the contractor's primary obligation to assure proper compliance with the contract.

> Only the failure of the Government to discover an obvious error in construction would have relieved plaintiff of its responsibility to insure that the tower and the derricks were properly constructed.

Therefore, the court ruled that the contractor was not entitled to any equitable adjustment.

CASE 17-3   Guaranty Survived Approval

A contractor was held responsible for the removal and replacement of three fan motors because they did not conform to the contract though the government had previously approved them [*Appeal of Klefstab Engineering Co., Inc.* VACAB, 704, 68-2 BCA 7241 (1968), aff'd on reconsideration, 68-2 BCA 7389 (1968)].

The contractor had contracted to install an air-conditioning system in an existing Veterans Administration hospital. The plans and specifications were prepared for the government by an independent architect-engineer and were furnished to the contractor as part of its contract. The contract required that the three fan motors comply with certain details. In addition, the contractor was required to submit to the government data describing the motors it intended to furnish and install. These data were to be checked against the contract and either approved or disapproved for installation.

The contractor submitted the requested data. Though the government did not spot the discrepancy, the data indicated that the proposed motors did not conform to the contract requirements. The contractor's data were approved, and the nonconforming motors were installed.

Subsequently, during the guaranty period, the government discovered that one of the motors was defective. This led to the disclosure that all three motors were nonconforming. The government then demanded, pursuant to the guaranty provision, that the motors be removed and replaced.

The Veterans Administration Contract Appeals Board said that in order for the government to establish the validity of its demand under the guaranty clause, it must prove that the unsatisfactory condition was discovered during the guaranty period and that the cause was the contractor's use of nonconforming materials.

The contractor claimed that it should not be held responsible because the government had approved the data submittal proposing the use of the motors. The board noted that this would be true if the contractor specifically and affirmatively put the government on notice that its submittal included a particular proposed contract modification. However, the contractor's failure properly to notify the government of the nonconforming motors prohibited it from claiming that the government should have found the discrepancy, it said.

The board concluded that the nonconforming motors constituted an unsatisfactory condition within the guaranty clause.

CASE 17-4   Contractor Not Liable for Cost
             of Correcting Patent Defects

The Armed Services Board of Contract Appeals ruled that even though a contractor did not comply with contract requirements, it was not responsible for costs to correct a construction defect because the defect was patent and not latent [*Appeal of Federal Constr. Co.,* ASBCA 17599, 73-1 BCA 10,003 (1973)].

The dispute involved the contractor's failure to saw expansion joints in a concrete runway to a contract depth of 6 inches. The government says it did not discover the shallow joints until the final inspection because they were covered immediately with a joint sealer.

The government sued for reimbursement of its costs to correct the defect. The improper joints, it claimed, were latent defects that fell under a contract clause that stated, "Acceptance shall be final and conclusive except as regards latent defects. . . . " The contractor argued it was entitled to rely on trade practice which, it said, calls for an expansion cut equal to only one-sixth of the runway depth.

The board said that the contract was clear and sustained the government's claim of the required 6-inches depth. But, it said, no latent defect existed because the deficiencies were readily discoverable by placing a sharp object in the cuts. In fact, it says, evidence shows that the government's on-site inspector did this and "thus knew or should have known of the alleged deficiency." The board concluded that "since the deficiency was patent, the government's acceptance was final and conclusive."

EIGHTEEN

Releases

There are numerous means by which a claimant can be found to have released, waived, or forfeited its rights. Contractors seem to come up with new ones every day. There are many technical and procedural means by which claims can be lost, even before starting. Obviously, as has been stated throughout this book, the contractor is under an obligation to preserve and reserve its claims; otherwise, like breaches, they may be waived. Nonaction can be fatal. The protest document is an essential item for maintaining rights. There are other statutory and contractual considerations the contractor must also be aware of else, again, it will have lost its rights.

Statutes of limitations or other legislative enactments prescribe specific time periods and often the method by which a suit can and must be commenced. Each state has its own statutes of limitations.

If the lawsuit is not started within the statutory time, the cause of action is legally barred. Most states have separate time periods for the commencement of actions for breach-of-contract actions, negligence actions, breach of warranty, and other legal actions. In New York, for example, a lawsuit based on the theory of breach of contract must be commenced within six years from the date the cause of action accrued. This creates a separate problem: When did the cause of action accrue? Did the cause of action accrue on the date the event occurred, the date when notice was given, the date when the other party rejected the claim, the date of final completion of the work, the date of final acceptance of the project, the date of final payment for the project, the date of the termination of warranty, or some other date? To avoid the tremendous legal involvement, the contractor should consider, with its counsel, the commencement of legal proceedings as soon as possible so as to avoid another obstacle. The questions of statute of limitations are further complicated by the fact that in New York the period by which legal action must be commenced for negligence is three years, with the same legal problems involved. This places the burden upon the claimant to determine what basis of liability it is going to assert, and if it asserts one basis as against another, the entire action will have to be commenced within a different time frame. If the matter arises out of a sale of a commodity, e.g., from the manufacturer to the supplier, and the product is defective and not suitable for the intended use, there is a Uniform Commercial Code action, which in New York carries a four-year statute of limitations. It seems to be the general principle that arbitrations, although not in the court system, are bound by the same statutes of limitations. If the arbitration had been commenced in court and would have been precluded by a statute of limitations, the arbitration is subject to being barred by the court.

A New Jersey statute of limitations, which started to run on the date of completion of construction and precluded liability for defective and unsafe conditions for the performing or furnishing the design, planning, and supervision of construction or construction of such improvement of real property more than ten years after the performance or furnishing of such services and construction, was upheld [*O'Connor v. Altus,* 335 A.2d 545 (N.J. Sup. Ct. 1975)].

These statutory time limitations are not the only limiting enactments. As part of their enabling legislation many, if not most, public authorities have separate statutory enactments, their own statute of limitations. In fact, when dealing with a government, the first consideration is whether or not the doctrine of sovereign immunity applies. The doctrine of sovereign immunity bars all actions against the government. Although the doctrine of sovereign immunity is pretty well eliminated in most contractual matters, it cannot be ignored. If a right to commence an action does exist, the specific legislative enactment relating to that particular governmental entity must be carefully reviewed. Most governmental entities have limitation periods which are shorter than those included with the general limitation provisions.

What is initially as important as the statute of limitations is the requirement by many contractual or statutory provisions that *notice* be furnished within a specified period of time. This notice may be called a notice of claim or have some other label. Most of the statutes involving public authority preclude filing the eventual lawsuit, even though it might be within the statutory period, if the statutory notice of claim has not been properly filed. These notices of claim often have very short time spans, e.g., thirty, sixty, or ninety days. They are also subject to the obligation requiring the notice to be filed within so many days of a given event. Even though the party is intending to arbitrate, as specified by contract, and the notice-of-claim requirement seems to apply to court proceedings, contractors have been denied the right to proceed in arbitration when they have failed to comply with the notice-of-claim provisions.

The disputes procedures set forth in federal contracts have been the subject of untold dispute. Suffice it to say that the contractor is obligated to file an appeal from the contracting officer's final decision within the specified time period, else it will be precluded from further rights. It must be remembered that contracting officers often render final decisions during performance, substantially before the job is anywhere near completion. The contractor cannot sit on these, putting them on the corner of its desk, hoping to see its lawyer in a month or two to review them. The courts are very strict in interpreting these provisions and are reluctant to extend or modify their strict requirements.

In addition to the various statutes of limitations and special legislation, there may be what is commonly called the *short statute of limitations*, a statutory period or claim procedure prescribed by the contract where there is no legislative enactment. By actual contractual agreement the parties may legally reduce the specified statute of limitations to a time substantially shorter than that which would otherwise govern. These short contractual statutes of limitations are generally recognized as being valid and enforceable provided they are not unreasonably short or unconscionable [*Stanley R. Benjamin, Inc. v. Fidelity Casualty Co. of New York*, 72 Misc.2d 742 (1972)]. The most typical and often missed statutory period is that which appears in a surety bond. All too often a subcontractor will assume that it has the "normal" statutory period in which to sue the bonded contractor for damages. This may well be true, but the subcontractor going on the assumption that a surety company stands behind a payment bond or other collateral and that it has no real risk of loss as long as that surety company is around may be in for a rude shock. In many instances, if not the vast majority, most bonds specifically state that for bond coverage to be applicable *notices of claim must be filed* within a specified limit and that actual litigation must be commenced within a specified time. This time is typically one or two years from a given date, whereas the notice of claim might be thirty, sixty, or ninety days from a given date.

A labor-and-material-payment bond provision stating that in order for a subcontractor to have any enforceable right against the surety company it must commence its action within one year after the principal (prime contractor) ceased work is not void as against public policy [*Sam Finley, Inc. v. Interstate Fire Ins. Co.*, 217 S.E.2d 358 (Ga. Ct. App. 1975)].

While the subcontractor contemplates commencement of an action, the surety company is relieved of all liability, the bonded contractor becomes financially insolvent, and the subcontractor is unsecured.

Other forms of contractual waiver or release are specified in the contractual documents (Cases 18-1 and 18-2). Specific reference is made to the acceptance of final payment. Many contract forms expressly state that the contractor's acceptance of final payment shall constitute a release of all claims. These clauses are generally valid and enforceable. Unilaterally scratching off the words "final payment" from the check normally would not result in a contractor's reservation of rights unless it was with the express signed acknowledgment of the other party. There appears to be some dispute over whether the mere certification of the check will amount to acceptance thereof, which will then be tantamount to a waiver and release. Other releases may result from the failure to comply with a contractual obligation to submit a complete list of all open claims with the final requisition (Case 18-3). This type of clause is often used by owners to ascertain whether any potential claims will be asserted against it before it releases its major settlement lever, final payment.

The law-form publishers are loaded with standard forms for general releases. In many words they simply indicate that the claimant releases the other party from any and all rights it may have had from the day God created the heavens and earth until the day of execution and even possibly thereafter. Unless fraud, duress, misrepresentation, or some unconscionable act can be asserted and proved, these releases are valid. Most courts do state, however, that if at the time of execution of the release the parties were not aware and *should have not been aware* of the facts upon which another cause of action is based, such a release might not preclude a subsequent action for those given facts. This creates the major litigation question whether the claimant knew or should have known of the possible cause of action at the time the release was executed.

From the very title *general release* one should be able to comprehend its scope. The all-inclusiveness of such a release can be and should be limited in the vast majority of factual situations. That release should refer to the particular contract between the parties, especially when the parties have several contractual arrangements. At that juncture the general release has taken on a limitation, and thus becomes a *limited release*. The release should specify its intended scope. If it relates to a particular change order, it should be so specified. If it relates only to labor and materials of a given change order but does not relate to idle time, impact, or delay damages, the parties should not only indicate what it relates to but limit the release to indicate what it does not relate to. The more hurdles you place in front of your attorney, the greater your chances of losing. Limit your release; otherwise you must take the chance that the court will conclude that you have released rights, including those you did not intend to release.

Contract forms have gone as far as indicating that the acceptance of any progress payment will amount to a release of any and all claims covered by that progress payment. The validity of such a clause may well be questioned. It could be attacked on equitable grounds that it is unconscionable, on the basis of economic duress, or other basis, but it is far wiser to eliminate the argument by negotiating such a clause out of your contract or specifically reserving rights when requisitions are submitted. This may require showing your hand before the last card is drawn; however, if the "claim" is as it is defined, one being based on right, too much should not be lost.

Releases can take all forms; they may be by the execution of change orders, contract modifications, or some other document which can act as an accord and satisfaction of the claims. When a change order is executed, be scrupulous in reserving rights for delay and impact costs if that is what you want. If an extension of time is going to be sought for a change order, say so. Most forms indicate the amount of time being requested by the contractor for the change, and unfortunately most of the time it is left blank. Few things are harder to fight for than delay or impact changes and extensions of time resulting from change orders when, in fact, numerous changes have been executed without the reservation of any rights. As with the interpretation of any other contract document, say what you mean: say it clearly and succinctly.

CASE 18-1   Contract May Limit Redress

A subcontractor was denied the right to sue its prime contractor in a state court because it had agreed by contract to another form of relief [*Humphreys & Harding, Inc. v. Pittsburgh-Des Moines Steel Co.*, 397 F.2d 227 (4th Cir. 1968)].

The contract between the two contractors provided for processing disputes under the federal administrative appeal procedure set forth in the prime contract. A federal court said that this procedure took precedence over other avenues of relief. It enjoined the subcontractor's state court action.

The prime contract involved construction of an airport terminal building in Virginia. The subcontractor was to furnish and erect steel mullions and related work required for the installation of curtain walls. During its performance the subcontractor discovered that a preceding independent contractor had improperly performed its work. The openings for the mullion installation were not uniformly dimensioned. The subcontractor alleged that it was now required to perform substantial extra work since it was unable to work in the modular method anticipated.

The contract between the prime contractor and subcontractor provided that in these circumstances the subcontractor's claim was to be submitted to the architect through the prime contractor via the government contracting officer. The architect's interpretation was to be final and conclusive.

This procedure was followed, and the contracting officer, on consultation with the architect, granted a small part of the total claim as an extra. The major portion of the claim was denied, based on the architect's determination that the remaining work was part of the contract. The prime contractor was advised of its right to appeal the final decision to the Board of Contract Appeals.

While the prime contractor was appealing the contracting officer's decision, the subcontractor started a lawsuit in the state court. The subcontractor alleged that it was not required to follow the prime contract's administrative procedure since the prime contractor had breached the subcontract by failing to furnish uniform mullion openings.

Relying on these facts, the prime contractor filed a petition in the federal district court seeking to enjoin the subcontractor from continuing with its breach-of-contract action.

The specific merits of the subcontractor's breach-of-contract claim were not presented to the court for final decision. However, the court expressed the view that the subcontract was not breached since the subcontractor had contractually agreed to perform this type of work as an extra and to submit claims for extras to the architect for final decision. It was further noted that this dispute involved the government as well as the two contractors.

The court held that the subcontract had incorporated by reference that part of the prime contract which provided for the administrative appealing of the contracting officer's decision to the board. By accepting the prime contract's administrative appeal procedure, the subcontractor was bound to complete this procedure before pursuing other avenues of relief either defined in the contract or allowed by law, the court said.

CASE 18-2   Contractor Lost Right to Sue

The Supreme Court of Arizona has held that a subcontractor lost its right to sue for an alleged wrongful termination of contract because it admitted failing to make proper progress and acknowledged the general contractor's right to take over the work.

A highway construction subcontract was let without a specific date for commencement or completion. Initially the prime contractor told the subcontractor it could start work about October 1, but the subcontractor did not receive notice to begin until December 30. Another three weeks passed before work actually began.

When the subcontractor did start working, only two months remained before the completion date of the prime contract. The subcontractor said it could not complete the job within that time. The prime contractor then told the subcontractor that it was taking over the work and cited a subcontract provision: "If Subcontractor fails to prosecute the work required diligently or fails in any way to perform the conditions hereof . . . Contractor shall have the right . . . to take over all work [in subcontract] or any part thereof."

The prime offered a termination agreement to the subcontractor as an alternative to legal action it said it would take, if necessary, to acquire the work. The subcontractor signed the agreement which said, in effect, that the subcontractor, having failed to increase progress, agrees that the prime shall take over all work in the subcontract.

The subcontractor filed a wrongful termination suit after the prime completed the work under the subcontract. It charged that the prime did not comply with an agreement allowing the subcontractor four months to complete the job from the date it received notice to begin.

The question before the court was the interpretation of the termination agreement. The subcontractor argued its intent was not to forfeit any legal rights for breach relating to wrongful termination but that it only intended to mitigate its damages since it could not complete the work on time.

The court said there was no evidence that the subcontractor had signed the agreement under duress. And it concluded that by the agreement the subcontractor admitted to the conditions of the termination of the contract, namely the failure to make proper progress. The court said,

> by signing the agreement, acquiescing in the termination and, most significantly, permitting Vinnell [prime contractor] to complete the project, Skousen [subcontractor] cannot now nullify this conduct by claiming that he was not permitted four months time to finish the project. The two positions are inconsistent and the present

action is barred under the doctrine of waiver [*Vinnell Corp. v. State ex rel. Bob Skousen Contractor, Inc.,* 505 P.2d 547 (1973)].

CASE 18-3   Release Rules Out Nonexcepted Claims

The U.S. Court of Claims has ruled that existence of a valid and binding release rules out consideration of any contractor claims other than those listed as exceptions to the release [*Adler Const. Co. v. United States,* 423 F.2d 1362 (1970), *cert. denied,* 400 U.S. 993 (1971)].

The case arose during construction of a dam for the U.S. Department of Interior, Bureau of Land Reclamation. After completion of a substantial portion of the work, and in consideration of payment of certain sums, most of which was retainage, the contractor signed an official release form. The release provided, in part, that the contractor "remises, releases and forever discharges the United States of and from all manner of debts, dues, sum or sums of money, accounts, claims, and demands whatsoever, in law or in equity, under or by virtue of the said contract, except contract items and quantities as listed on the reverse side hereof."

In accordance with the terms of the release, the contractor listed thirteen specific exceptions. After submitting the release, the contractor sought recovery for claims not included in the list of exceptions.

The question presented by the appeal was whether the court has any right to review the contractor's claims omitted from the list of exceptions. The court indicated that the substantive merit of the claims was of no concern in determining its right to hear the claims. "No matter how meritorious may be the claims not excepted by a contractor from the operation of a full, valid release under a Government contract, they may not be judicially entertained later unless the release is found invalid or waived by subsequent conduct of the Government," the court said.

The court then took up the question of the release's validity. In denying the contractor's argument of alleged invalidity on grounds of economic duress, the court noted that the contractor had signed the release of its own free choice and that there was no evidence the government would have denied final payment had the contractor listed additional exceptions. . . .

"Irrespective of [the contractor's] dire financial predicament," the court said, "no conceivable economic coercion can invalidate a release where, as . . . here there is no evidence that [the contractor] was restricted in the scope of his exceptions to the release."

NINETEEN

Arbitration Versus Litigation

The pros and cons of arbitration versus formal court litigation create many opposing opinions and controversies. The pros and cons of arbitration have been the subject of many heated battles between construction attorneys. There is no one right answer. To make generalized statements can only lead to exceptions.

There is no unilateral right of choice whether one arbitrates or not. The right to arbitration is a contractual right and is strictly governed by the contractual and statutory arbitration provisions. Either an arbitration clause exists, or there is no right to arbitration. However, this statement must also be tempered in that some statutory regulations specify the procedural means for settlement of disputes, which might preclude or require arbitration (Case 19-1). If the parties do not have an arbitration provision in their contract, they can subsequently agree to arbitration, again subject to jurisdictional statutory limitations.

The fact that at the time of contract a party may have an initial choice in the means of resolution of disputes is an advantage unique to our legal system. Arbitration is looked upon with great favor by the courts, and the arbitration statutes and contract clauses are normally liberally construed to sanction and compel arbitration. However, the right to arbitration may be lost if the contractor fails to comply with statutory notice provisions. Recently, a contractor's arbitration claim was dismissed on the grounds that it failed to comply with statutory requirements that a notice of claim be presented within three months after accrual of the cause of action. The failure to comply with this condition resulted in the rejection of all claims, including the right to arbitration [*Board of Education v. Wager Constr. Corp.*, 333 N.E.2d 353 (N.Y. 1975)].

A contract required the general contractor to file its demand for arbitration within thirty days from the receipt of the written decision by the architect denying the claim, provided such decision indicated that the decision was "final but subject to appeal." The general contractor failed to file the demand for arbitration within thirty days after the architect had denied its claims; however, this claim denial did not indicate that the decision was "final but subject to appeal." After the contractor filed its demand for arbitration, the owner objected, claiming that arbitration had been waived. The court ruled that the language of the contract was clear and that the architect's decision was not in compliance with the contractual condition precedent to arbitration. The contractor's right to demand arbitration was not bound by the thirty-day period from the date the architect rendered its decision since the architect's decision failed to comply with the requirements of the contract as to "final but subject to appeal" format for compelling arbitration [*In re Niagara Mohawk Power Corp., Respondent, and Perfetto & Whalen Constr. Corp.,* 52 App. Div.2d 1081 (41) (4th Dept. 1976)].

The scope, effect, and enforcement rights of and to arbitration should be part of the arbitration clause and again may be subject to statutory pronouncement. Assuming that an arbitration clause exists, the right to arbitration is limited by the scope of the arbitration clause. If the arbitration clause solely relates to determination of prices on change orders, one party cannot require arbitration on delay claims. Most arbitration clauses now are broad in scope in order to include any and all claims, controversies, or disputes which might arise out of, or relate to, the contract or breach thereof. The parties often do not take advantage of the beauty of arbitration, namely that while they are negotiating the contract, the parties can specify, within certain broad limitations, what type of arbitration procedure they wish. It is normally within their power to say whether they want one, three, or even more, arbitrators. They can usually specify particular procedures or limitations they want to abide by.

The right to compel arbitration is bound by certain statutory limitations. Each state with an arbitration act has its own restrictions or interpretations of the law. Not all states have a modern arbitration act, although most do. Modern arbitration acts seem to cover a wide gamut of procedural topics. In addition to modern arbitration acts, other statutory provisions may exist. For states with arbitration statutes it can be generally stated that if there is an arbitration clause, and if one party commences a lawsuit in court instead of arbitration, the other party normally has the right to go into court, stay the proceedings, and compel the submission of the dispute to arbitration. In like fashion, it is normally provided by statute that if a party is seeking arbitration when there is no proper arbitration clause, the other party has the right to go into court, stay the arbitration, and compel court jurisdiction.

Arbitration procedures often become extremely time-consuming and cumbersome if the parties perform their own administration. For that reason, as well as the establishment of rules, reliance on the American Arbitration Association is highly recommended. The association has not only commercial arbitration rules but also construction industry rules. Although there is no great difference, the real benefit of the construction industry rules and procedures is that the list of arbitrators from whom the parties select are normally representatives of the construction industry. Not all states have an American Arbitration Association office, although the association will try to accommodate arbitrations not within the particular state of their office.

In that the right to arbitration is normally determined at the time of the contract, and not at the time of the eventual dispute, it is strongly recommended that the respective parties consider the pros and cons of arbitration for their given situation at the very outset, as they may not have any choice at the time of the dispute.

The following considerations are argumentative but should be reviewed by each party so that they can make their own initial decision. These paragraphs and positions reflect the author's collation of differing views of construction attorneys as well as the author's personal view after having spent many days in arbitration. It should be noted that the author is in favor of arbitration.

SPEED

It seems to be a consensus among arbitration attorneys on major construction claims that arbitration is not guaranteed to be any faster than formal litigation. In many instances, arbitration can, in fact, extend the final judgment date. On small matters arbitration probably does offer a means to a faster verdict. The larger matters are normally held up while various motions are made concerning whether arbitration is applicable or not, and the scope of the arbitrators' authority. Then comes the delay in the actual scheduling of arbitration dates, which can often be weeks, and finally come the legal motions and proceedings to compel and vacate the arbitration award. Arbitration on major claims, as against litigation, should not be determined solely by the belief that arbitration will substantially reduce the judgment day.

COSTS

Legal fees and other incidental costs for arbitration are not necessarily less than legal fees for formal litigation. In fact, in many instances arbitration costs are higher. It is true that litigation in most jurisdictions involves extensive pretrial discovery procedures, including depositions, interrogatories, bills of particulars, production of books and records, and other procedural steps which are not normally involved in arbitration. The reduction of these steps reduces counsel's time and possibly legal fees. However, these legal procedures are claimed to better acquaint attorneys and parties with the arguments of the respective sides and represent part of the time for the attorneys' preparation. Many attorneys oppose arbitration on the basis that they walk into arbitration without meaningful background knowledge and are then faced with a surprise. But many times it is believed that the parties already know the respective positions of each other and that these various legal maneuvers are procedural and not substantive concerns. Arbitration procedures normally involve the bare minimum of initial disclosure. However, substantial discretion is given to the arbitrators to direct disclosure.

It is the author's personal experience, as well as that of many arbitration attorneys, that actual witness preparation for arbitration is substantially more time-consuming than litigation preparation. In court the experienced trial attorney knows the rules and regulations before setting foot in the courtroom. In arbitration, since the rules are subject to total flexibility and nearly absolute discretion of the arbitrators, the properly prepared case requires preparation from every possible angle and the procedure of court is effectively nonexistent. There are obvious pros and cons to both positions. Many attorneys take the position that the procedural guidelines should be clearly established so that the ground rules are known to all before the game begins. On the other hand, many arbitration attorneys believe that since each arbitration is a totally separate matter, procedural rules for one case might have little or no application to another. They are willing to leave it up to their particular arbitrators' discretion. Therefore, since the preparation time for arbitration may substantially outweigh the preparation time for litigation and whereas the pretrial discovery time of litigation would outweigh the disclosure time for arbitration, the final effect seems to be a balancing of costs and time.

Other items of cost which must be given consideration are the fact that in arbitration a rather large fee may be required when the itemized claim is set forth. This fee might be thousands of dollars, whereas few courts require filing fees in excess of several hundred dollars. In addition, it is normal procedure for arbitrators to receive compensation for their time. If three arbitrators are sitting, even assuming they are not receiving any remuneration for the first two days of hearing, if the arbitration should go ten, twenty, or more days, the fee for the arbitrators, paid to and through the American Arbitration Association, could become substantial. Further costs which must be considered relate to the transcript. Often when an arbitration is to run several days or weeks over an extended time, transcripts are kept. Though transcripts are also kept in court, many times they are not ordered. The necessity for them in arbitration is different, since if the time between arbitrations is three or four weeks, the transcripts may be necessary to give continuity. This is normally left to the parties to determine.

EVIDENCE—PRESENTATION—APPEAL

The rules of evidence in arbitration are greatly relaxed, if not nonexistent. This creates a more open round-table procedure. However, many times the arbitrators can pursue trains of thought which have no bearing whatsoever, and there is no right to object. In court, the establishment of certain guidelines and rules of evidence keeps the testimony to the relevant issues; however, this might be overly restrictive.

Essentially, arbitration rulings are final and binding. Reasons for decisions are normally not required of the arbitrators (Case 19-2). If the arbitrator is wrong or gives a ruling based upon submitted evidence which might not be legally admissible, the decision is still final and binding. The arbitrator's primary obligation with regard to evidence is to receive all proper evidence. Insofar as many arbitrators are not legally educated and are unaware of what would be legally admissible evidence, normally whatever the evidence is, it is accepted for whatever it is worth. A bad decision has no right of appeal, whereas in court, there is normally a second place to go, the appellate court. In arbitration since there is no prior legal precedent or rule, the arbitrators have nearly unlimited discretion in applying various principles. This prohibits an attorney from advising a client properly about its legal rights, case law, and precedent. In a like fashion, many attorneys express the strong feeling that once they have an agreed upon contract, that is the contract they want to have interpreted. Whereas, in arbitration, again, the limitations of authority are usually unspecified, and often the specific contract language is not even referred to. Sometimes arbitrators might enforce clauses in a contract whereas in court the clauses might be dismissed or voided as being against public policy.

Most statutes indicate that the only way to overturn an arbitrator's award is by attacking the arbitrators. This attack is normally based upon an arbitrator's fraud, willful misconduct, undisclosed relationships, bias, or possibly other arbitrary and capricious acts.

An arbitration award has a presumption of validity, and the party attempting to reverse it on the basis of fraud must sustain its burden by clear allegations and proof of such misconduct [*Mork & Associates, Inc. v. Jackson,* 231 N.W.2d 303 (Minn. S. Ct. 1975)].

Courts attempt to foster the concept of impartial arbitration. Once the impartiality is lost, the arbitration is subject to being declared invalid (Case 19-3). Courts have held, even where the decision possibly seems to be against existing case law, that this is not a sufficient reason for overturning an arbitration, as arbitration is normally not bound by the law. The few instances where awards have been overturned are when arbitrators have stated what they believe to be the law, have set forth the wrong law, and then have applied that law. When the stated law is, in fact, wrong, the courts will possibly take a look at the decision. The other major area for overturning an arbitration is if the arbitrators have exceeded the scope of their authority. This goes back to the original question of what the arbitration agreements specify and what powers the parties granted to the arbitrators. The result is that the right to appeal in arbitration is less than those rights in court.

Another basis for overturning an arbitration award is if there is a palpable mistake of fact.

> It is well settled that while an award may be set aside for a palpable mistake of fact in the nature of a clerical error, such as a miscalculation of figures, still, in general,

such mistake to be available must appear on the face of the award or in some paper delivered with it [*Sweet v. Morrison,* 116 N.Y. 19 (1889)].

An arbitrator's decision granting the contractor relief was not properly vacated and dismissed since the award did not evidence any mistake on its face. Without clear mistake on its face, the award should be affirmed. In reaching its decision, the court held:

> The general rule is that arbitrators, when acting under the authority granted them by the contract between the parties, become the judges of both the law, and the facts. Unless the award on its face shows the adoption of an erroneous rule or mistake in applying the law, the trial court should not vacate or modify the award [*Moen v. State,* 533 P.2d 862 (Wash. App. 1975)].

The courts do not like to look behind the award to determine whether mistakes have been made. They believe that this would be infringing upon the arbitration right and would undermine the very purpose of arbitration.

In a nonconstruction case, the highest court of the State of New York has ruled that in an arbitration proceeding the arbitrator has no power to award punitive damages. The court stated:

> An arbitrator has no power to award punitive damages, even if agreed upon by the parties. . . . Punitive damages is a sanction reserved to the State, a public policy of such magnitude as to call for a judicial intrusion to prevent its contravention. Since enforcement of an award of punitive damages as purely private remedy would violate strong public policy, an arbitrator's award which imposes punitive damages should be vacated [*Garrity v. Lyle Stuart, Inc.,* 40 N.Y.2d 354 (1976)].

WAIVER

The right to arbitration can be waived and must be carefully watched (Cases 19-4 and 19-5). The commencement of a legal action might be deemed a waiver of the right to arbitration, and it would preclude that party from asserting its right to arbitration. It is then up to the other party to determine whether it wishes to force the matter back into arbitration or take part in the legal proceedings and thereby waive its rights. The involvement of the defendant in legal proceedings might be deemed waiver of arbitration, and thereby both parties will have been deemed to have waived their rights.

It is up to the party who wants arbitration to seek it. It has the initial burden of going forward and seeking its enforcement. However, the party who is seeking arbitration should be aware that the arbitration will not bind parties who are not parties to that arbitration. Therefore, a subcontractor's arbitration against a general contractor may have no effect on the general contractor's surety company because the company is not a party to the arbitration agreement. There is great controversy over the question of triparty arbitration. If a subcontractor should sue a prime contractor for a change which originally emanated from the owner and the general contractor then commences an arbitration against the owner for that exact change, many states will not force the two arbitrations to be held together and therefore one arbitration will have no effect on the other. The question of common rights and facts, or the consolidation of arbitrations, is a major area of concern, and before an arbitration is commenced the parties should consider whether a third party's interests will be involved. The jurisdictions appear to be split on the question of court-directed consolidated arbitration.

As an attorney in favor of arbitration, the author is the first to indicate that on major arbitrations, arbitration is no faster, no cheaper, and no easier than court litigation. The arbitrators may avoid legal precedent and the contract documents and have wider discretion and greater powers than most trial judges. The real question is whether the client will gain greater justice from three arbitrators who are knowledgeable in the field relating to the scope of the arbitration or whether the judge, who probably is not familiar with the construction industry but who would interpret a specific provision of a given contract according to prescribed precedent and procedures, would be better. The choice is not an easy one, and it depends upon the facts and circumstances of each particular case. Carefully review your rights, if the choice is yours, before making a decision between arbitration and litigation. Before engaging in either, negotiation should be fully explored.

CASE 19-1 Arbitration Law Enforced
as Part of Public Contract

The Rhode Island Supreme Court ruled that although a public contract had no arbitration clause, an owner was compelled to arbitrate a dispute because a state statute governing public contracts required arbitration [*Sterling Engineering & Constr. Co., Inc. v. Town of Burrillville Housing Authority*, 279 A.2d 445 (1971)].

A contractor was awarded work on a housing project for the elderly under a public contract that provided the contractor be given the site free from prior tenants. The housing authority was unable to evict a property owner, and construction began with part of the site occupied.

The contractor claimed that the housing authority hindered its performance and demanded arbitration of the dispute. The authority claimed arbitration was improper since the contract did not contain an arbitration clause.

The contractor then pointed out that a state statute existed that made arbitration compulsory on public contracts.

The court, noting the wording of the statute, held that "the legislative mandate cannot be ignored" and that it "is included as a matter of law within the terms of the . . . contract."

CASE 19-2 Arbitration Awards Need Not
Go Beyond Bare Essentials

An arbitration award that answers the question submitted cannot be challenged because it does not contain the arbitrator's reasoning, the Supreme Court of Connecticut has ruled [*Gary Excavating Co. v. Town of North Haven*, 279 A.2d 543 (1971)].

The case grew out of a dispute over allegedly undisclosed subsoil conditions encountered by a contractor on sanitary sewer laterals for the town of North Haven, Connecticut. The dispute went to arbitration. The award was in favor of the contractor. The town appealed, claiming that the award was not sufficiently definite and final.

In upholding the award, the court said, "The arbitrators are only required to render an award in conformity to the submission and an award need contain no more than the actual decision. . . . The means by which they reach the award, unless the submission requires, is needless and superfluous."

CASE 19-3   Lack of Impartiality Voids Arbitration Award

The U.S. Supreme Court has held that if an arbitrator fails to disclose fully his relationship with one of the arbitrating parties, the arbitration decision must be set aside [*Commonwealth Coatings Corp. v. Continental Casualty Co.,* 89 Sup. Ct. 337 (1968), *rehearing denied.* 89 Sup. Ct. 848 (1969)].

A painting subcontractor had claimed that it was entitled to be paid for performing certain painting work. The subcontract provided that disputes of this type must be submitted to arbitration.

Three arbitrators were to be selected, one by the subcontractor and the prime contractor and a neutral arbitrator by the first two arbitrators.

After the arbitration ended and the arbitrators had unanimously denied the subcontractor's claim, the subcontractor learned for the first time that the neutral arbitrator was an engineering consultant who had rendered services to the prime contractor on numerous construction projects, including the construction project from which the subcontractor's claim arose. The relationship with the prime contractor was sporadic, and no dealings had occurred for at least one year before the arbitration.

Prior to that time the arbitrator had received fees amounting to about $12,000 from the prime contractor over a five-year period.

The subcontractor did not claim that the arbitrator was in any way guilty of fraud or bias in reaching his conclusion in the arbitration. The subcontractor argued that the mere failure to disclose this business relationship by either the arbitrator or the prime contractor was grounds for setting the arbitration aside.

The court first noted that the law governing its decision was the U.S. Arbitration Act, 9 U.S.C. § § 1-15. The court then stated that § 10 of this law authorizes setting aside an award "where it was procured by corruption, fraud or undue means or where there was evident partiality in the arbitrators. These provisions show a desire of Congress to provide not merely for any arbitration but for an impartial one."

In vacating the arbitration decision because of the undisclosed pecuniary interest and past business relationship of the third arbitrator with the prime contractor, the court concluded: "We can perceive no way in which the effectiveness of the arbitration process will be hampered by the simple requirement that arbitrators disclose to the parties any dealings that might create an impression of possible bias."

CASE 19-4   Contractor Waived Right to Arbitration by Its Actions

A contractor is deemed to have waived the right to arbitration when it failed to stop an owner's lawsuit and defended its position in court, the U.S. Court of Appeals for the Fifth Circuit has ruled [*Burton-Dixie Corp. v. Timothy McCarthy Constr. Co.,* 436 F.2d 405 (5th Cir. 1971)].

The case involved a building contract. The standard American Institute of Architects contract form was used. The contract clause relating to faulty workmanship provided that "all questions arising under this article shall be decided by the Architect subject to arbitration." The contract also stated that "the decision of the arbitrators shall be a condition precedent to any right of legal action."

About a year after the building was completed, the roof blistered. The contractor tried to repair it over a period of time. Eventually, the owner asked that the roof be removed and replaced. The contractor denied liability and refused. The owner hired another contractor and sued for the cost of replacement.

The contractor claimed the owner was barred from suing as a matter of law because it had failed to arbitrate the dispute. The owner claimed the contractor had waived its right to arbitration by not demanding it sooner.

The court noted that the contractor had not denied liability before the demand that the roof be replaced, had not demanded arbitration, and had let the case go to litigation. The contractor accordingly had waived its right to arbitration, the court ruled.

CASE 19-5   Owner Can Demand Arbitration after Contractor Files Lien

The Supreme Court of Nevada has ruled that an owner retains the right to demand arbitration even after a contractor has sued to settle a dispute [*Lane-Tahoe, Inc., v. Kindred Constr. Co.,* 536 P.2d 491 (1975)].

An owner let a number of site-preparation and construction contracts for a condominium project in Nevada. All the contracts contained arbitration clauses, providing "All claims, disputes and other matters in question arising out of, or relating to, this contract or the breach thereof . . . shall be decided by arbitration." The clauses further stated that "the demand for arbitration shall be made . . . within a reasonable time after the claim, dispute or other matter in question has arisen. . . ."

However, when disputes did arise, the contractors ignored these provisions and filed liens against the project. At this point, the owner went to court to stay the legal proceedings and to compel the contractors to submit their disputes to arbitration.

In court, the contractors argued that the owner had waived its right to arbitration by failing to exercise it until after they had filed their liens. They also claimed that the owner had not filed its demands in writing within a reasonable amount of time.

Noting that the contractors had not tried to arbitrate their disputes before bringing suit against the owner, the court said state law favors the use of arbitration when it is provided for in a contract.

Rejecting the contractors' argument that the owner had failed to demand arbitration within a reasonable time, the court said the burden of demanding arbitration was theirs, not the owner's.

"Absent express language in the contract placing the initial burden on either party, that responsibility [to demand arbitration] rests with the party seeking relief," the court said. "We hold only that the burden to initiate arbitration is upon the party seeking relief and does not shift to the opponent absent a clear waiver of arbitration by the opponent."

The court concluded that nothing in the record of the case indicated that the owner had waived arbitration. It added that "the passage of time after the disputes arose, without more, does not point to a waiver of the arbitration provisions."

As a result, the court prohibited the contractors from continuing their legal actions against the owner and ordered them to arbitrate their disputes.

TWENTY

Mechanic's Lien

The rights, limitations, scope, procedure, and nearly all other considerations regarding mechanic's liens are set forth in the statutes. The mechanic's lien, so far as the construction industry is concerned, is a creation of statute. No general statement can be made regarding mechanic's liens, other than making it perfectly clear that every state is different. There may be different rules and procedures governing private contracts and public contracts. There may be different procedures and statutory provisions relating to whether the official contract has to be, or should have been, filed of record or not. This chapter can do no more than discuss a few points.

Most mechanic's-lien statutes define who has the right to file such a lien. This right normally applies to contractors and subcontractors, and suppliers and materialmen of the owner and prime contractors. The suppliers and materialmen of subcontractors and of other suppliers and materialmen, however, become questionable parties and often have no right to file liens (Case 20-1). With each change in position, different procedures may apply. No right or procedure can be assumed.

The question of when the lien must be filed has many variations. In some jurisdictions the party seeking the protection of the mechanic's-lien law must file its notice of intention to file a mechanic's lien before performing the work. The mechanic's lien may attach only on the work *to be performed*. In other jurisdictions the mechanic's lien is filed within a prescribed period after the work is performed and applies only to work *already performed*. In New York, for example, a notice of intention to file a mechanic's lien must be filed within four months from the last date on which the lienor furnished materials or labor. However, this relates only to a private lien. On a public lien the New York statutes provide that the lien must be filed within thirty days of the completion of the project. This might be substantially beyond the four-month period allowed in the private lien, or it might be less. The determination of the last date on which work, labor, or services were performed can become a major dispute in litigation. It seems that the performance of corrective work is distinguished from that of extra work or completion of unperformed work.

For private liens, it generally appears that the lien attaches to the property and/or the existing funds. Public liens are basically restricted to attaching to the existing funds and not to the physical property, the rationale simply being discomfort at the idea of the local subcontractor's ending up owning the local police station after a foreclosure action. The enforceability of each lien is again a creature of statute. The lienor usually has to notify those persons it wishes to have bound by the lien after the lien has been properly docketed according to the applicable statute. Apparently most jurisdictions do not require a party who acts in good faith and who paid once without any knowledge of the lien to pay a second time. However, once the lien has become of record and properly noticed to that party, seemingly that party would be acting at its own risk by paying proceeds to the liened party.

The duration of the lien is still another detail that cannot be taken for granted. Most statutes provide when and how a lien is to be renewed and state that it must be renewed in order to continue. This period varies from state to state, and even within a given state for public or private liens. Whether a party has a right to waive its right to file a mechanic's lien by contract again depends upon the particular jurisdiction involved (Case 20-2). Although some jurisdictions have been faced with the question whether such a clause would be against public policy, other jurisdictions have specifically provided, by statute, the means by which the right to waive a mechanic's lien can be accomplished. Some states specifically provide by statute that it is illegal to require the waiver of mechanic's liens.

The laws relating to mechanic's liens require a complete treatise for each state. In addition, various states have other related statutes. Some states place statutory limitations on the use of the money received for a given project. This might come under embezzlement statutes or under some form of trust-fund theory. The trust-fund concept, again as exemplified by New York, places great restriction on the use of the money, on the records required to be kept relating to those funds, and on the right of beneficiaries of the trust to review and inspect the trust records and stipulates the penalties for diversion of trust assets.

The right to a mechanic's lien on federal projects is statutorily prohibited. The Miller Act specifically provides the procedure to be followed by would-be lienors on federal projects. In essence, the Miller Act mandates that the contractor furnish labor and material payment bonds for its subcontractors' and suppliers' benefit. It is only the prime contractor who is totally precluded of rights, other than reliance on the stability of the federal government.

It is strongly recommended that the contractor ascertain the extent of the lien law in the state in which it is to perform the work and in which the project is located before work starts. After that it may well be too late to look to the law for protection.

CASE 20-1   Supplier's Lien Denied

The leasor of equipment and drivers to a supplier of the prime contractor on a New York state highway project was not entitled to file a lien against the prime contractor because the supplier was a materialman and not a subcontractor, a New York court has ruled [*A & J Buyers, Inc. v. Johnson, Drake & Piper, Inc.,* 25 N.Y.2d 265 (1969)].

The prime contractor had issued several purchase orders to a supplier for delivery of stone and gravel to the jobsite. The material was needed for construction of the roadbed and also as backfill. Since the supplier did not have sufficient equipment to deliver the material, it leased equipment and drivers from the plaintiff. The plaintiff, not having been fully paid by the supplier, sued the prime contractor and its surety pursuant to the New York Lien Law.

The question on appeal to the New York Court of Appeals was whether the plaintiff had the right to file its claim under the Lien Law. Section 5 of the law states, "A person performing labor for or furnishing materials to a contractor, his subcontractor, or legal representative, for the construction . . . of a public improvement pursuant to a contract by such contractor with the state . . . shall have a lien. . . ."

There was no question that the prime contractor's supplier would have a valid lien if monies were due and owing because it furnished materials directly to the prime contractor. Since the plaintiff, however, had no direct contract with the prime contractor, the validity of its lien depended upon proving that the supplier was, in fact, the prime contractor's subcontractor and not a materialman. Under New York law, the plaintiff would have no right to a lien if it merely leased equipment to a prime contractor's materialman.

The law defines a subcontractor as "a person who enters into a contract with a contractor and/or with a subcontractor for the improvement of such real property or such public improvement or with a person who has contracted with or through such contractor for the performance of his contract or any part thereof." A materialman is defined as "any person who furnishes material or the use of machinery, tools, or equipment . . . either to an owner, contractor or subcontractor."

In determining whether the supplier was a subcontractor or a materialman, the court first noted that most of the material delivered to the site was merely dumped in piles. In delivering the remaining material, the truck was driven onto the roadbed being constructed, the truck body was tilted, and the tailgate was partially opened. The truck then proceeded slowly, unloading and spreading controlled amounts of material onto the right-of-way. On the basis of this controlled spreading, the plaintiff alleged that the supplier was more than just a materialman.

The court, however, denied the plaintiff the right to file a lien by determining that the supplier was a materialman and not a subcontractor. It stated, "Something more than the mere furnishing of materials which happen to become part of the permanent improvement must have been contemplated by the Legislature in order to achieve subcontractor status."

There was no evidence indicating that the supplier did any work away from the site that would classify it as a subcontractor, the court said. The supplier merely loaded and delivered material. The fact that it was required to deliver material that met the state's standard specification did not change its status. As for the controlled dumping, the court found that this did not constitute performing labor on the jobsite. This was merely a standard method of delivering material.

CASE 20-2   Mechanic's-Lien Waiver Legal, Not Contrary to Public Policy

A Maryland Court of Appeals has ruled that a provision in a subcontract specifically waiving the subcontractor's right to file a mechanic's lien was valid, and not contrary to public policy [*Port City Constr. Co. v. Adams & Douglass, Inc.*, 273 A.2d 121 (1971)].

One of the provisions on the face of the subcontract form in question stated: "This Subcontract is subject to and includes the terms and conditions set forth on the other side of this page." A condition on the reverse side provided that: "Subcontractor hereby expressly waives the right to file any lien or claim against the property of the Owner or Contractor or Contractor's payment bond, if any, or against money due Contractor under the Prime Contract."

The subcontractor argued that to be enforceable this waiver of a lien provision must be clear and unambiguous. The court agreed, but after reviewing the waiver provision determined that it was, "plain, clear and unambiguous," and therefore, enforceable. In addition, the court stated, "There is no public policy against the waiver of the right to file a mechanic's lien. . . ."

Although the subcontractor's right to file a mechanic's lien was denied, the subcontractor's right to sue for the money allegedly due it still existed.

TWENTY-ONE

Surety Law

Surety law is a separate and vast area of law, rules, and exceptions directly related to the construction professions. This chapter will touch on some common disputed and litigated areas. It must be remembered that most surety obligations are direct contractual obligations, and the rights, obligations, and restrictions are normally found in the specific bond. The concept of suretyship is a security against a loss, whereby the surety undertakes to guarantee the fulfillment of the obligations of another. Since the surety company comes in to stand in the shoes of another, the courts have traditionally said that the person who is seeking to take advantage of the surety company's performance must comply strictly with the surety agreement and bond limitations. However, this has resulted in the agreements becoming over restrictive and a law of technical defenses. This strict technical-defensive area of the law has been changing, some modern liberal decisions denying technical defenses and holding surety companies liable. The trend is

> under modern American surety law, a mere technical breach of a surety contract, not resulting in damage or prejudice to the surety, will not release it from its obligations [*Winston Corp. v. Continental Casualty Co.*, 508 F.2d 1298 (6th Cir. 1975)].

The three major bonds in the construction industry are the bid bond, the performance bond, and the payment bond (sometimes called a labor and material bond). The bid bond usually accompanies the contractor's bid to guarantee that it will accept and perform the contract. The surety company is liable up to the face amount of the bond. The bid-bonds penal amounts vary in the normal range of 5 to 15 percent, but the contractor cannot automatically assume that that is the total extent of its liability if it refuses to accept the contract. The contractor's liability is technically the difference in price between its bid and the next lowest proper bid. This may be substantially more than the penal amount of the bond. The contractor may be liable under an indemnification agreement to the surety company when the bond is forfeited, but also for the difference above that amount to the bid of the next bidder. It is strongly recommended that the bid documents be reviewed carefully. Many bid documents are written in which the total liquidated damage and liability of the contractor are the amount of the bid bond. This would seem to limit the liability to that specific amount. Other contract bid documents have been written whereby the bid bond is basically a guarantee that the performance bond will be supplied, or is nothing more than a partial guarantee of the total damages the contractor would otherwise be liable for. The contractor should carefully review the bid documents and see that its bid bond conforms to the bid requirements. Otherwise, the contractor may be giving more than required; if it gives less, it may become nonresponsive.

The performance bond is written for the owner's protection. In many cases subcontractors are required to have performance bonds, which are for the contractor's protection (Case 21-1). The bonding of subcontractors can often result in the prime contractor's having a higher bonding capacity. In essence, subject to variations, the performance bond tells the owner that if the contractor should default the surety company will either (1) complete, (2) obtain another to complete, or (3) pay for the cost of completion. The owner is warned that its right to call on the surety to complete is filled with technicalities. Most bonds require that the contractor first be held formally in default, and there can be substantial battles between the contractor and owner over the propriety of the termination. Most surety companies will back the contractor in these fights. In addition, before the owner can go out and complete the work itself, many bonds require the owner to give the surety company the right or option to complete. Although the purpose of the performance bond is different from that of the payment bond, in a recent decision a court held that the performance bond, which called for completion of the prime contract and proper payment of subcontractors, could be used by the subcontractors (Case 21-2). Thus, the performance-bond surety became liable for payment to subcontractors and suppliers.

The payment, or labor and material, bond is written so that the subcontractor is the beneficiary of the bond; if the prime contractor does not pay, if the conditions of the bond are satisfied, the surety company will pay. Depending upon the bond or the statutory provisions governing it, there are questions about how far down the line the bond will apply. It normally applies to the subcontractors and suppliers to the principal (prime contractor), but the real question is whether it applies to the second-tier subcontractors, or to the suppliers and materialmen of the subcontractor, or to the suppliers of the suppliers. Case law relies on the wording of the particular bond. Under the Miller Act payment bond, the materialmen of the materialmen do not have protection.

Depending upon the wording of the payment bond, there is a major question about what the payment bond covers. It normally encompasses the labor and materials furnished. The word "furnished"may or may not involve items manufactured but not supplied. It generally appears that these bonds do not include lost anticipated profit on unperformed work or legal fees (Case 21-3). They do not include unexpended items. Most cases to date have refused to apply the bond to delay claims, but under the recent trend of enlarging liability, the surety companies are being held liable for increased costs, material increases, extended loss-of-efficiency costs, and other direct out-of-pocket costs which are part of delay claims (Case 21-4). Thus, what is happening appears to be that surety companies are becoming liable for far in excess of the contract price for a given portion of the work, although still within the penal amount of the bond. Questions are being raised in court about what happens and whether the surety pays if the subcontractor has to *redo* work due to theft or vandalism. After all, although the work was put in twice, it was labor and materials furnished and installed in the project. The contractor should seriously consider the possibility of requiring the owner to earmark construction funds in escrow accounts or furnish payment bonds for its benefit, especially if the contractor is required to furnish a performance bond.

The payment bond presents another legal and factual problem. Under most bonds, even though the principal contractor under the payment bond has paid the subcontractor once, the principal may still be liable a second time if the subcontractor has not paid its suppliers or subcontractors. This results in a dual liability and payment. For this reason many contractors require their subcontractor to furnish affidavits and other data and security assuring the contractor that the subcontractor's subcontractors and suppliers have been paid to date before making further payment. This could become a cumbersome procedure; however, the contractor must give consideration to potential double liability. This can be done by requiring an accounting of the books every month, personal indemnification from the principals of the subcontractor, or possibly some type of surety obligation from the subcontractor to the contractor.

The beneficiaries of the bond must be specifically forewarned that the liability of the surety company depends upon the terms of the bond. In many cases the beneficiary of the bonds must give required notice of claim to the surety within a specified period of time (Case 21-5), but giving notice may not be the only requirement. Most bonds have a short statute of limitations. This necessitates instituting legal procedures by filing formal litigation, usually not arbitration, within a specified time period or in a specified jurisdiction. The Miller Act calls for a one-year limitation period. "The payment bond is an independent contract which is enforceable according to its own provisions." Thus, a party seeking to enforce the provisions of the bond must abide by the terms of the bond. In a lawsuit commenced against the surety company who provided a payment bond for the general contractor, the court held that the payment-bond provision which required the lawsuit to be commenced in the jurisdiction in which the project is located was reasonable.

Forum-selection clauses have historically not been favored by American courts. Many courts, federal and state, have declined to enforce such clauses on the ground that they were "contrary to public policy," or that their effect was to "oust the jurisdiction" of the court. . . .The modern trend, however, is to give effect to such clauses where the forum chosen is reasonable [*St. Paul Fire and Marine Insurance Co. v. Travelers Indemnity Co.* 401 F. Supp. 927 (D. Mass. 1975)].

In that there are so many restrictions and limitations on coverage, the party who believes it has a right under a bond better be sure that it has a copy of the bond in its possession at the very beginning of work. It is often nearly impossible to find out who has a copy of the executed bond when one wishes to put in a claim. It is much more readily available before the actual contract is signed, and a formally executed copy should, if possible, be incorporated as a part of the contract.

CASE 21-1   Surety Liable on Bond Even after Limitations Date

A surety company was liable on a subcontractor's performance bond even though a claim was filed after the statute of limitations appeared to have expired because the limitations period had not become effective, held the Supreme Court of New York [*Stanley R. Benjamin, Inc., v. Fidelity Casualty Co. of New York,* 72 Misc.2d 742 (1972)].

A subcontractor had furnished a performance bond to the general contractor to insure against loss caused by the subcontractor's faulty performance. The subcontractor abandoned the contract in October 1966, and in October 1972, the prime contractor began proceedings against the surety.

The performance bond provided that "any suit under this bond must be instituted before the expiration of two years from the date on which final payment under the subcontract falls due." The surety argued that the contractor's action was late and improper.

But the court held the action was proper. It said that final payment never became due because the subcontractor never completed its work under the subcontract. Therefore, the court said, there was no date from which the two-year period of limitations could be measured.

CASE 21-2   Owner's Performance Bond May Permit Subcontractor Recovery

The Superior Court of New Jersey, Appellate Division, has ruled that a performance bond issued to a general contractor for the protection of the owner may be used to pay a subcontractor [*Amelco Window Corp. v. Federal Insurance Co.,* 317 A.2d 398 (1974)].

A prime contract for a university project provided that the owner could require the general contractor "to furnish bonds covering the faithful performance of the Contract and the payment of all obligations. . . ." Although the contract further stated that the contractor would pay for all labor, materials and tools, the owner only required the posting of a performance bond.

The bond, obtained from a surety company, was issued "in accordance with the terms and conditions of said [prime] contract," which were incorporated in the agreement.

After entering into several subcontracts, the general contractor went bankrupt.

The question before the court was whether the subcontractor could sue the surety company for payment of its unpaid claims even though the bond contained no express provisions for payment of any subcontractor claims.

Noting that this was a case of first impression, the court said that the rights of the subcontractor were dependent upon the contractual relationship that existed in the surety agreement. If the bond promised "either in express words or by reasonable implication" to pay the subcontractor, it would be a beneficiary to the surety agreement.

Stressing that the wording of the bond did not expressly exclude subcontractors from its coverage, the court stated "the surety bond incorporates the prime construction contract by reference, the two being integrated must be considered together."

The court concluded that the bond was conditioned on the full performance of the contract and so the subcontractor was permitted to sue the surety company for its claims.

CASE 21-3   Miller Act Surety Not Liable for Subcontractor's Legal Bill

A federal court has ruled that a subcontractor who had furnished labor and material for work on a federal project in Texas cannot recover his attorneys' fees from the prime contractor's Miller Act surety [*Transamerica Insurance Co. v. Red Top Metal, Inc.*, 384 F.2d 752 (5th Cir, 1967)].

In reversing a lower court decision, the U.S. Court of Appeals applied federal law, departing from the usual line of decisions that have applied the law of the state where the federal project was located to determine the subcontractor's rights.

The case involved a situation where the subcontractor sued the surety after the general contractor refused to pay the subcontractor for various delays and extras.

The subcontractor's claims had all been settled before the appeal except for attorneys' fees.

In reaching its decision, the court noted that a subcontractor suing on a Miller Act bond is denied the right to sue in a state court and must seek relief in the federal district court where the federal project is located. The court said it was not faced with the problem of construing the construction contracts, but with interpretation of a federal law (Miller Act) and of the bond issued in compliance with that law. For this reason, the court explained, the dispute must be governed by federal law if such law is found to exist.

The court found that no federal law presently exists on this point and incorporated Texas state law as part of the federal law.

Under the terms of Texas law, the subcontractor lost its action for attorneys' fees because the materials were not delivered to the surety. Though Texas law permits recovery in certain instances, no recovery is allowed against a surety unless the suretyship documents are obviously worded to allow recovery. The judgment of the lower court was accordingly reversed.

The fact that the court looked to federal law for the guiding principle is important. In recent years there has been quite a lot of discussion about the need for federal legislation to allow recovery of attorneys' fees in Miller Act cases.

CASE 21-4   Miller Act Bond Covers Delay-Claim Costs

A U.S. district court in Washington, D.C., has allowed a subcontractor to recover on a prime contractor's Miller Act bond for additional labor and material costs the subcontractor claimed were caused by extensive delays.

A dispute between the General Services Administration and its general contractor delayed construction of the Joseph H. Hirshhorn Museum in Washington, D.C., for nineteen months. When work resumed, the subcontractor found that its labor, material, and administrative costs had increased substantially. To recover these extra costs, the subcontractor sued the general contractor's surety company, claiming that these costs should be paid under the contractor's Miller Act bond.

The Miller Act requires contractors on federal projects to put up a surety bond to guarantee payment to all persons supplying labor and material to the contractor. Congress passed this law to protect subcontractors and suppliers because lien rights do not exist on federal projects.

In court, the surety argued that it was not liable for these additional costs because its bond stated: "If the . . . [general contractor] . . . shall promptly make payment to all persons supplying labor and material in the prosecution of the work provided for in said contract, and any and all duly authorized modifications of said contract that may hereafter be made . . . then the above obligation . . . shall be void and of no effect."

Because the subcontractor had already been paid its full subcontract price, it could not recover on the bond, the surety claimed.

The court said that the real issue in the case was whether the delayed costs were expenses for labor and material under the Miller Act.

Finding that the additional costs were actually out-of-pocket expenses, the court said that "the Miller Act surety is liable to a subcontractor for increased costs actually incurred due to delay for labor and material, to the extent that such delay is not attributable to the subcontractor." To rule otherwise, the court said, would place the contractor in the position that Congress was trying to avoid when it passed the Miller Act.

> The proper test under the Miller Act is whether the claim for relief is based on actual expenditures for labor or materials utilized in the performance of the subcontract [the court continued. The subcontractor's] cause of action is not defeated by such technical exercises as analyzing whether the claim arose within or without the contract or by determining if the added costs were indispensable to the satisfactory

contractual performance [*United States of America ex rel. Leonardo Mariana v. Piracci Constr. Co., Inc.,* 405 F. Supp. 904 (D.C. 1975)].

CASE 21-5   Filing of Miller Act Claim
Held to Be Timely

A materialman's notice to the general contractor of a Miller Act claim over ninety days after inspection, acceptance, and possession of the premises by the government was valid because material required by the contract was furnished after possession, a federal court has ruled [*United States of America ex rel. Noland Company v. Andrews,* 406 F.2d 790 (4th Cir. 1969)].

In this case, a materialman sued both the general contractor and its surety under the Miller Act for the unpaid balance on an open account for materials supplied to one of the subcontractors. Under the Miller Act the materialman may hold the general contract liable for its subcontractor's debts provided written notice is given to the general contractor within ninety days "from the date on which such person [materialman] . . . supplied the last of the material for which such claim is made. . . ."

The general contractor claimed that the materialman's action must be dismissed since notice was not given within the required ninety days. It argued, with respect to the work for which the materialman had supplied materials, that the government had performed a final inspection, accepted the work on correction of deficiencies, and taken possession of the premises more than ninety days before the materialman gave any notice of its claim.

However, the U.S. Court of Appeals found that after possession by the government, the subcontractor visited the site and while there noticed that two required valves had been omitted from the work. There was no question but that the valves were part of the original contract requirements. The government directed the installation of the valves.

Within ninety days after furnishing the two valves but well over ninety days after the government took possession, the materialman notified the general contractor that it was looking to it for payment of the entire unpaid balance owed by the subcontractor. The court had to determine on what date the ninety-day period started to run.

The general contractor argued that furnishing the additional valves was not done in the prosecution of the contract work but was a mere correction of a defect which did not extend the time for giving notice. The materialman replied that the valves were part of the original contract and that the work was not finished until the valves were installed. The fact that the general contractor, owner, and others might have erroneously thought the work was finished was of no importance, it said.

The court noted that the legal principles presented by both parties were correct in that the mere correcting of defects does not extend the ninety-day notice period. However, on these facts, the court held,

> It seems plain to us that the installation of the two missing valves cannot be characterized as a mere correction of a defect. The fact that the valves were called for by

both the primary contract and the subcontract and were not furnished . . . is dispositive of the issue, notwithstanding the Government's acceptance of the premises at an earlier date under the mistaken impression that the work had been completed.

The court concluded that the contract was not completed until the valves were installed and that notice by the materialman within ninety days from the furnishing of the valves was proper.

TWENTY-TWO

Damages

Being legally right is only the beginning. Proving that you are right is the second problem. The third and equally important step is being able to prove your damages. Liability and damages are separate and distinct items. Damages without liability theoretically lead to a loss. Liability without provable damages results in a paper victory, which more often than not amounts to a loss. The idea that a damaged party is entitled to recover whatever it claims or even whatever it knows it lost is a mistaken belief. Construction contracts and claims require *proof* of damages and *proof* of a specific dollar and cents loss.

If you cannot substantiate your damages and tie the specific damage to the specific default, you will often have a futile, expensive litigation (Case 22-1). Construction-contract damages do not include pain and suffering compensation. Construction contracts relate to nuts and bolts and the cost of each. Unless the contractor is prepared and able to prove the cost of each item of damage by facts and evidence, the chances of being a winner are slim.

The most accepted method, and often the only approved one, for computing damages is by clear and convincing proof of what specific damages were incurred by that particular default. Each breach requires separate proof of specific damages. You must substantiate each dollar. The mere cry of the contractor, whether founded or unfounded, that but for the other's default it would not have lost money on this contract falls on deaf judiciary ears. The mere allegation that one anticipated the contract to cost x dollars, that the defaulting party caused it damages, that the total cost of the contract was $2x$ and therefore it seeks the difference of x dollars is seldom accepted by the courts. This is called the *total-cost method.*

The total-cost approach to damages is not looked upon with favor by the courts. This approach has led to successful recovery in court only where the contractor is able to prove its original anticipated cost for the work, that the anticipated cost was reasonable, that the sole cause for the increased cost in the performance of the work was the other party, who committed a default, that the total cost was y dollars, and therefore the total difference between actual costs and anticipated costs are the claimed damages. The total-cost approach fails to pinpoint damages on a given day or show that each specific damage was the result of each specific individualized default. The total-cost approach lumps together as a single item (or into categories) the damages or the defaults or both and seeks the difference in cost. This approach has, on occasion, been successful but more often leads to defeat.

When the total-cost approach is successful, the court normally requires the contractor's substantiation, by clear proof, that it was not in any way the cause of the default; that it was not in any way the cause for increasing the costs; and that it cannot in any reasonable way prove the actual specific damages arising from the specific default.

A court indicated that the use of the total-cost approach can be justified by circumstances in particular cases when, as a practical matter, the court could find that no other method was feasible, the supporting evidence was fully documented, the damages were incurred, and

> no excess charges were run up by Moorhead [contractor] and that its bid was more realistic than the estimate prepared by the City's own engineer. The contractor was obviously confronted with a situation not of its own making, but one induced by the City's delay and failure to prepare the site properly. The total amount expended under these circumstances was reasonably used by the Court as a basis for figuring the damage award [*Moorhead Constr. Co., Inc. v. City of Grand Forks*, 508 F.2d 1008 (8th Cir. N.D. 1975)].

In other words, many times before the total-cost approach will be accepted, the contractor must go through all the mathematical computations and attempts to prove specific damages and then must demonstrate that the proof that specific damages are related to specific defaults is a near impossibility. Inability to do this will be likely to result in a failure of claim.

The *jury-type method* of computing damages has often been equated to the total-cost approach, but there are differences. The jury-type approach permits the judge or jury to consider the reasonableness of the figures and to compare responsibilities and degrees of fault. It permits a "reasonable estimate" of total damages based upon submitted evidence. This approach is favored over the total-cost approach when a distinction is made. It is still not a preferred method by the courts and is subject to dismissal.

One of the items the claimant must be able to prove, under all theories of damages, is the fact that it has attempted to mitigate the overall damages being sought. Every party is under a legal and moral obligation not to build up the damages after there has been a default by the other party; instead the injured party is *required* to take reasonable steps to try to keep potential damages as low as reasonably possible (Case 22-2). An injured party will be denied recovery from the defaulting party for the amount of damages which the court may reasonably determine could have been mitigated and avoided. If a contractor knows that work is going to be suspended for six months, and work is suspended with a predetermined established six-month period, for the contractor to maintain rented equipment on a daily basis on the jobsite for the six-month interval when it could have been returned and reacquired before work started again, or paid for by a monthly instead of a daily rental rate, will probably result in a decision that the contractor did not properly mitigate damages and is not entitled to the damages in excess of what the court determines to be a reasonable amount. However, merely because there is a six-month delay does not mean that the contractor was obligated to return the equipment. If the facts indicate that the delay was believed to be a short one, and if the owner continuously advised the contractor to be prepared to resume work on short notice, and/or if there might reasonably be a several-week lead time to remobilize the equipment, maintaining equipment on the jobsite for the eventual six-month period of time will probably result in all the damages being compensable. The obligation and responsibility of being able to prove that it has mitigated damages rests on the claimant. Bonanzas are seldom, if ever, realized by claimants as a result of a lawsuit.

Daily records, kept in the regular course of business by the project manager, field or job superintendent, or other authorized person, are probably the most important documents in proving damages. Strong auditable accounting records are essential. The era of working out of the hip pocket is gone.

The type of damages a contractor is entitled to recover is governed by various theories and applications by the courts. If the contractor is performing contract work and payment is denied, most courts seem to restrict recovery to the contractual amount specified for that work.

"While a plaintiff may simultaneously *sue* upon theories of express contract and, alternatively, implied contract . . ., he cannot *recover* on a quantum meruit where an express contract exists." Thus, if an actual contract exists, the party is bound by the contract and cannot disregard it and sue on the basis of reasonable value for quantum meruit [*Venture Constr. Co. v. Great American Mortgage Investors*, 214 S.E.2d 683 (Ga. App. 1975)].

Other courts have raised the argument that where the owner has materially breached the contract, the owner should not be entitled to take advantage of a clause in the contract as a defense. Thus, the contractor would have the right to sue either for the contract price or for the reasonable value of that portion of work. If no contract exists, recovery might be based on reasonable value (Case 22-3) or on unjust enrichment for implied contracts (Case 22-4). The reasonable value might be substantially higher than the actual contract price for that work. Even under the theory of reasonable value, or quantum meruit, there is a question whether the contractor is entitled to profits on top of its actual costs. This may be the case where a unit price is provided in the contract for a certain type of work, which the contractor does not want to live with, preferring to sue for the reasonable value. It would appear that in the majority of instances the contractor is still limited to the acknowledged contract value, but in certain instances it may be entitled to its additional damages.

Another type of relief involves specific performance in lieu of damages. Specific performance is an equitable argument whereby when one party refuses to perform a given function and the other party indicates that damages would not be sufficient to compensate it, and that the harm caused by the failure to act would be irreparable, the injured party may seek the court's directive requiring performance of the act. Specific performance is unusual in construction contracts but has been applied in special circumstances. Other equitable arguments would be the seeking of restitution, rescission, unjust enrichment, promissory estoppel, equitable estoppel, etc.

When the contractor seeks damages as a result of a breach, other than a specific enforcement of a contract price, it is generally recognized that a contractor is entitled to receive all its direct damages flowing from and as a result of the breach (Cases 22-2 and 22-5). There seems to be a question of semantics when it comes to indirect costs. Many courts will not allow indirect-cost elements. Whether or not they are in accord with those courts which allow indirect costs actually depends upon a given situation and the semantics involved. A majority of decisions seems to allow indirect damages which result from the given breach. What are indirect damages to one court may be direct damages to another. When it comes to speculative and consequential damages, those which truly could not be foreseeable, the vast majority of decisions denies compensation (Case 22-6).

Direct allowable costs normally include increased wage rates; performing work in different wage periods; increased material prices; increased and extended storage charges; increased and extended nonproductive personnel; increased and extended equipment charges, rentals and fees; increased supervisory costs; extended supervisory costs; loss of efficiency and productivity of workers and equipment; increased and extended field overhead; increased engineering costs; increased and extended home-office overhead; general and administrative expenses; idle-equipment charges; financing charges; interest (Case 22-7); having to work in a disjointed manner; having to work under adverse conditions; having to work in different seasons; the increased costs of performing unchanged work; and lost anticipated profits [see *Appeal of Sovereign Constr. Co., Ltd.*, 75-1 BCA 11,251 (1975); *Southern New England Contracting Co. v. State of Conn.* 345 A.2d 550 (1974); and *Appeal of Aerojet-General Corp.*, 74-2 BCA 10,863 (1974)].

A contractor's failure to complete the project by the contract stipulated date resulted in the owner's having to alter financing arrangements. The new financing caused the owner to incur substantial damages for which claims and counterclaims were asserted. The court granted the owner the right to collect extended financing costs as a direct damage but denied it the increased interest rate, which it was obligated to pay on refinancing, in that it is a consequential damage. The court discussed the right to collect damages and stated:

There are two broad categories of damages *ex contractu:* direct (or general) damages and consequential (or special) damages. . . . Direct damages are those which arise "naturally" or "ordinarily" from a breach of contract; they are damages which, in the ordinary course of human experience, can be expected to result from a breach. Consequential damages are those which arise from the intervention of "special circumstances" not ordinarily predictable. If damages are determined to be direct, they are compensable. If damages are determined to be consequential, they are compensable only if it is determined that the special circumstances were within the "contemplation" of both contracting parties. Whether damages are direct or consequential is a question of law. Whether special circumstances were within the contemplation of the parties is a question of fact. . . .

As a general rule, contemplation must exist at the time the contract was executed. . . . However, that rule is not absolute. When the breach alleged is an unexcused delay in completion, if the completion date has been altered by consensual amendment, contemplation is to be determined as of the date of amendment. . . .

We agree with the owner and the trial court that the extended financing costs are direct damages. Customarily, construction contracts, particularly large contracts, require third-party financing. Ordinarily, delay in completion requires an extension of the term of construction financing. The interest costs incurred and the interest revenue lost during such an extended term are predictable results of the delay and are, therefore, compensable direct damages.

We agree with the trial court that the damages resulting from increased interest rates are not direct damages. Increases in interest rates are not caused by delays in completion of construction contracts. Rather, they are caused by variable pressures and counter-pressures affecting supply and demand in the money market. . . . For that reason, increases in interest rates are "special circumstances," and damages resulting therefrom are consequential and not compensable unless such circumstances were within the contemplation of the parties [*Roanoke Hospital Ass. v. Doyle & Russel, Inc.,* 214 S.E.2d 155 (Va. Sup. Ct. 1975)].

Items which are generally recognized as not being compensable are the costs for claims preparation and presentation (Cases 22-8 and 22-9). This would necessarily include the attorney's fee (Case 22-10). The only right to collect attorneys' fees is in an exceptional instance (Case 22-11) or when it is so provided in the contract or by statute. Statutes are exceptional instances. Therefore, one of the most important clauses to be inserted in any contract, when it can be included, is the right to collect attorneys' fees. If you are able to have attorneys' fees included, you may as well try to include costs of litigation preparation and presentation. Another item of damage generally not allowed is lost prospective profits on contracts not yet entered. This is deemed to be too speculative, although in one recent case recovery has been allowed (Case 22-12).

Interest is often forbidden or limited by statute (Case 22-13); however, financing charges may be a direct cost, which is reimbursable (Case 22-7).

Under contracts with the federal government "interest is only allowable under a contract or Act of Congress expressly providing for payment." In the case before the Interior Board of Contract Appeals, no interest clause was in the contract, nor was one incorporated by reference. The board noted that if interest were to be permitted, it would have to be under the *Christian* doctrine, which stands for the proposition that if the clause is required by statute, but was omitted from the actual contract, it will still be inferred as if it were incorporated therein. In the instance before the board,

> The record does not disclose whether the omission [of the interest clause] was by design or through inadvertence. Federal Procurement Regulations, this Board has held, have the force and effect of law. [After reviewing the statutory interest clause, the Board concluded:] The language in the . . . regulation is a mandatory direction to the Government procurement officials to include an interest clause in contracts. To allow the official charged with this Governmental responsibility to ignore this unequivocal direction through either design or inadvertence would allow the total frustration of declared Government policy. The mandatory requirement that the interest clause be included in Government contracts cannot be dependent upon the capriciousness of the official awarding the contract. The policy of the Government is to include an interest clause and this Board can do no less. Under the *Christian* doctrine the interest clause quoted above is incorporated into this contract and is applicable to this appeal [*Appeal of Commonwealth Electric Co.,* 77-2 BCA 12,649 (IBCA 1977)].

One area of considerable debate and controversy relates to extended general and administrative expenses, i.e., continuing home-office nonallocable expenses. Tradition shows that the contractor merely adds a percentage of direct costs for its overhead. This overhead percentage, which normally runs between 5 and 15 percent, may or may not include field supervision, project management, or other overhead items. This again depends upon the contract terms and tradition. Even when the factor is representative of the home-office general and administrative expenses, the use of a percentage factor normally has little resemblance to actual costs. This can be shown more clearly by a simple example. A contract which is supposed to last one year is suspended during a heated debate. There is no indication when the people will come back to work, but the owner has ordered all workers and materials and equipment off the site. For the next six months there are daily administrative arguments and battles, rescheduling contractual commitments, arranging receipt of materials and new orders, maintaining job security, continuous meetings with the architect and engineer, and much aggravation. In actuality very little direct field cost is incurred but, as with all bad jobs, there is a disproportionate amount of home-office overhead and general and administrative expense. Taking even a 15 percent factor of the small increased direct field costs, assuming a default on the owner, will have little or no relationship to the actual general and administrative expense. What is needed is some reasonable accounting basis for the distribution of nonallocable expenses. The courts and boards on federal contracts have recognized the contractor's right to receive extended general and administrative expenses based upon sound accounting principles, whatever they might be, rather than a pure percentage of the direct costs. No uniform set formula can be given, although several have been used; it will depend upon the contractor's financial records, its accountant, and its testimony.

The problem out of which this dispute arises is how to allocate home office expenses incurred during a period of suspension of work. These expenses continue during temporary or partial suspensions, and it was in this case not practical for the contractor to undertake the performance of other work which might absorb them. There is no exact method to determine the amount of such expenses to be allocated to any particular contract or part of a contract. It has been held a number of times that it is not necessary to prove a specific amount, but only to determine a fair allocation for the purpose of compensating a contractor for delay by the Government [*Appeal of Eichleay Corp.*, 60-2 BCA 2688 (1960)].

In computing the compensation a contractor was entitled to for damages resulting from impact for delay on general administrative expenses, the court indicated that in determining the per diem overhead charge the actual contract price, as adjusted, should be used rather than the original bid contract price. In computing the increased and extended general and administrative expenses, the lower court had determined this cost factor as a percentage of the sales

> multiplied this by the original contract price, and then divided by the original contract period to determine the general administrative expense allocable to the contract on a per day basis. This figure was then multiplied by the . . . delay found by the district court to arrive at damages chargeable. . . .

This was now modified to insert the actual adjusted contract in lieu of the original contract price [*United States ex rel. H & S Industries, Inc. v. F. D. Rich Co., Inc.*, 525 F.2d 760 (7th Cir. 1975)].

The entire realm of damages is based upon what you can reasonably *prove* as being direct and possibly indirect costs as the result of given facts. Damages are limited to the liability (Case 22-14). Your success in receiving just and proper compensation is directly proportionate to your knowledge of your rights and your ability to document them.

CASE 22-1 Contract-Change Costs Must be Substantiated

The General Services Board of Contract Appeals denied a contractor's claim for damages because it failed to sustain the burden of proof and sufficiently substantiate actual cost increases resulting from a contract change [*Appeal of B. D. Click Co. Inc.*, GSBCA 3007, 70-1 BCA 8335 (1970)].

The contractor, performing various alterations to a U.S. Post Office, became involved in a dispute relating to the dollar amount it was entitled to receive for performing a certain contract change. The contractor submitted a cost breakdown for the work, which the government refuted. The contractor neither challenged the government's basis for denying its cost breakdown nor offered any additional evidence to substantiate its version.

The board denied the contractor's cost breakdown and allowed it to recover only the amount indicated by the government. The board held that "although precise proof of actual cost is not necessary, the appellant [contractor] has the burden of proving the dollar amount of equitable adjustment to which it is entitled. . . ."

CASE 22-2   Prime Contractor's Cost of Completion Reduces Subcontractor's Award

The Court of Appeals of Michigan has ruled that a prime contractor may reduce its payment to a subcontractor in default in order to offset the actual costs of completing a project [*Maraldo Asphalt Paving, Inc., v. Harry D. Osgood Co., Inc.,* 220 N.W.2d 50 (1974)].

A paving subcontract provided that the work would be completed by a set date. When the paving subcontractor failed to make proper progress toward completion, it was discharged and another subcontractor was retained to finish the job. The original subcontractor brought suit to recover for the work it had performed.

Although a lower court found that the subcontractor had been properly discharged, it ordered the prime contractor to pay the subcontractor for its expenditures before termination.

On appeal, the prime contractor argued that payment of this award would leave insufficient funds in the original subcontract to cover the actual cost of completing the project. Noting that an injured party is under obligation to mitigate damage and minimize its actual loss, the appeals court said, "It is equally clear that the burden of proof is upon the the party who breached the contract to show that the injured party has not used every reasonable effort within his control to minimize damage."

The appeals court found that the subcontractor had breached the contract and that the prime contractor had acted reasonably in obtaining a subcontractor to complete the work.

It awarded the prime contractor its total costs of completion, reducing the subcontractor's recovery to the difference between the cost of completing the project and the original contract price.

In its conclusion, the court stated, "The object of the measure of damages is to put the injured party in as good a position as he would have been in if the performance had been rendered as promised."

CASE 22-3   Subcontractor Recovers for Work Done under Unclear Pact

The Supreme Court of Idaho has ruled that a subcontract was so unclear and indefinite that it was unenforceable and that the subcontractor was entitled to recover for its work on the basis of its reasonable value [*Dale's Service Co., Inc. v. Jones,* 534 P.2d 1102 (1975)].

A subcontractor entered into a contract with a general contractor to provide and compact earthfill on a car-wash project. The agreement stated that the subcontractor was to perform all work necessary to "rough grade 4 in. of finish grade. These grades to be finally determined by paving contractor. . . . This [suitable grade] does not necessarily fit the plot plan. . . ."

After the work had begun, the general contractor became dissatisfied with the subcontractor's performance and terminated the subcontract. Another paving contractor was retained, and the general contractor sued the original subcontractor for the additional costs of completion. In turn, the subcontractor countersued seeking to recover the reasonable value (quantum meruit) of the work it had already completed.

The subcontractor claimed that there had never been "a meeting of the minds." It said there was no enforceable contract because of the uncertainty of the quantity of fill required.

The court agreed, stating: "It is essential to an enforceable contract that it be sufficiently definite and certain in its terms and requirements so that it can be determined when acts are to be performed and when performance is completed." Noting that the plans and specifications did not provide sufficient information to compute the quantity of fill required, the court ruled no contract had been consummated.

Even though the work had been performed under an invalid contract, the court said the subcontractor was entitled to recover the reasonable value of the services provided and materials furnished. The court based its decision on the general contractor's implied promise, in the contract, to pay the reasonable value of the services performed.

CASE 22-4 Implied Contract Is Basis for Additional Compensation

After a renegotiation clause in a contract was ruled to be legally unenforceable, the Supreme Court of Idaho permitted a contractor to seek additional compensation from a public authority on the basis of an implied contract [*McKay Construction Co., v. Ada County Board of County Commissioners*, 538 P.2d 1185 (1975)].

The contract stated that the contractor would truck waste to two sanitary-landfill sites. A clause in the contract provided that if the quantity of waste exceeded a certain number of tons per day "then the contract amount will be renegotiated." After the tonnage had been exceeded and attempts to renegotiate the contract had failed, the contractor sued.

A lower court held that the contract's renegotiation clause was too vague, and therefore legally unenforceable.

On appeal, the state supreme court assumed that the trial court's ruling on the enforceability of the renegotiation clause was correct and denied the contractor's claim under the specific contract clause.

However, the court went on to state that the clause was apparently inserted in the contract in good faith. It also accepted the unchallenged fact that the unit tonnage specified in the contract had been exceeded, and that the owner continued to accept the contractor's service.

In reaching its final decision that the contractor was entitled to seek additional compensation, the court said: "It is unchallenged that the Board of Commissioners had the power to make the express contract. . . . If the county had the power to make the express contract then in the proper circumstances it can be held liable on the theory of an implied contract. The rationale for the rule is that one party may not unjustly enrich itself at the expense of another."

The court said that the contractor "was not a volunteer and equity will not permit an unjust enrichment of the County at the expense of McKay [the contractor]."

CASE 22-5   Second Low Bid Was Proper
Assessment of Defaulted Work

The General Services Board of Contract Appeals held that an owner's acceptance of the second low bid for completion of a partially terminated contract was proper [*Blake Constr. Co., Inc.*, GSBCA 2887, 74-1 BCA 10,373 (1974)].

Part of a hospital construction contract let by the federal government called for installation of 31 special prefabricated rooms. The government's contracting officer found that progress on these rooms was unsatisfactory and terminated this portion of the contract.

The defaulted contractor appealed the owner's assessment of back charges for the unfinished work because the assessment was based on the price of the second low bid and not on the first bidder's price. The firm argued that only the low bid should have been accepted.

The board found that the government, in recalling for bids, had requested each bidder to submit a list of similar installations it had done. The low bidder failed to give any evidence. An investigation by the government of the low bidder's past performance showed that the firm received unfavorable comments on two similar projects.

The board concluded that acceptance of the second low bid and use of that price as the back charge for the reprocurement was proper. It said: "The record, in its entirety, discloses sufficient indications of unsatisfactory performance to support the conclusion that . . . [the low bidder] was not a qualified bidder."

CASE 22-6   Contractor Not Responsible
for Unforeseen Damages

The General Services Board of Contract Appeals has held that a contracting firm was not responsible for unforeseeable damages caused as a direct result of its work [*Appeal of I. Alper Co.*, GSBCA 2990, 70-1 BCA 8226 (1970)].

The case grew out of a contract awarded for the repair of a warehouse roof. After part of the roof had been removed, the contractor, acting quickly in a sudden rainstorm, covered the open area with protective coverings that leaked and caused the contents of the warehouse to become damaged.

The contract required the contractor to keep the inside of the building dry. In addition, the contract stated that the contractor would be liable for damages resulting from its negligence.

The contractor admitted responsibility and agreed to pay the actual cost of the damaged goods, sisal fiber. Unknown to the contractor, however, the fiber became highly combustible when wet and the owner (government) incurred additional costs in safeguarding the fiber and the warehouse against fire. The additional costs were assessed against the contractor and it appealed.

The board noted the contractor was unaware of the fiber's combustible nature. It held that the contractor's contractual obligations as to property damages were discharged upon payment for the sisal fiber damaged because of the leak.

Since the contractor was not told about the fiber, it could not have known of the risk. The board concluded that the claimed additional damages were improperly deducted from the contractor's payment.

CASE 22-7   Contractor Recovers Interest

The U.S. Court of Claims has allowed a contractor to recover interest costs under the changes clause of a contract with the federal government [*Bell, et al. v. United States,* 404 F.2d 975 (1968)].

The contractor's claim stemmed from the fact it had been forced to slow down its work because of defects in the government's specifications. It had originally financed its operations with a substantial bank loan, and the delay increased the interest costs of the loan.

The government contested any allowance for the increased interest costs and the Armed Services Board of Contract Appeals refused recovery.

In granting the claim for the increase in interest costs, the Court of Claims said, "The Board should have applied its own 'constructive change' doctrine by treating as done that which should have been done, namely the issuance by the contracting officer of a deceleration order. . . ."

Although a federal statute generally prohibits recovery of interest where it is based on a contractor's claim that the government delayed in making payments, the court stated that the statute was not applicable in this case. The contractor, it said, is neither seeking interest on money owed to it by the government nor is it asserting a breach of contract claim. Rather, it wants to recover the additional interest it had to pay on its loan over the extended period of time as a result of the slowdown caused by the defective specifications.

The court, in allowing recovery of the interest, held that the increased interest "was undoubtedly an increased cost of contract performance attributable to the change."

CASE 22-8   Proposal Expenses Not
Recoverable

The Armed Forces Board of Contract Appeals has ruled that a contractor has no right to collect costs incurred during preparation of a price proposal for changes in response to government solicitation.

The case involved a primary lump sum contract for the construction of 100 units of family housing in Mississippi. Several months after work had started the government contracting officer sent the contractor a letter accompanied by a list of "additional and revised work items" for which a price proposal was requested. About a month later the contractor submitted the price proposal and shortly thereafter conferred with the government contracting officer for the purpose of negotiating payment for the work involved in preparing the proposal. No agreement was reached, and the contractor subséquently withdrew its price proposal.

The contractor then sought reimbursement for the cost of preparing the proposal, citing time, travel and related expenses of $1500. Although the board admitted that certain circumstances might entitle a contractor to payment for a proposal, it found that the contractor's proposal in this case was not an undertaking of such magnitude or complexity as to suggest that the government intended to pay or otherwise compensate the contractor. The board held that the contractor's proposal was submitted without any expectation or intention on the part of either party that the contractor would be paid for the proposal if it were not accepted by the government.

> It is evident [the board said] that all the contracting officer did was invite an offer by the contractor which, if accepted by the government, would result in a bilateral supplemental agreement for performance of the proposed additional work for the offered price so that any action under the contract's changes clause would be rendered unnecessary. The contractor, therefore, was not under any contractual obligation to submit the requested proposal [*Appeal of Greenhut Constr. Co., Inc.*, ASBCA 14354, 70-1 BCA 8209 (1970)].

CASE 22-9   Negotiating Final Quantities Is Nonrecoverable Overhead Cost

The Corps of Engineers Board of Contract Appeals has denied a contractor recovery for costs incurred in negotiating final quantities of work performed under a government contract.

The contract called for various items of work relating to a water-protection system, including levees, channels, and a water-treatment plant in Kansas. Most of the work was excavating and filling.

After the work was completed, the contractor claimed "additional costs . . . for performing extra engineering for the purpose of determining actual quantities and to cause a correction of the inaccuracies of the government's final estimate of quantities upon which the appellant [contractor] was asked to accept final payment."

Before receipt of the government's final survey, the contractor had disbanded its workforce. After it discovered what it considered major and obvious errors in the survey, it reassembled its engineering force and hired a private consultant to recompute final quantities and to take part in further negotiations with the government.

In denying the contractor the right to recover these extra costs, the board said,

> We assume that the appellant is now contending that it did not anticipate engaging in any negotiation on final quantities. The cost of preparing for such a negotiation cannot be considered other than a normal overhead cost to the contractor . . . The extent to which he prepares himself . . . is the contractor's prerogative and the expenses should be absorbed by the contractor . . . It is well established that costs incurred in preparing a claim to the contracting officer or the board on appeal are not compensable." [*Appeal of Utilco Constr., a Division of McGrath Constr. Co.*, ENGBCA 2846, 69-2 BCA 7969 (1969)].

CASE 22-10 Legal Fees Not Recoverable

The Armed Services Board of Contract Appeals has ruled that a contractor cannot recover for legal fees incurred during negotiations and appeal procedures, even though the legal services led directly to a final settlement [*Appeal of Western General Services, Inc.*, ASBCA 18836, 77-1 BCA 12,278 (1976)].

The contractor had a fixed-price contract for the interior and exterior painting of a military dormitory. In the course of the project, the contractor performed certain work which it felt was beyond its contractual obligation and for which it should receive additional payment as provided in the changed-conditions clause of the contract.

The contractor hired an attorney on a time basis plus a contingent fee if a recovery resulted. Thereafter, the attorney was involved in negotiations with various government representatives, in addition to preparation and documentation of the claim.

During these negotiations, the contractor became financially unable to continue the project and stopped work. The surety took over and saw to its completion.

After the government contracting officer denied the claim for additional payment, the contractor, through its attorney, filed an appeal to the board. Negotiations continued and a settlement was reached. The contract was modified, granting the contractor a substantial increase for the additional work it had performed.

The settlement resolved all the claims with the exception of the contractor's demand for payment of its legal fees incurred during negotiations and the required appeal procedures.

The board noted that although the attorney played a substantial and active part in reaching the settlement, the contractor's claims for legal fees were neither presented on appeal nor settled by the parties as provided in the contract. It further noted that the legal expenses were not contemplated in the contract provisions.

Denying the claim for the attorney's fees, the board said: "With respect to the attorney's fees incurred in connection with the initiation of [the contractor's] claim before this board, and subsequent proceedings, such fees have been held to be unrecoverable."

The board also rejected the contractor's claim for legal fees incurred in connection with presentations to, and discussions with, the contracting officer, saying: "This board has customarily and consistently held that such attorney's fees are generally unrecoverable."

The basis for the board's ruling was that "such fees were incidental to the presentation of claims by [the contractor] against the government and were not expenses incurred in the performance of work."

CASE 22-11 Government Pays Legal Fees on Subcontractors' Claims

A contractor may be entitled to recover from the government its attorney fees incurred in settling claims with subcontractors. The Armed Services Board of

Contract Appeals ruled that where the subcontractor's claims were the direct result of government delays, the government is liable [*Appeal of Lea County Constr. Co.*, ASBCA 13964, 72-1 BCA 9298 (1972)].

In this case, the contractor had planned the construction of dock and hangar facilities to move from one site to another and complete them within time limits. The board found that the contractor's work was substantially delayed by the government's failure to coordinate properly the work of other contractors whose work affected the appellant's and unreasonably delaying approval of shop drawings. The government did not make two progress payments to the prime contractor, resulting in work stoppages and suits filed by subcontractors against the contractor.

The question was whether the contractor could collect from the government the legal fees spent in settling suits with subcontractors.

While the board acknowledged the general principle of law that attorney fees are not recoverable, it cited an exception that,

> Where a party . . . was involved in previous litigation with others because of some wrongful or compensable act of the presently defending party, reasonable compensation for expenses, including attorney fees, attributable to the former suit are recoverable where such expenses are the natural consequences of the defendant's wrongful act.

CASE 22-12   Unearned-Lost-Profit Claim
Upheld by Court

The Supreme Court of Montana has ruled that an owner's delay in furnishing a highway right-of-way was a breach of contract that caused the contractor to lose its bonding capacity, future jobs, and future unearned profits.

The contractor in the case had been given notice to proceed with grading and drainage work along 6.5 miles of road on October 20, 1964. The work, to be completed within 250 days, was not finished until November 1966.

The contractor sued, alleging that the owner delayed work by failure to furnish a required right-of-way. It claimed, "As a result of being tied up on this job, the plaintiff [contractor] lost his bonding capacity, and thereby lost future profits." The lower court determined that a breach did exist, and the jury awarded damages, including loss of future profits.

The owner appealed to the Montana Supreme Court, which concurred with the lower court's findings. It pointed out that the contract documents "provided that if the right-of-way had not been obtained at the time bids were opened, the award would not be made until the entire right-of-way had been obtained."

On the question of future profits, the owner claimed that they should be denied because future unearned profits have always been denied on the basis that they were too speculative and uncertain. While the court recognized the general principle of law precluding recovery of unearned profits, it also noted a change in the law allowing future unearned profits to be recovered when the contractor can prove, with reasonable certainty, what foreseeable profits would have been earned but for the breach.

In upholding its decision to award the plaintiff future profits, the court stated:

> In essence, the plaintiff alleges he was so entangled over this particular contract, and went so far in debt as a result of the delays in this contract, that he lost his bonding capacity and thereby lost profits in the years 1967, 1968 and 1969. He proved he had always been a successful contractor, had always made a profit on all his jobs over some 22 years, and on that basis, he lost anticipated or future profits for the three years in question to the extent of $250,000. The jury agreed with him to the extent of $78,000.
>
> This figure arrived at by the jury appears to us to be reasonable. Two accountants, one for each side, went into the plaintiff's income . . . his depreciation and all other facets were covered. Additionally, the period of time used was but three years. In other words, future profits on a speculative basis were not allowed. Rather, future profits for the immediately foreseeable period with a complete background were arrived at by the jury [*Laas v. Montana State Highway Commission,* 483 P.2d 699 (1971)].

CASE 22-13   Cash in Lieu of Bid Bond, No Interest Allowed

The government has denied a contractor interest on a cash deposit submitted in lieu of a bid bond even though the government delayed returning the deposit to the contractor [*Appeal of Hans Schmoldt,* ASBCA 12797, 68-2 BCA 7318 (1968)].

The contractor, having completed its contract for furnishing and installing a cathodic protection system at Davis-Monthan Air Force Base in Arizona, filed several claims, but the contracting officer denied most of them. Appeal was taken to the Armed Services Board of Contract Appeals, where the government counsel also sought to have the board reverse portions of the claims originally granted by the contracting officer. Both were partially successful in this case.

The contractor had posted a cash deposit instead of a bid bond with its bid. The invitation for bids provided that if a cash bid security was furnished in lieu of a bid bond, upon award of the contract the cash deposit would be returned promptly.

The cash deposit was not returned until two months after final completion of the project. The contractor claimed interest at 6 percent on the delayed refund from the date of contract award to the date of refund.

Although the contracting officer had originally granted a major portion of the interest claim, the contractor had not received any payment. Therefore, the entire amount originally requested was again being claimed. The government fought any interest payment.

The board noted that this claim must be regarded as a breach-of-contract claim. The claim, it said, neither arose out of a change to the contract nor was it related to contract performance. The basis of the claim was strictly the failure of the government to refund money when due. In such instances, the board said, the claim must be dismissed since the government is statutorily prohibited from paying interest unless specifically authorized by a particular law or by contract.

However, the board added that if the contractor had accepted the partial sum allowed by the contracting officer "as an accord and satisfaction in release of the claim, the government's right to challenge the settlement would have been barred, since the contracting officer is empowered in law to settle breach claims by agreement."

The contractor asserted another claim pursuant to the "Price Adjustment for Suspension, Delays, or Interruption of Work" clause of its contract. Here the contractor alleged that it was directed to locate underground utility structures that were not shown on the drawings. As a result, it said, its construction progress was delayed and it incurred additional costs.

The board held that "each hour of delay looking for the underground utilities which the government failed to show on its plans was unreasonable." The contractor was allowed recovery of its increased costs of performance caused by this delay.

CASE 22-14   Liability for Repair Costs Limited by Court

A contractor is liable only for the reasonable cost to correct a specific defective condition and not for the cost of performing total corrective and protective measures beyond the area in which the defect was located, according to the Armed Services Board of Contract Appeals.

The contract called for the construction of a hospital facility at an Air Force base in Florida. After construction was completed and the government had taken occupancy, it was discovered that rainwater had leaked into the building. The government held the contractor responsible, under its contract, for the repairs of the apparent construction deficiencies. For several years the contractor attempted to locate the cause of the leak and performed corrective repair work.

Although most of the leaks were stopped by the contractor's repair work, a small portion of the total building still leaked. At this point the government suggested installation of a specially designed flashing system around the entire perimeter of the building. The contractor denied responsibility for this repair work. The government contracted with another firm for the installation of the flashing system and sought to hold the contractor liable for the entire cost of the work. The contractor appealed from the holding.

The Armed Services Board of Contract Appeals first determined that the leakage problem was neither caused by nor was it the fault of the government. It said no design deficiency existed and that the leaks were the fault of the contractor's faulty construction. Therefore, it concluded, the contractor was liable for the cost of correcting defects.

However, the board noted that before the government contracted for the repair work, the contractor had eliminated most of the leaks. In fact, the area which still leaked represented the need for extra flashing for only about 61 feet. The repair contract called for the installation of over 1200 feet of the specially designed flashing system.

In holding the contractor liable for a small portion of the repair contract cost, the board said:

The claim for applying the corrective measure to the entire perimeter of the roof does not represent a reasonable measure of damages to correct the deficiencies remaining uncorrected at that time. Accordingly, the measure of damages for which we find appellant [contractor] responsible is that proportion of the total cost incurred in the repair contract . . . which is equal to the proportion that the 61 feet . . . bears to the total footage [over 1200 feet] for which repair was made [*Appeal of Acme Missiles & Constr. Corporation,* ASBCA 13671, 69-1 BCA 7698 (1969)].

TWENTY-THREE

Documentation

An attorney who claims never to have lost a case is either a wishful thinker or has had only one case. However, few cases are lost because of the attorney. Most cases are lost because of the client. The client does not have the documents the attorney *needs* in court. There is a difference beween the type of documents the contractor may occasionally need in house for cost control, the type of documents engineers may want, and the type of documents *needed* for court. An attorney needs legally admissible documents for court: without them the contractor cannot win. The best way to stay out of court is to be prepared for it, and that means full and complete documentation.

Generally, a client cannot walk away with a good settlement without good documentation. Cases are more favorably settled when the contractor goes to the negotiating table, sits down, and says, "We've got all these documents in support of our claim," and is able to respond to questions with documents. When the adversary has a reasonably intelligent and educated attorney, architect, engineer, or other representative, and it sees the documents you are prepared to present in court, you will settle your case more often than not. If you go in with a story and nothing more, you are not going to get a satisfactory settlement; you will end up in court, and you will probably lose. No adversary is properly representing itself or its client by settling a matter which you cannot prove now, but that you can and will substantiate in court later.

The old belief that attorneys create litigation is false. Attorneys represent the interests of the client. Clients put a lot of faith in attorneys. Clients put a lot of faith in the judge. Clients often believe that an attorney can do what they cannot.

Gentlemen, this is a case which should be settled between the parties. In present day thinking, it seems to be the idea that any problem can be cured in a Federal District Court. This, I assure you, is an erroneous approach. There is not a lawyer in this courtroom capable of operating the Providence Hospital. There is not a lawyer in this courtroom capable of running Manhattan Construction Company; there is not a lawyer in this room capable of running McCauley Associates; nor a lawyer in this room capable of running Fairbanks-Morse; nor a lawyer capable of running Ernst, and I assure you there is not a Judge in this courtroom capable of doing so. All of you litigants are successful operators or you would not be participating in a six million dollar contract. Lawyers in their zeal to represent their clients many times fail to see but one side of the litigation and that is the side of his client. This litigation is not a one-sided bit of litigation, it is a five-sided bit of litigation.

I stated at the outset that this was a case that should be settled between the parties. . . .

Yes, litigation is expensive, but remember the courts do not create litigation, it is created by the litigants. I have asked that you representatives of the litigants be here today. Although I know you have been kept abreast of this litigation by your attorneys, I wanted you to hear directly from the trial judge his thoughts on this matter. You litigants are in a fairly closely related field. Being trained in this field, you are in a far better position to adjust your differences than those untrained in these related fields. As an illustration, I, who have had no training whatsoever in engineering, had to determine whether or not the emergency generator system proposed to be furnished . . . met the specifications, when experts couldn't agree. That is a strange bit of logic. . . .

The object of litigation is to do substantial justice between the parties litigant, but the parties litigant should realize that, in most situations, they are by their particular training better able to accomplish this among themselves [*E. C. Ernst, Inc. v. Manhattan Constr. Co. of Texas*, 387 F. Supp. 1001 (1974)].

Lawyers do not create claims. They present them. This is done through evidentiary facts and documentation.

The single most important document for claims review, preparation, and proof is the contractor's daily business record, e.g., the daily field report. The claim must exist, but all too often, without daily reports, the client does not know what claims exist, learns of their existence too late, or cannot prove them. The contractor must have complete and accurate daily field reports setting forth all occurrences and events, even though problems are not known to exist at present. Daily records cannot be put together after the fact. In fact, the daily record is legitimate precisely because it is not prepared specifically for litigation but is prepared for the proper running of a business.

Clients are nearly unanimous in knowing that they are right and that they have been wronged. According to the client, it is always the other side which has committed the default. The client's principal, who runs the firm from the office, has heard all the problems from the project personnel. The principal has coordinated the fact finding during the contract and knows how all the opinions of its personnel fit together and how and why they are right and the other firm is wrong. During the period between the event which caused the claim, the completion of the project, and the day in court, several years have passed. The project superintendent has gone on to greener pastures. The field personnel have disappeared. The principal of the contracting firm is ready to testify for the cause and wants his chance in court. Unfortunately, it cannot testify from personal knowledge. It cannot testify. It is hearsay. Where are the documents? Where is the proof? With only limited documents to present to the judge you may not be able to put a winner together in negotiation even when you are right. Your chances in court are severely limited. Lack of proof not only affects your affirmative claim but places you at great disadvantage when you are defending an action.

When they satisfy the requirements of applicable jurisdiction's statutes, daily records are an exception to the hearsay rule. They can be used as evidence without the person who prepared them. They are the basis for all future testimony.

Although the lack of daily records may not automatically defeat a claim, it is tantamount to defeat in many instances. In the remaining instances, it will affect the risk of loss. As stated in a recent New York case:

> We reject the State's contention that claims under public construction contracts must be proved by written business records which would be subject to audit by the State. We know of no statute, rule or decisional law which requires proof in such form. It may well be imprudent and hazardous for the claimant not to maintain detailed business records. He runs the substantial risk that his oral testimony may be disbelieved to a lesser or greater extent and that accordingly his claim may be disallowed in whole or in part for insufficiency of proof. Most claimants would seek to avoid such risks [*D'Angelo v. State of New York*, 39 N.Y.2d 781 (1976)].

Normally records are not admissible as evidence to prove the truth of the statements contained in them without the original author. However, daily records are often a statutory exception and can become evidence in and by themselves. As stated in a case cited before,

> Business entries have long been recognized as an exception to the hearsay rule provided (1) the entries are made in the regular course of business; (2) the entries are made contemporaneously with the events recorded; (3) the entries are original entries; and, (4) the entries are based upon personal knowledge of the person making them [*Ray D. Lowder, Inc. v. North Carolina State Highway Commission*, 217 S.E.2d 682 (1975)].

The specific rule of evidence is usually set forth in the state statute. For example, Missouri is one of the majority of states which has a business-records statute patterned after the Uniform Business Records as Evidence Act. The Missouri Statute provides:

> 490.680. Records competent evidence, when
> A record of an act, condition or event, shall, insofar as relevant, be competent evidence if the custodian or other qualified witness testifies to its identity and the mode of its preparation, and if it was made in the regular course of business, at or near the time of the act, condition or event, and if, in the opinion of the court, the sources of information, method and time of preparation were such as to justify its admission [L. 1949, p. 275, § 3)].

The various states do not have identical statutes covering these types of documents, and therefore each state's statute must be reviewed for wording and court interpretation. The Texas Statute is a good example of a statute which follows the basic concepts of the uniform statute but has added new twists. It provides:

> Art. 3737e. Memorandum or record of act, event or condition; absence of memorandum or record as evidence.
>
> Section 1. A memorandum or record of an act, event or condition shall, insofar as relevant, be competent evidence of the occurrence of the act or event or the existence of the condition if the judge finds that:
>
> (a) It was made in the regular course of business;
>
> (b) It was the regular course of that business for an employee or representative of such business with personal knowledge of such act, event or condition to make such memorandum or record or to transmit information thereof to be included in such memorandum or record;
>
> (c) It was made at or near the time of the act, event or condition or reasonably soon thereafter.
>
> Sec. 2. The identity and mode of preparation of the memorandum or record in accordance with the provisions of paragraph one (1) may be proved by testimony of the entrant, custodian or other qualified witness even though he may not have personal knowledge as to the various items or contents of such memorandum or record. Such lack of personal knowledge may be shown to affect the weight and credibility of the memorandum or record but shall not affect its admissibility.

Substantial discretion is left to the judge's decision on points like the following:

1. What is the regular course of business?
2. Were the documents kept in the regular course of business, and does that mean daily, weekly, or monthly?
3. Are tape recordings permissible, and what about the transcript of the recordings?
4. If a transcript of a recording exists, must it be signed by the original author, and if so, when?
5. Was the document signed at the time of the event "or reasonably soon thereafter"?
6. Is eight hours, twelve hours, or one week after the event a reasonable time for execution of the documents?
7. Are the documents trustworthy and reliable?
8. Are the documents prepared from personal knowledge?

What happens if an alleged event is not recorded in the daily reports? Do we or can we just overlook the absence of records? The answer is not easy. It depends (1) on the existing statute, (2) on court decisions, and (3) assuming no statute, on the argument of counsel. The Texas, Wisconsin, Utah, and other state statutes provide a specific answer. The Texas Statute provides:

Sec. 3. Evidence to the effect that the records of a business do not contain any memorandum or record of an alleged act, event or condition shall be competent to prove the non-occurrence of the act or event or the non-existence of the condition in that business if the judge finds that it was the regular course of that business to make such memoranda or records of all such acts, events or conditions at the time or within reasonable time thereafter and to preserve them.

If it is your regular course of business to keep daily reports (and you are the first person to call it a daily record), and if you do not have on a given date the event you say occurred (e.g., giving oral notice to the owner), that is evidence of the nonoccurrence of that event. This is a powerful statute. However, even in the absence of the statute, attorneys will argue the same theory. This means that if you keep records, they had better be right and complete, because if they are incomplete, they will be used against you.

From the attorney's point of view, no single group of documents is more important than a daily business record. The author is repeatedly asked: "How do we get the field personnel to keep accurate daily records?" The answer is simple: Fire them! Too many contractors are unable to prove and collect their claims simply because of the lack of proper daily records. When you are legally right but cannot prove liability or damages, or both, the importance of daily records will surface very quickly. If you are averse to firing project superintendents because you "make too much money from them," such people are so valuable to you that you can afford to hire a record keeper for each project to assist the superintendent. This is a business decision, but without the documentation required, the legal decision is going to be a foregone conclusion.

The daily records should not smell "lawsuit." They must be complete and accurate. You do not know who you will be in court with, if anyone, at the end of the project. Honest and complete reports are the only way to go. No one expects that the job will run without some problems or complications. No one expects the contractor to be error-free. It is mandatory that all true facts be written down and noted. Without full documentation, no intelligent analysis can be made.

When was the last time you wrote the architect about the small problems you were having on the job? The answer is probably never. Most contractors do not write, although they should, even when it is a minor problem. You do not want to cause an architect to become agitated or aggravated. You may not have given proper notice. However, you may have complained to the architect when you encountered the problem in the field. *Put it in your daily records.* The minor problem goes on for three months, no letter has been written, and that minor problem has now turned into a major claim. Since you seldom know in advance the future scope of a problem, it is important to keep a record of all events. Where is the notice that you were required to give the owner? There is no notice. You never wrote a letter or protested in writing; after all, it was a minor problem. Although proper protest does not exist, some courts will hold that constructive notice existed. Constructive notice might be found in the daily record indicating that you showed the problem to the architect. The owner no longer can claim surprise or prejudice. If that is in the daily record, you may have notice. It is a start; without it, you have nothing. All events should be duly noted in the daily records.

The Lowder case, cited above, stresses the importance of daily business records. The case involved a grading utility contractor. One of the unit-price items in the bid documents called for removal of 12,000 cubic yards. The actual quantity of material removed represented an increase of in excess of 2000 percent. The trial judge found that the contractor had made a reasonable site inspection and that the condition it encountered could not have been discovered by a reasonable inspection. (By the way, who did the site inspections on your projects? Do you have detailed records of them?) Remember, that in the Lowder case they did not know that they would need the site-inspection documents later or that they would have to prove they made a reasonable site inspection. Be prepared. Relying upon the facts, the court ruled that a changed-conditions claim existed as a result of the excess of undercut excavation required. However, the court was now faced with the question of damages. The court stated:

> This bring us to the second critical issue raised by this appeal: Did Lowder's compilation of damages report qualify as a record made in the regular course of business so as to permit its admission into evidence as an exception to the hearsay rule?
>
> The compilation of damages report, which the Commission argues was improperly admitted, is divided into three parts. Part A is a claim for additional compensation by reason of rental of extra equipment for undercut excavation in the amount of $94,310.14. Part B is a claim for additional compensation for labor in the amount of $24,343.67. Part C is a claim for additional compensation for expenses incurred between 1 October 1966, the original deadline, and 30 March 1967, two days after the project was accepted by the Commission. Labor costs in Part C are listed as $91,504.94; bond, insurance, and tax as $14,755.98; miscellaneous expenses as $36,540.70; and equipment rental as $219,796.30. The Part C total is $362,597.92. The aggregate total, less the $129,874.64 paid at the unit price by the Commission to Lowder for the overrun is $351,377.09.
>
> The compilation of damages summary was taken from an analysis of daily reports prepared by Grady Meisenheimer, Lowder's superintendent during most of the construction of project 8.11618. Meisenheimer testified by deposition that he kept daily records of "laborers, machinery, and the type of work that we were doing on the job. We kept records of all of the equipment, how many hours it would run, the kind of work we're doing . . . whatever we were doing, we kept a record of it." These reports were filled out each day after work had stopped, and were mailed each night to Lowder home office in Albemarle. After lying "fallow" for several years in Lowder's files, the reports were used to prepare the compilation of damages report. Mrs. Nell Poplin, secretary-treasurer of Lowder and "custodian of financial records," stated that Lowder compiled its information from the daily reports and from an analysis of the reports which had been prepared by Meisenheimer. Poplin testified that "we would take the equipment that was used on the undercut excavation, the men who were the operators of that equipment, and the number of hours each worked, equipment, and men." "We took off the equipment, the materials that he received, the number of people on the payroll, the total of skilled, total of unskilled; all the information he had. . . ." Part A of the compilation of damages "came from the daily

reports made by Grady Meisenheimer." Part C was taken "directly from our job cost records." Part B "came directly from our payroll accounts." The cost records, which rely on the daily reports also, were compiled by Mrs. Poplin [*Ray D. Lowder, Inc. v. North Carolina State Highway Commission*, 217 S.E.2d 682 (1975)].

The damage summaries were a direct result of the daily reports. Therefore, the court had to examine carefully the daily reports prepared by Lowder's superintendent to determine whether the contractor's documents were reliable. The daily reports were made on a loose-leaf preprinted form. The front side of the form had

> spaces for reporting weather conditions, the work day, and the number of skilled and unskilled laborers present. The majority of space is allocated to three headings: "Road Way," "Pipelines," and "Clearing." Some space is reserved for "Remarks." On the back side of the form there are two spaces: One is reserved for the listing of "Material Received, Borrowed Or Rented"; the other is reserved for "List of Equipment Nos." [ibid.].

Although similar to many daily reports and probably better than most, these reports were deemed insufficient by the court. Even though the court noted that ample remarks were set out, progress of work was recorded, and equipment on the jobsite was listed on many reports there was, in the majority of reports, insufficient specific indication of equipment actually in use or broken down. The specific hours that the equipment was in operation were not set down. There was no way to tell what equipment was in operation. When equipment appeared as "down" in the remarks section, it might also appear in the equipment list on the jobsite. "Although we regard these reports as incomplete, the reports filed after Meisenheimer's departure are practically devoid of information. Little is reported about the nature of the work done, and no equipment is listed as being on the jobsite." The entire foundation for the damage calculation was in question.

The court concluded:

> Had the daily reports not been incomplete, we might not express reservation about the finalized report. . . .
> It is not our intention to require copious entries in business records. But we are of the opinion that entries should be so complete and in such detail as to indicate that they are reliable and accurate. To report that 36 machines are on a job site on a given day is unsatisfactory. It would be better practice to report not only the number of machines on the job but also the number of machines operating, the task each performs, and the length of time each operates. The product of that kind of record keeping is more likely to bear the earmark of reliability. . . .
> [W]e refuse to find reports admissible when they lack minimum requirements of trustworthiness and reliability. The compilation of damages report was prepared for this litigation; it was based on incomplete daily reports; it was not contemporaneous but was the product of Meisenheimer's personal judgment, discretion and memory some four years later. It simply is not the product of an efficient clerical system, and it has not been made in the regular course of business [ibid.].

Lowder's claim of liability was acknowledged, but due to its poor daily reports it was unable to prove its damages. The court reversed the lower court's decision, which had awarded Lowder damages, and ordered a new trial.

The evidence submitted in a Texas case, in support of a subcontractor and prime contractor's claim for extras against the owner, were summaries of voluminous business records. The owner objected to the admission of these summaries on the basis that they were hearsay, that the records upon which they were based were not actually submitted to the court as evidence, and that the underlying business records were not established as being admissible by themselves. The court indicated

> It seems to be the settled rule in Texas that a summary of voluminous records may, in the discretion of the trial court, be admitted into evidence provided that all of the source records are shown to be admissible and are produced in court or are otherwise available to the opposing party for purposes of audit and cross-examination.

However, the evidence on the appeal indicated that many of the records supporting the summaries were prepared not at the time of the event, but long after the events recorded therein. Many of the underlying documents were prepared in support of the summaries, at the time of the summaries, and others were based upon oral statements and assumptions. In addition, some of the underlying records were not produced at the time of trial, and no proof was submitted showing that the supporting documentation was made available to the owner. The summaries were deemed not admissible evidence. [*Black Lake Pipe Line Co. v. Union Constr. Co., Inc.,* 520 S.W.2d 486 (Tex. App. 1975)].

The question of legal admissibility of evidence and documents should not be the reason for failing to document events during contract bidding or performance. There is negotiation before litigation and possibly arbitration in lieu of litigation. One of the first things an arbitrator is told is that a basic reason for overturning an arbitration award is the arbitrator's failure to hear and receive proper evidence. Arbitrators are normally selected because of their knowledge in construction, not necessarily in the law. They do not know such terminology as the dead man's rule of evidence, the hearsay rule, or the parol-evidence rule. They are knowledgeable in the substance of what is being arbitrated. They want to see documents. What may or may not be inadmissible in court may be absolutely admissible in arbitration and a necessity in negotiation.

Documentation does not stop with daily reports. Letters should be written confirming all oral agreements. Memories change with time. Set it down in writing. This is true, even though the letter may be self-serving. The existence of self-serving confirmation letters often forms the basis for avoiding litigation.

When the contract or applicable statute requires notice be served, do it in writing. In this instance do it by a certified letter, return receipt requested. Time limitations must be met, and the best way to prove compliance is with a return receipt.

Write; it should not hurt. Remember, there are different ways of writing or protesting. You can label a person "a no-good S.O.B."; that is one type of protest letter. You can also say, "Dear Joe, We would like respectfully to indicate disagreement with your ruling." You can even write letters so as not to ruffle an architect's feathers. It is not the writing that bothers most people; it is the style and how you say what you say. Documents are an essential part of effecting a successful resolution and disposition of claims. When you should protest, protest.

Remember, it is the contractor's money and business that are being protected. You may not have to go to court and can probably settle the case amicably by negotiation if you have proper documents. It only costs a small additional amount to be properly documented; but if you do not keep records, it may cost you your company.

Table of Cases

A

B

	Case No.	Page
Ballou v. Basic Constr. Co., 407 F.2d 1137 (1969)	15-5	189, 193, 194
Appeal of Baltimore Contractors, Inc., GSBCA 3425, 72-2 BCA 9622 (1972)	11-11	127-128
Appeal of Baltimore Contractors, Inc., GSBCA 37A, 73-2 BCA 10,032 (1973)	8-3	64
Barash v. State, 154 N.Y.S.2d 317 (1956)		71
Barr & Sons, Inc. v. Cherry Hill Center Inc., 217 A.2d 631 (N.J. Super. Ct. 1966)		196
Appeal of T. C. Bateson Constr. Co., GSBCA 2656, 68-2 BCA 7263 (1968)	14-9	174
Appeal of Baxter Constr. Co., Inc., ENGBCA 2870, 69-2 BCA 7893 (1969)	14-24	178
Beacon Constr. Co. v. United States, 314 F.2d 501 (1963)		72
Appeal of Beagle-Chilcutt Painting Co., 60-2 BCA 2731 (1960)		68
Bell, et. al. v. United States, 404 F.2d 975 (1968)	22-7	249
Stanley R. Benjamin, Inc. v. Fidelity Casualty Co. of New York, 72 Misc.2d 742, 340 N.Y.S.2d 578 (1972)	21-1	212, 234
Chris Berg, Inc. v. United States, 455 F.2d 1037 (1972)	11-8	126
Bergstedt, Wahlberg, Berquist Associates, Inc. v. Rothchild, 225 N.W.2d 261 (1975)	5-6	45-46
Best v. Fred Weber Constr. Co., 525 S.W.2d 102 (Mo. Ct. App. 1975)		7
Bethlehem Steel Co. v. Turner Constr. Co., 2 N.Y.2d 456 (1957)		70
Black Lake Pipe Line Co. v. Union Constr. Co., 520 S.W.2d 486 (Tex. App. 1975)		117, 263
Appeal of Blake Constr. Co., Inc., GSBCA 2887, 74-1 BCA 10,373 (1974)	22-5	248
Blum v. City of Hillsboro, 183 N.W.2d 47 (1971)	11-3	121-122
Board of Education v. Wager Constr. Corp., 333 N.E.2d 353 (N.Y. 1975)		217
Brown Bros. Electrical Contractors, Inc. v. Beam Constr. Corp., 41 N.Y.2d 397 (1977)	5-4	44-45
Drew Brown Limited v. Joseph Rugo, Inc., 436 F.2d 632 (1st Cir. 1971)	10-12	108, 160
Appeal of Browning Constr. Co., ASBCA 17708, 73-1 BCA 9913 (1973)	9-10	82-83
Burgess Constr. Co. v. M. Morrin & Sons Co., Inc., 526 F.2d 108 (10th Cir. 1976)		155
Burgess Mining & Constr. Corp. v. City of Bessemer, Alabama, 312 So.2d 24 (1975)	10-2	101, 137
Burton-Dixie Corp. v. Timothy McCarthy Constr. Co., 436 F.2d 405 (5th Cir. 1971)	19-4	225
Appeal of Clyde Burton & Sons Constr. Co., Inc., GSBCA 3227, 71-2 BCA 9152 (1971)	14-25	178-179
A & J Buyers, Inc. v. Johnson, Drake & Piper, Inc., 25 N.Y.2d 265 (1969)	20-1	229-230

C

	Case No.	Page
Cable-Wiedemer, Inc. v. A. Friederich & Sons Co., 71 Misc.2d 443, 336 N.Y.S.2d 139 (1972)	9-15	86-87
Calumet Constr. Co. v. Bd. of Education of City of Hoboken, 76 Atl. 970 (1910)		70
Peter A. Camilli & Sons, Inc. v. State of New York, 245 N.Y.S.2d 521 (1963)		34
George Campbell Painting Corp. v. Reid et al., Members of N.Y. City Housing Authority et al., 392 U.S. 286 (1968)	1-1	3
Carter v. Sherburne Corp., 315 A.2d 870 (1974)		156
G. C. Casebolt Co. v. United States, 421 F.2d 710 (1970)	15-2	190-191
Centric Corp. v. Barbarossa & Son, Inc., 521 P.2d 874 (Wyo. 1974)	3-9	19-20, 26-27
Chaney and James Constr. Co., Inc. v. United States, 190 Ct. Cl. 669, 421 F.2d 728 (1970)	14-1	154, 161-162

D

E

F

G

K

L

Index